NEW YORK

à la Cart

RECIPES & STORIES
from the Big Apple's
BEST FOOD TRUCKS

SIOBHAN WALLACE
& ALEXANDRA PENFOLD

FOREWORD BY ZACH BROOKS
FOUNDER OF MIDTOWNLUNCH.COM

RUNNING PRESS
PHILADELPHIA · LONDON

"ALL THAT I AM, OR HOPE TO BE, I OWE TO MY ANGEL MOTHER."

—ABRAHAM LINCOLN

FOR OUR MOTHERS. —A.P. & S.W.

© 2013 by Alexandra Penfold and Siobhan Wallace
Published by Running Press,
A Member of the Perseus Books Group

Printed in China

Books published by Running Press are available at special
discounts for bulk purchases in the United States by
corporations, institutions, and other organizations. For more
information, please contact the Special Markets Department
at the Perseus Books Group, 2300 Chestnut Street, Suite 200,
Philadelphia, PA 19103, or call (800) 810-4145, ext. 5000, or
e-mail special.markets@perseusbooks.com.

ISBN 978-0-7624-4682-7
Library of Congress Control Number: 2012954314

E-book ISBN 978-0-7624-4824-1

9   8   7   6   5   4   3   2   1
Digit on the right indicates the number of this printing

Design by Joshua McDonnell
Edited by Jennifer Kasius
Map by Drew Willis
Typography: Avenir, Bembo, Governor, and Print

Running Press Book Publishers
2300 Chestnut Street
Philadelphia, PA 19103-4371

Visit us on the web!
www.runningpress.com

CONTENTS

DOWNTOWN

MIDTOWN

UPTOWN

ALL AROUND TOWN

OUTER BOROUGHS

Foreword by Zach Brooks

I honestly can't remember when or how I met Siobhan and Alex, or as they're known to their close friends (and ardent followers) Blondie and Brownie. But I do remember when I started linking to their blog. It was a little bit over 5 years ago, around the time they made it their mission to eat every single thing on the Treats Truck's menu. You know . . . for "science." Of course, when VendrTV launched their YouTube show with an episode about the Treats Truck, it surprised nobody to see them hovering in the background, eyeing the brownies . . . and blondies.

Years later, when my family's move to Los Angeles forced me to hand over the reins of Midtown Lunch, "Blondie" and "Brownie" were the two very first people I asked to contribute. From eating a Walgreens cheeseburger that I refused to eat, to finding the best fried fish sandwich from a cart for Lent, their fearless attitude towards scoping out the best things to eat in NY has always impressed.

And their commitment to the New York street food scene is second to none. Every year Midtown Lunch holds a showdown called Street Meat Palooza, to determine the best plate of chicken and lamb over rice with white sauce and hot sauce in Midtown. They've been to all five (and Siobhan actually ran this past year's contest!) And I can't remember the last Vendy Awards they weren't at as volunteers.

A New York without street food is unimaginable, and in the years since Alex and Siobhan started their blog, Blondie and Brownie, the scene has only gotten better and better. From halal street meat and Mexican tacos, to belgian waffles and jerk chicken, there has never been a better time to step outside for meal in New York City. And it's not just the food that's amazing, but the vendors themselves have amazing stories to tell and recipes to share (some for the first time ever!) And I can't think of two better people to share their creations than them. I hope you enjoy this book, and let it inspire you. Not just to make the recipes yourself at home, but to come to New York and try the street food!

INTRODUCTION

Our mothers did not look kindly on street food. A second-generation New Yorker and a thirteenth-generation New Englander, they couldn't have had more different life experiences, but their reaction to New York City cart food? The same.

"Where do they wash their hands?"

"They touch the money *and* your food."

"No, you can't have a pretzel. I said *no* pretzel. That's it, we're leaving!"

Fast-forward a couple of decades to two young (and broke) junior editors who bonded over a love of adventurous eating on the cheap. Tired of over-priced deli salads and sad excuses for sandwiches, we began venturing out for the sort of lunches that would give our mothers heart failure. Kati rolls from the Biryani Cart, falafel from Moshe's, lamb over rice from Kwik Meal.

Delighted by the new cuisines we discovered and emboldened by our failure to catch the plague—or any of the other maladies we'd been cautioned against—soon we were breaking the first commandment of street food eating: *Thou shalt not eat fish from a cart.* Perfectly crispy, golden fried fish proved to be a gateway into raw fish. Before long we were looking forward to ceviche Saturdays at the Red Hook Ball Fields (*shhhh*, don't tell Mom).

In time, we became regulars at several carts around midtown, and through the friendships we formed with the owners, we began to hear the stories behind the food—tales of the good (and the bad) old days in the city. Every plate of chicken over rice came with a story.

In recent years trendy food trucks selling everything from Korean tacos to crème brûlée have

captured the popular imagination, but street vending is far from new in New York City. Numerous waves of immigrants have found the promise of a better life in street vending, bringing a bit of the old country to the New World.

Prior to the Civil War, Irish women known as "Apple Marys" hawked apples in the Financial District, while Hot Corn Girls sold roasted corn on streets of the infamous Five Points alongside sweet cake vendors and fruit peddlers. As the German, Italian, and Jewish populations swelled, they brought sausages, vegetables, ice cream, bread, and

smoked fish, among other delicacies. Lower East Side stalwarts Russ & Daughters, Guss' Pickles, and Yonah Schimmel Knish Bakery all had their beginnings in pushcart vending. In more recent years, Latin vendors of all stripes have introduced pan-American fare from icy cold *horchata*, sweet fried plantains with *queso* and *crema*, and mammoth chorizo *huaraches*, while Egyptian and Afghanis have found opportunity in selling fiery hot sauce–doused halal chicken and lamb pitas and platters to hungry cabbies and office dwellers alike.

A city of old and new immigrants, New York offers unparalleled dining diversity. Where else in the world can you find Korean, Jamaican, Austrian, Taiwanese, Greek, Israeli, Belgian, Indian, Bangladeshi, Trinidadian-Pakistani, Moroccan, and Mexican street food within a ten block radius? The city streets abound with deliciousness that is begging to be explored. There's street food for every budget and for eaters bold and timid alike (the aforementioned moms are even beginning to come around on a case-by-case basis).

As we swapped stories with vendors, one thing became clear: behind every cart and every truck were the hopes and dreams of a fellow New Yorker by birth or by choice. With this collection of stories and recipes, we hope to honor the tireless vendors who came before and those who rise each day before the sun to feed the soul of the city one meal at a time.

—SIOBHAN & ALEXANDRA

T he history of street food in New York City is a tapestry woven from the threads of the immigrant experience. Street vending has been a part of the city since at least 1691, when the first regulations on sidewalk vending hit the books. And in the intervening centuries, it's followed a cyclical pattern of expansion and contraction as allowed by law.

In the earliest days, street food was confined to whole foods like fruits and vegetables as well as other groceries items, rather than meals-on-the-go. Today's carts and trucks trace their roots to the mid- nineteenth century and the Hot Corn Girls, barefoot and starving teenagers from the city's immigrant tenement slums who sold roasted hot corn to augment their families' meager incomes. These young girls unknowingly started a tradition that new immigrants follow to this day, using food vending as a means to make a living and a stepping stone to success.

New York's food vendors often came from marginalized populations. When the city grew flush with Irish immigrants fleeing the Great Famine, many of the women turned to selling apples in the bustling Financial District, earning the nickname of "Apple Marys." New York's two most iconic street foods, the hot dog and the pretzel, were introduced by German immigrants. In 1871 Charles Feltman put a sausage on a bun in Brooklyn and the hot dog was born. Pretzels were originally sold on sticks or out of baskets by poor German women. Vending has even made its mark on the streets themselves—modern day Pearl Street in downtown Manhattan takes its name from bivalve refuse left behind by carts hawking oysters fresh from New York Harbor.

As the city's population swelled and sprawled, workers could no longer count on returning home during their lunch hour. This difficulty was especially prevalent among the financiers and newspaper writers, who needed quick, convenient lunch spots. Street food vendors popped up along "Newspaper Row" (the modern Park Row) and Wall Street, eager to cater to this new market. On Wall Street, three deluxe food stands appeared across from Jay Cooke & Company, then one of the biggest banks in America. By 1890, the first of Manhattan's now ubiquitous hot dog carts had begun to vend on Downtown's Frankfort Street by a man named Louis Haims. He would go on to sell from a window in the now-demolished World Building on Park Row.

In the hot summer months, when New York's sweltering masses sought a cool, refreshing treat, they bought ice cream on the city streets. The late

"A vendor at an accustomed spot becomes a familiar neighborhood asset, part of the community fabric."

—NEW YORK CITY 1991 TASK FORCE ON GENERAL VENDORS

19th century peddlers' calls were a harbinger of today's noisy ice cream trucks. Vendors in this era sold shallow glasses of ice cream known as penny licks. Customers would lick their portion clean then the vendors reused glasses after a quick water wash. Another "cooling" culinary innovation that can be traced back to pushcart vendors is the ice cream sandwich. One genius Bowery peddler began selling these frozen treats for a penny in 1899, and they quickly became a street food trend.

By the turn of the twentieth century, the street food options reflected the diversity of the expanding city and streets in the immigrant enclaves of the Lower East and West Sides teemed with vendors peddling their offerings at daytime markets. The first of these markets began on Hester Street in 1886 with four vendors; by 1920, approximately thirty such markets were in operation. Jewish and German neighborhoods were home to carts selling homemade pickles, hot knishes and pretzels kept in special warming drawers. In an attempt to control and profit from the burgeoning surge of vendors, the city began selling vendor licenses. In 1897 New York boasted 2,000 licensed vendors; by 1917 that number had soared to 7,000.

The street markets would continue well into the twentieth century. During the Great Depression legions of unemployed New Yorkers turned to vending to scrape by. Streets packed with carts could be found throughout Manhattan in the 1930s,

including a thriving market in East Harlem where seven hundred licensed carts selling everything from hot yams to buttons could be found along Park Avenue during the summer months. By 1934 there were 14,000 vendors and a growing movement to take the vendors—whose carts frequently created unsafe pedestrian and traffic conditions—off the streets. Mayor Fiorello La Guardia and others in power felt that street vending was chaotic and unsanitary. Mayor La Guardia sought to "abolish all itinerant peddling from the streets." La Guardia, in an effort to move the pushcarts and their customers indoors, opened nine market buildings in 1940 including the Essex Street Market which is still going strong today. The mayor went so far as to ban Good Humor ice cream carts from peddling to children in the seaside community of Rockaway Beach, Queens. With the vendors' move indoors and the number of licenses reduced to 1,200, ownership of the few outdoor, prepared-food carts slowly shifted from predominantly Jewish and Italian vendors to newer immigrant groups.

The period following World War II brought about massive changes in New York City's cultural and social dynamics. As upper- and middle-class white New Yorkers fled the metropolis for the suburbs in the post-War boom, their departure was off-set by growing populations of Puerto Ricans and African-Americans migrating to New York from the South. Despite this population shift, in this era New Yorkers no longer looked to street vendors to fulfill their increasingly global food cravings. New York street food mostly consisted of hot dogs, Danishes, and coffee; tastier meals could be found at cheap lunch counters around the city. One of the few innovations of this period came when Horn & Hardart, the company behind the automats dotting nearly every block, opened a "Mobile-Mat" in Bryant Park in the summer of 1966. Except it just served the same dishes found directly across the street at another of their automats.

However, New York City and its palate saw another rapid change when the 1965 Immigration Act opened the borders to increased immigration from Asia, southern Europe, and the Caribbean. To find success in their newfound home, the new wave of immigrants did what many generations had done before: they began selling food on the streets. Greeks opened carts selling gyros and souvlaki, grilled chicken and lamb pita sandwiches; with time, they came to own the majority of the working food carts. Their success allowed them to employ other immigrants to actually man the carts. A 1970 *New York Times* article highlighted the changing demographics of Midtown Manhattan's far west side neighborhood, Hell's Kitchen, mentioning that food carts depots on West 49th Street from Eighth to Tenth Avenue. Also, a vital street rule had emerged: do not ever compete for the same corner with other vendors from your garage. One popular street food debuted at this time were the candied peanuts now found throughout the city. Latin American cart employees began cooking peanuts in a sweet syrup right on the cart, letting the smell of

roasting nuts waft to hungry passersby.

But City Hall and the police department still weren't willing to allow street food vendors to take over the city. Vendors faced tickets, fines and court battles. The summer of 1977 saw the "Great Hot Dog War," play out when John Zervas, the "hot dog king" of Central Park, lost his five-year contract with the city. Zervas had paid $80,000 for the right to vend from sixty different locations in Central Park, but after being charged with assault by other vendors, his contract was revoked. In response, Zervas sued the city; his case ended up in State Supreme Court, where his contract was reinstated.

It wasn't just hot dogs being sold in Central Park anymore. Street food had officially upgraded. By the early 80s, vendors still congregated in areas of high demand, which as in bygone days, meant the financial centers of Downtown and Midtown, with a few areas of high concentration spread throughout Brooklyn, Queens and the Bronx. Sixth Avenue in Midtown, a stretch which remains popular today saw a demand for inexpensive meals after new construction replaced diners with plazas. Vendors gladly rolled in to provide affordable breakfasts and lunches for legions of office workers, including being able get a thick slice of quiche Lorraine for a dollar, with fresh orange juice on the side. In a May 1981 article, even *New York Times* restaurant critic Mimi Sheraton commented on the scene; she advocated picking up the Chinese Fu Manchu stew on the corner of 52nd Street and the fried ground beef kofta from the "Little Afghanistan" cart on West 43rd Street.

By 1982, Mayor Koch's Office of Operations estimated that ninety percent of the city's active food peddlers were working in Manhattan south of 59th Street. With that many vendors competing for customers, they had to find ways to be unique. It was around this time that the forerunner of now "standard" chicken over rice dish first appeared. Najib Popal, a refrigerator salesman from Afghanistan vending across from Radio City Music Hall, began grilling marinated chicken thighs, dicing them, and serving them in pitas with lettuce and tomato. On the same corner as Popal, the Egyptian vendor Said Abdelghani sold deep-fried falafel, hummus and baba ghannouj. A few blocks over, you could find a vendor hawking baked potatoes. Chinese carts selling plump pork dumplings, rich scallion pancakes, crispy traditional cookies and even tender roast duck appeared in Chinatown and on 42nd Street, vending items comparable to, and sometimes better than, restaurants occupying the same block.

Just as with Mayor La Guardia and Mayor Koch, in the late 1990s and early 2000s, Mayors Rudy Giuliani and Michael Bloomberg enacted their own vendor crackdowns. As part of his "quality of life" campaign, Mayor Giuliani enforced restrictions limiting where vendors could sell; parking options were also limited for street vendors depending on foot traffic to find customers, with the busiest areas placed off-limits. Carts came and went as licenses expired and operators moved onto other careers, but by the beginning of the 21st century, morning coffee carts, hot dogs, shish kebabs, and "chicken over rice" carts once again became the rule rather than the exception.

As in years past, many vendors are still newly-arrived immigrants, often relying on help from family and friends to maneuver the city's legal trappings. In 2002, the Urban Justice Center, a non-profit organization that provides legal representation and advocacy to various marginalized groups, started the Street Vendor Project to assist vendors with legal and financial issues, helping them understand their rights, fight unwarranted tickets and heavy fines. In 2005, the Street Vendor Project organized the inaugural Vendy Awards, a fundraiser to support vendor advocacy that has gained renown as "the Oscars of street food." What started as a small event now draws crowds in the thousands and includes awards for "Best Dessert Vendor" and "Best New Vendor," in addition to the coveted Vendy Cup.

The Vendys raised the profile of vendors, garnering the lucky finalists local and national media coverage, foodies around the city and abroad began to seek out exceptional carts, reveling in the incredibly good, incredibly cheap food that could be found if you knew where to look. Threads began popping up on sites like Chowhound.com extolling the wonders of the pan-Latin cuisine at the Red Hook soccer fields, or the outstanding lamb shoulder over rice served at the Kwik Meal cart (page 84).

Yet, no one was prepared for the late 2000s. Food trucks and carriages had existed before in and around New York, but social media would change everything for New York's vendors. As Twitter and Facebook went mainstream and the economy tanked, mobile food flourished. Food trucks and carts could tweet their hours and locations. They were no longer chained to a consistent spot to attract customers and could make use of their wheels, hitting different neighborhoods and cultivating a wider customer base. Specialized trucks and carts serving everything from Belgian waffles and artisanal grilled cheese sandwiches, to schnitzel and seasonal gelato, could find and maintain a following via the internet. Websites jumped on the trend, feeding massive and loyal followings with reviews of new vendors as soon as they hit the streets. While the price point for some of the fancier street food options nudged up considerably, it was still cheaper than dinner out at a sit-down establishment—and for economizing New Yorkers, street food felt like an affordable indulgence.

Despite the growth in street food options the future for New York's food vendors is uncertain. Vending remains highly regulated, with recent city administrations cherry-picking which regulations they want to enforce and when. The number of licenses for vending is still capped at 1983 levels and the waiting list to get a license from the city is years, perhaps decades, long. Without the option of gaining a license from the city, new vendors must seek out current license holders and "rent" their license on the black market.

Notwithstanding the challenges, there is hope.

Vendor run associations like the New York City Food Truck Association have formed to promote and advocate for members to the city government and general public. A number of early-to-market new-wave food trucks like Van Leeuwen Ice Cream (page 180), Treats Truck (page 123), Schnitzel and Things (page 199), and Mexicue (page 194) expanded their presence with brick and mortar locations that complement their trucks, and vice versa. While public support for food trucks is strong, with the high cost of vending and long hours that the business demands, only time will tell which of today's vendors will still be around to serve the next generation of street food enthusiasts.

TEN QUESTIONS WITH STREET VENDOR PROJECT FOUNDER AND DIRECTOR, SEAN BASINSKI

1) What inspired you to start the Street Vendor Project?

I was inspired by vendors I met during the summer of 1998, when I sold burritos from a cart in Midtown Manhattan. Mayor Giuliani tried to kick vendors off hundreds of streets, and we held a big march down Broadway. After that, I was lucky enough to go to law school, where I learned what role lawyers can play in social justice movements.

2) How many food vendors belong to SVP?

We currently have 1,500 members, about half of whom sell food. Many others come to the meetings we hold in our office and around the city. Most of our vendors sell typical NYC street fare like hot dogs and roasted peanuts, but we have many members who could be five-star chefs.

3) How is the group run?

By our Leadership Board, which is elected every year from our general membership. They are all experienced vendors who are respected in their communities. The board makes the big decisions and does a lot of the organizing work. We also have a great staff of four people who keep tabs on our day-to-day operations.

4) How has vending changed in the time you've been heading up the SVP?

The perception of vending has changed, at least in certain circles. Vending has become trendy. But on the street, I don't think much has changed. Vendors are still mostly immigrants who work hard every day, in spite of great obstacles, and provide a great benefit to our city. It's been that way for nearly 200 years.

5) What issues do vendors most commonly face?

They face many challenges that are inherent to vending, like bad weather and pollution and the physical demands of standing on your feet all day. In terms of policy, vendors have a very hard time getting licenses, finding legal places to vend, and avoiding harassment from the police and health inspectors. They come to our office every day with these issues.

6) What have been the biggest achievements for the Street Vendor Project?

I think we have been successful at raising awareness, with New York policy-makers, that vendors are an important population that can and will no longer be ignored. We have forced the city to provide legal notice to vendors before changing the rules, and to give them translators when they go to court. But our biggest achievement is to survive for ten years, and still be growing and making a difference every day.

7) How is the Street Vendor Project different from other vendor associations?

We have been around a lot longer than other vending organizations in the United States, so we are somewhat bigger and more experienced. There are vendor associations getting started in cities all across the country, and we would like to help them, based on what we have learned. Compared to vendor associations in parts of Asia, Africa, and Latin America, we are tiny.

8) How did you come up with the idea for the Vendy Awards?

One of my jobs is to raise money to keep SVP running. We were planning our first fundraiser, in 2005. We knew that we would have vendors there, cooking food. The Food Channel was already big, and shows like *Top Chef* were already proving that food competitions are a big draw. So it did not take a genius to put those ideas together. One of our interns came up with the name.

9) How have the Vendy Awards changed over the years?

The New York event has gotten bigger, and we've expanded to Los Angeles and Philadelphia. We have many more categories. And corporate sponsors. But the basic format is the same. And the basic message is the same: we walk past these people every day, and don't think twice—let's take one day to honor them.

10) What's the best part about running the Street Vendor Project?

I am part of a big, close-knit community. And I have many friends. Wherever I go, I run into our members. This makes New York City feel like a very small town. And it never fails to impress my parents when they come to visit.

For more information on the Street Vendor Project, visit streetvendor.org

KELVIN™ NATURAL SLUSH CO.

On blazing hot summer days, a big blue oasis can be found parked in the Flatiron District. Named for the thermodynamic scale that expresses absolute cold, Kelvin Natural Slush Co.'s industrial-grade slush machines churn out cups of frosty goodness in spicy ginger, puckery citrus, and a mellow mixture of green and black tea. The lightly sweetened base slushes are then customized with a rotating menu of mix-ins—fresh chopped mint and basil, and seasonal fresh fruit purées including white peach, guava, and caramelized pineapple. All the brain-freeze bliss you remember from childhood (sans the high-fructose corn syrup and tongue-tinting Red 40 dye).

Owner Alex Rein loved slushes and slurpees as a kid, but at a certain point he stopped drinking the sugar-laden, truck-stop staples. "The thing is slushes can be really refreshing. They aren't as heavy as a milkshake. . . . I wanted to offer a lighter, more grown-up version." He began dreaming of a more sophisticated, crave-worthy slush while working as a corporate attorney, brewing up batches of tea and ginger beer in his apartment kitchen then freezing and blending them to create the recipes that ultimately became their three signature drink bases.

With less than two months of street experience, Kelvin Slush was the decided dark horse at the 2010 Vendys against a field that included The Big Gay Ice Cream Truck (page 184) and The Dessert-Truck (page 188)—both established vendors with massive followings. The scorching late September heat on the day of the awards made for ideal conditions to showcase their chilly treats and when the last vote was counted, the people had spoken. The newbies from Kelvin took home the coveted Dessert Vendy title and cemented their reputation in the foodie community as a summer-must.

With their fan base secured, it wasn't long before Kelvin took the next step in sophisticated slushie-dom: frozen cocktails. While New York's open container laws prevent Kelvin from bringing boozy slushes to the streets, Alex's business partner, Zack Silverman started noticing some rogue behavior from their customers "People would show up at our truck with flasks and mini-bottles all the time to make their own, what we call, 'prohibition style' slush on the street." In 2012 they launched a restaurant and bar partnership program working with select restaurants and bars to offer Kelvin "frozen cocktails." Now you can get boozy slushes at some of the coolest spots around the city or make your own Kelvin-style cocktail from the comfort of your own home.

| GF V

FROZEN AND STORMY
Adapted from Alex Rein's recipe

Traditional Dark and Stormy® cocktails while the call for ginger beer, this frozen rendition uses a home-brewed, spiced syrup. Kelvin Slush owner Alex Rein recommends splurging on a top-shelf dark rum like Gosling's Black Seal® Bermuda Black Rum. This drink gets its rich molassesy-flavor from cane sugar, an unrefined sugar. If you can't find cane sugar or an equivalent like *panela*, use dark brown sugar.

"When I'm on the truck I'll have at least one slush a day. It's hard to resist when you have the machines right there."

—ALEX REIN

YIELD: SERVES 4 TO 6

½ cup cane sugar like *panela* or dark brown sugar

1 piece (approximately 4 inches long) fresh ginger, peeled and roughly chopped into approximately ½ x ¼–inch pieces

8 cloves

1 star anise

½ cup dark rum

⅓ cup fresh lemon juice (about 2 lemons)

8 cups ice

In a small saucepan bring ½ cup water to a low simmer over medium heat. Add the sugar and stir until it dissolves. Add the chopped ginger, cloves, and star anise. Remove from heat and steep uncovered for 25 minutes. Strain syrup mixture into a small bowl or airtight container, squeezing out as much liquid as possible from the ginger, cover and chill the syrup in the refrigerator for at least 20 minutes.

Add the spiced ginger syrup, rum, lemon juice, and ice to a blender. Blend until smooth. Serve in lowball glasses.

FROZEN LEMON MINT JULEP

Adapted from Alex Rein's recipe

This bright and light julep is perfect for Derby Day or any summer day. The recipe will work well with your favorite bourbon. Kelvin Slush owner Alex Rein personally favors Knob Creek®.

....

YIELD: SERVES 4 TO 6

½ cup granulated sugar

½ fresh lemon, sliced as thick rounds

⅔ cup fresh mint leaves (about 40 leaves), divided, plus additional for garnish, if desired

½ cup bourbon

⅓ cup fresh lemon juice (about 2 lemons)

8 cups ice

In a small saucepan, bring ½ cup water to a low simmer over medium heat. Add the sugar and stir until dissolved, about 2 to 3 minutes.

Remove mixture from heat and add the sliced lemons (do not squeeze lemon juice) and 30 mint leaves. Steep mixture uncovered for 10 minutes.

Strain into a small bowl or airtight container (squeeze out as much liquid as possible from the lemon and mint). Cover and chill strained syrup in the refrigerator for at least 20 minutes.

Add the lemon mint simple syrup and remaining mint leaves to blender. Blend until mint is finely chopped.

Add the bourbon, lemon juice, and ice to blender. Blend until smooth. Serve in lowball glasses garnished with fresh mint leaves, if desired.

In 2004 when Mario Batali opened the Gelōtō Cart, a mobile, gelato-only offshoot of his popular pizzeria, OTTO, the first specialty dessert trucks were several years off, and buying high-end desserts from a cart was unheard of in New York. And, as hard as it might be to believe, there were few places selling authentic Italian gelato in the city at the time. Fast-forward a decade, and gelato has moved from the specialty shop to the grocery case as the American appetite for ice cream's luxe Italian cousin has grown. While the options for gelato-on-the-go have multiplied, the Gelōtō cart remains a warm-weather gem for dessert hunters and gatherers in Greenwich Village.

The setup is decidedly old school. From late spring to mid-fall the red, yellow, and green painted pushcart commutes just a couple blocks from its specially made wee garage at the mothership, Batali's casual Neapolitan pizza eatery where pastry chef and gelato master extraordinaire, Meredith Kurtzman churns out small batches of heaven.

Seasonal produce and top-notch ingredients drive the dessert program at OTTO. The crown gem of the rotating menu is the olive oil gelato, an earthy yet intensely buttery and smooth concoction made with Sicilian olive oil that's been on the menu since they first opened their doors. While Americans love their mix-ins—from candy to nuts to cookie pieces—Meredith, for the most part, keeps things traditional. "I've tried to steer clear of putting *stuff* in my gelato, but it seems to be popular. . . . Honestly I like the idea of doing simple things, and I *love* working with fruit."

Several years before food carts and trucks became trendy, Batali wanted to create an authentic street gelato experience. "It was Mario's idea when he opened the place," says Meredith. Initially parked on the northwest corner of Washington Square Park, the cart found early success. "It was a unique product," Meredith explains. But over the years the Gelōtō Cart has faced its fair share of challenges, especially with all the red tape that comes along with permitting for vendors. "I don't think anyone who goes into it knows what they're getting into," sighs Meredith. Since the cart opened, Washington Square Park has undergone an ambitious and protracted renovation that has kept various areas of the park fenced off to foot traffic for long stretches of time. Even without the construction, the cart's previous locale on the northwest corner was a sleepy spot. In 2012, the cart moved to the northeast cor-

"From the get-go, I wanted to make something really delicious—that's why I went into the food business. My main thing is I want to make delicious food." —MEREDITH KURTZMAN

ner, where Waverly Place becomes Washington Square North and University Place becomes Washington Square East, a far livelier thoroughfare, regularly traversed by thousands of NYU students making their way to and from classes.

Meredith's passion for ice cream was born in her childhood: "I grew up chasing the Good Humor Man," she says with a laugh. But her path to the kitchen wasn't a traditional one. Before donning chef's whites, she spent years as a freelance textile designer specializing in silk-screen painting. "With the advent of computer-aided design, the work disappeared, and I was bored with it anyway.

I'd always been interested in food and cooking, and started volunteering as a kitchen assistant at a local cooking school," Meredith says. An International Association of Culinary Professionals (IACP) scholarship brought her to the New York Restaurant School for pastry arts. Meredith was working as the pastry chef at Esca when Batali tapped her to develop the gelato program for the not-yet-opened OTTO, where she's since created a name for herself with inventive flavors from the likes of sweet-corn gelato to avocado gelato to concord grape sorbetto with fennel. "Gelato has less overrun than ice cream. That is, it takes on less air [volume], when it is churned," Meredith explains. The end product is denser than ice cream, making each bite a more intense flavor experience.

Like the restaurant, the cart has a rotating menu of flavors. "In an ideal world, having a cart where you really could assemble things would be great. The trouble in New York is that people are impatient, and it takes time." Due to space limitations, they can only offer four or five flavors at a time from the cart, from which they sell both small and large servings for prices that are less than at the restaurant. "It's an expensive product, and when people eat street food they don't necessarily want to spend $8 on gelato. So we lowered it to $4 and $7." For years the cart didn't serve the famous olive oil gelato, but recently Meredith relented, "The thing I used to say is, *I want people to taste good gelato in the park, but eventually I want to lure them into the restaurant.* This year I said, *the hell with it. Give the people what they want.*"

BANANA TARTUFO
(BANANA GELATO COVERED WITH CARAMELIZED WHITE CHOCOLATE)
Adapted from Meredith Kurtzman's recipe

Also known as a *bomba*, *tartufo* is a ball of ice cream covered in a crunchy chocolate shell. When directly translated from Italian, *tartufo* means *truffle*, and as far as desserts go, it's about as close as Italians get to the Good Humor Man. Meredith's plays with convention by studding her tartufo with peanuts and chocolate cookies and subbing caramelized white chocolate for regular chocolate in this sweet and salty treat. While the cart version of this treat includes homemade sugared peanuts and brownie cookie crumbles, you can simplify preparation by substituting ½ cup dark chocolate chips and ½ cup salted peanuts.

YIELD: 4 TO 6

FOR THE GELATO:

7 egg yolks

¼ cup granulated sugar, divided

¾ cup nonfat dry milk powder

2 cups whole milk

½ cup heavy cream

½ cup sweetened condensed milk

¾ teaspoon salt

2 very ripe bananas

FOR THE TARTUFI:

1 cup Sugared Peanuts (page 30)

1 cup Brownie Cookie crumbles (page 31)

1½ cups Caramelized White Chocolate Glaze (page 29)

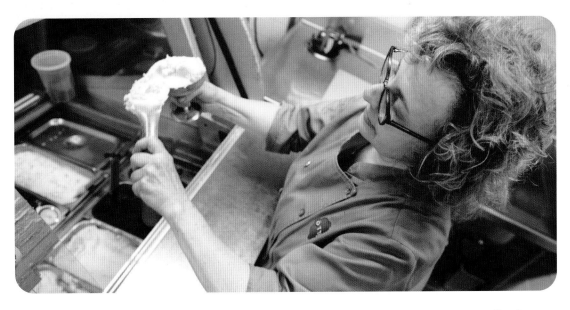

Whisk together the egg yolks, 2 tablespoons sugar, milk powder and cream in a large heat-proof bowl. Set aside.

In a medium saucepan warm the whole milk and the rest of the sugar over medium heat, stirring occasionally to dissolve the sugar. When tiny bubbles begin to form around the edge of the pan, remove mixture from heat.

While whisking constantly, temper eggs with the hot milk mixture, adding a tablespoon of hot liquid at a time. Return to medium heat, stirring constantly. When steam starts to rise in pot, immediately strain into a heatproof bowl. Whisk in the condensed milk and salt. Place bowl over an ice bath (see page 153 for instructions) and whisk to cool mixture to room temperature. Chill covered in refrigerator for 2 to 3 hours.

Thoroughly mash bananas and blend into chilled gelato mixture. Strain gelato to remove any banana solids and churn in an electric ice cream maker according to the manufacturer's directions. Transfer gelato into an airtight container and place in the freezer for 1 to 2 hours, or until gelato has set. Using a large ice cream scoop, form 6 large round balls of gelato and place in ramekins or serving dishes. Chill uncovered in freezer until hardened in freezer, about 1 to 2 hours, or until hardened.

Alternately, you can form the gelato balls and place in a parchment-lined jelly roll pan or rimmed baking sheet to freeze then just before serving use a metal square spatula to remove gelato balls from pan and place into serving dishes or cups.

TO ASSEMBLE TARTUFI:

Remove gelato balls from freezer and stud with Sugared Peanuts (page 30) and crumbled Brownie Cookies (page 31) or ½ cup salted peanuts and ½ cup semisweet chocolate chips.

Quickly ladle cooled Caramelized White Chocolate Glaze (page 29) over gelato; it will harden in a minute.

Serve immediately or store covered in freezer for up to a few hours before serving.

CARAMELIZED WHITE CHOCOLATE GLAZE

Adapted from Meredith Kurtzman's recipe

White chocolate lacks the cocoa solids found in milk and dark chocolate, and the flavor and workability can vary greatly between brands. For this recipe, Meredith always uses Valrhona® white chocolate fèves (oval-shaped pieces), which are ideal for melting. The secret to caramelizing white chocolate is to use a spatula to constantly move the chocolate around in the oven so it doesn't get the chance to burn. When you pour the white chocolate mixture over the ice cream, it will harden to form a crunchy shell.

....

YIELD: ABOUT 1½ CUPS GLAZE

10 ounces white chocolate fèves, or coarsely
    chopped pieces
⅓ cup coconut oil

TO CARAMELIZE CHOCOLATE:

Move oven rack to center position and preheat the oven to 300°F.

Spread fèves or chopped chocolate, on ½ sheet pan covered with a silicon baking mat.

Melt the chocolate for 5 minutes, opening the oven and pulling out the rack to stir occasionally with a heat-resistant spatula.

Continue to check and stir chocolate in 3-minute increments, until the chocolate has completely melted and is light tan in color.

Remove the chocolate from the oven and scrape into a bowl.

Whisk in the coconut oil. Pour mixture through a fine sieve set over a clean medium-sized bowl to strain out any sediment. Whisk the strained mixture until it reaches room temperature, about 3 to 5 minutes. Once mixture reaches room temperature you can use it to glaze gelato balls. Cover and store leftover glaze for up to 2 days in a heat-resistant container. Reheat glaze by microwaving on medium heat in 30-second bursts, stirring after each until glaze has returned to liquid form and has reached room temperature.

SUGARED PEANUTS
Adapted from Meredith Kurtzman's recipe

Candied nuts are a classic New York street food. At Mario Batali's Gelōttō Cart they use them for their Banana Tartufo (page 27), but you might want to make extra for snacking.

YIELD: 1 CUP

¼ cup light corn syrup

1 tablespoon dark brown sugar, firmly packed

¼ teaspoon salt

1 cup peanut halves

Move oven rack to center position and preheat the oven to 350°F.

In a large metal bowl whisk together corn syrup, brown sugar, and salt. Add peanuts and stir to coat with syrup.

Spread nuts out onto a small sheet pan lined with a silicon baking mat or parchment paper.

Bake for 25 to 30 minutes or until peanuts are a warm brown color. Remove from oven and using a greased offset spatula immediately scrape peanuts onto a cool metal or glass surface. Use a fork to poke peanuts apart, allowing them to separate and cool, about 30 minutes. Once peanuts are no longer too hot to handle, break up any remaining peanut clumps and store covered for up to 5 days.

BROWNIE COOKIES

Adapted from Meredith Kurtzman's recipe

These dark chocolate cookies make an appearance as cookie crumble pieces on the Banana Tartufo (page 27) at Mario Batali's Gelōttō cart. Intensely chocolatey and oh, so soft, it seems almost sinful to sacrifice them to crumbling. We won't tell if you snag one for munching.

....

YIELD: 2 DOZEN COOKIES

¼ cup all-purpose flour

¼ teaspoon baking powder

pinch of kosher salt

5 ounces bittersweet chocolate, coarsely
    chopped

2 ounces unsweetened chocolate, coarsely
    chopped

3 tablespoons unsalted butter, cut into
    ½ tablespoon pieces

2 large eggs

⅔ cup granulated sugar

1 teaspoon vanilla extract

Move oven rack to center position and preheat the oven to 350°F.

In a medium bowl, whisk together flour, baking powder, and salt. Set aside.

Combine chocolates and butter in a microwave-safe bowl. Cover with waxed paper and microwave on high for 30 seconds. Stir and if the chocolate isn't completely melted, cover, and microwave in 10-second bursts, stirring in between until chocolate and butter are completely melted. Let cool, about 15 minutes.

Add eggs and sugar to the bowl of an electric stand mixer and using the whisk attachment, beat until frothy. Add vanilla extract, and beat until soft peaks form.

Fold beaten eggs into cooled chocolate. Gently fold flour mixture into chocolate mixture until batter is thoroughly combined.

Stir to cool mixture slightly and using a tablespoon or 1-inch ice cream scoop, portion out cookies on a sheet pan lined with a silicon mat or parchment paper sheet pan, spacing the cookies approximately 2 inches apart. Allow shaped cookies to dry out for 5 minutes before baking.

Bake for 8 to 10 minutes, interior of cookie should be slightly soft. Cool on pan for 2 minutes then transfer to a wire rack to cool completely. Store in an airtight container for up to 3 days.

Cousins Danny Che, David Sat, and Kenneth Sa are no strangers to working together. They've been doing it their whole lives at Deluxe Food Market, an enormous Chinatown grocery and butcher shop owned by all three of their dads. "It's our family's market," says Danny. "I've worked there since I was nine or ten years old . . . during the summer my dad would bring me out to work, and I'd do anything he told me to."

The seeds of Wooly's Ice were planted when Danny and David studied abroad in Beijing in 2009 and traveled throughout Asia before returning home. On a trip to Taiwan they discovered *xua hua bing*, which translates roughly to "snow flower ice." Unlike Hawaiian shave ice or Taiwanese *bao bing*, the flavoring in *xua hua bing* is frozen into the ice, instead of just poured on top as a syrup. "The ice was flavored already, so that was a huge difference and that blew my mind." In Taiwan, *xua hua bing* is served family style, and when Danny, David, and a few friends got their massive plate of ice piled high with toppings and drenched in syrup, they were convinced they'd never be able to finish it—until they started eating and had to order a second one in rapid succession, "It was that good. People were, like, literally fighting for the last spoonful."

A year later, after Danny and David had returned home, they learned that Ice Monster, the place where they discovered *xua hua bing* in Taiwan, had shut down. "When I read the article I e-mailed it to my cousin, joking, we should start this thing," Danny says. "And he was like, *yeah, haha*." But the more Danny played with the idea, the more serious he became about it. *What's the worst that can happen if I fail?* he thought. "I'm still young. I have nothing to lose," Danny says. Soon David was on board, too.

It took a whole year of recipe development, which involved "eating a lot, a lot of ice" to get a product that they were proud of. With limited capital to start their business, they decided to jump on the mobile food trend, opting for a cart rather than a more costly food truck. Danny and David realized they would need more help, so they brought another cousin, Kenneth Sa, on board. All three had grown up working together at the family store, so it was a natural fit.

When it came time to name their business, Danny wanted "something that doesn't really mean anything. Something really abstract." He heard David's sister call him Wooly. Though the name was intended to be nonsensical, it's oddly fitting "it's like Wooly Mammoth, icy, Ice Age, and also the texture is kind of Woolyish," Danny says.

The cousins launched the Wooly's Ice cart in the summer of 2011 with two flavors: "original" and green tea. The original flavor is dairy-based, lightly sweetened, and very similar to what they had in Taiwan. Their light and fluffy snow-like ices come in two sizes: "the Wooly" and "the Mammoth" (you can guess which one is the bigger of the two). In addition to their ices, they also developed a menu of syrups and fresh fruit toppings, as opposed to the canned, syrupy stuff they found in Taiwan. For those who want to indulge, they serve brownie bites and *mochi*, sweet little balls of glutinous rice. Twitter followers get exclusive alerts

"It's the best job I've ever had. And it is the toughest job I've ever had. It's a grueling day just standing outside in the heat, but even then it's really fulfilling, too." —DANNY CHE

about their "secret menu," which changes daily and might include other ice flavors, like their mango or strawberry, as well as secret toppings.

Setting up the cart wasn't without challenges. "When we got into the business, we thought 'Oh my God, this is going to be the next Pinkberry,'" says Danny. "This is going to be the easiest thing. We'll just put it out there, and everybody is going to come. No." Their first location at City Hall had a busy lunch crowd, but was a ghost town after 3:00 p.m. They tried other spots with some success, but hadn't anticipated the challenge of getting people to try a new food, no matter how good it was. "Just breaking into the food scene is really hard," Danny admits.

Slowly but surely, the buzz started growing and growing. Two months after opening, they garnered a coveted Dessert Vendy nomination. All of their cousins pitched in on a hot Saturday in late September of 2011 as they served up thousands of ices to attendees at the annual Vendy Awards. The crowd (and the judges) fell in love with their light and refreshing ices, which proved the perfect antidote to the late summer heat. "It's not easy doing your own thing, but it's very fulfilling because you see your business growing before your very eyes. Like when we won the Vendy, it was like, *Oh my God*. It was like the best thing that ever happened to me."

With major award recognition and a season's worth of experience under their belts, they found a new home on the pier at the South Street Seaport in the spring of 2012. They serve tourists and locals there seven days a week from noon until 7:00 p.m. from April through October. "My dad's worked seven days a week for the past thirty years. Every single day. It's amazing to have a great role model that's so hardworking. When I'm working hard and I'm really tired, I'm like, *what about my dad, he's been working twice as hard as me for the past thirty years, so shut up and put your head down*." And when Danny, David, and Kenneth put their heads down and get to work, they're unstoppable.

GREEN TEA ICE

Adapted from Danny Che's recipe

When Wooly's Ice took home the 2011 Dessert Vendy Award, one of their special combos for the day was "The Green Man," featuring their signature green tea ice with chopped mango, mochi pieces, and Sea Salt Leche (page 37). You can use any type of green tea for this recipe. The guys at Wooly's prefer the green tea from Ten Ren (www.tenren.com) . For those who love a stronger and earthier flavor, try this recipe with matcha. The Wooly's crew has a heavy-duty ice shaver that gives their ices the consistency of light, soft snow. For at-home cooks, they recommend preparing the recipe granita-style which requires only a fork, patience and a watchful eye. You can customize this dessert to match your sweet tooth adding more (or less) sweetened condensed milk, if desired.

YIELD: SERVES 6

6 green tea bags
6 tablespoons to ½ cup sweetened
  condensed milk
Sea Salt Leche (page 37), for serving

In a large bowl, brew 6 cups of your favorite green tea. If you are using tea leaves, be sure to strain out all tea leaves after brewing.

Stir in the desired amount of sweetened condensed milk. Stir to blend mixture well.

Pour into a 8 x 8 glass baking dish, cover and let freeze for 30 minutes. Remove the pan from the freezer and use your fork to breakup any ice that has formed and stir it back in. Continue this process every 20 minutes for about 2 to 3 hours or until all of the liquid has crystalized—the more frequently you scrape and stir the ice, the finer your crystals will be. Just before serving vigorously scrape the ice and serve topped with Sea Salt Leche (page 37).

STRAWBERRY ICE

Adapted from Danny Che's recipe

Fresh, sweet, and summery, this ice is all about the strawberries you use, so you'll want to make sure your berries are at peak ripeness. Serve topped with Sea Salt Leche (page 37) and sliced strawberries, if desired.

YIELD: SERVES 6

½ pound fresh strawberries

5 tablespoons simple syrup (recipe follows)

Sea Salt Leche (page 37), for serving

Place strawberries in a food processor and purée. Transfer strawberries to a large bowl and add simple syrup along with 5 cups water.

Stir to blend mixture well.

Pour into a 8 x 8 glass baking dish, cover and let freeze for 30 minutes. Remove the pan from the freezer and use your fork to breakup any ice that has formed and stir it back in. Continue this process every 20 minutes for about 2 to 3 hours or until all of the liquid has crystalized—the more frequently you scrape and stir the ice, the finer your crystals will be. Just before serving vigorously scrape the ice and serve topped with Sea Salt Leche (page 37).

SIMPLE SYRUP

Simple syrup can be used to add sweetness to drinks like coffee, tea, or cocktails.

YIELD: MAKES ABOUT 1½ CUPS

1 cup sugar

In a small saucepan over medium heat, add the sugar to 1 cup water, and stir until dissolved, about 1 to 2 minutes. Increase heat to medium-high, bring to a boil, then reduce the heat to low and simmer until mixture has reduced to a slightly thick syrup, about 20 minutes. Store in the refrigerator in a sterilized glass jar or bottle for up to 2 weeks.

SEA SALT LECHE SYRUP

Adapted from Danny Che's recipe

Salty and sweet, this syrup is great on shave ice, and the leftovers also work well over ice cream or stirred into coffee.

YIELD: APPROXIMATELY 1 CUP SYRUP

1 cup sweetened condensed milk
2 tablespoons evaporated milk
1 teaspoon sea salt

Whisk all ingredients together to mix well. Pour into a squeeze bottle for serving. Drizzle over ice just before serving. Store covered in the refrigerator for up to a week.

When Taiwanese-born Doris Yau took over A-Pou's Taste in January 2011, she lacked both an extensive culinary background and any experience running a food cart. The petite woman, who reminds you of a friend's grandmother, had been recently forced to leave her career in the fashion industry due to illness and didn't "want to just stay home and do nothing. I always wanted to have a business in the Chinese food truck for a long time because before all I saw on the streets [was] hot dog, pretzel, nothing interesting." With her health on the mend, she answered a newspaper advertisement put out by A-Pou's former owner, Wen Pin, when he decided to sell the cart in order to focus on his new restaurant. Mr. Pin and A-Pou's Taste had already gained citywide attention when it was nominated to the 2010 Vendy Awards. This meant Doris knew the cart's good reputation would now be lying on her shoulders. She bought the carts—the original located in a plaza at Broadway and Liberty Street downtown and another located in Astor Place—and relied on the cooking skills she had acquired throughout her life when making traditional Asian meals. Doris kept the cart's menu intact from the four types of dumplings—beef, pork, chicken, and vegetable—to the "Chinese Spaghetti" aka lo mein. The only change was the addition of refreshing, tapioca-pearled bubble tea—a milky drink found throughout New York City's more Asian neighborhoods.

But taking over a well-established cart wasn't as easy as just learning the recipes. During that first year, various vendors, including Doris, had to deal with the Occupy Wall Street protests in Zuccotti Park—directly across the street from Liberty and Broadway. Thankfully, the protest never jumped the street to her plaza, but most of the Occupiers never thought to support their fellow "99%ers" by buying from the slew of carts found there. Despite the protestors and police presence, her regular customers continued frequenting the cart for lunch. "The employees that [were] stuck working there, it [didn't] bother them at all." Other beginning hassles included a few hot dog vendors who tried to intimidate Doris and her workers. While trying a new spot in Midtown on East 55th Street and Lexington Avenue, another vendor approached her cart stating

that it was his spot and began threatening her workers, "I don't really want to fight. I really don't want to argue." She took the cart elsewhere. Yet, there are times when the vendors look out for each other. During the colder months, she's known to give tea to neighboring vendors without shelter from the elements, especially when it's a newly-arrived immigrant simply manning the cart for work. At her downtown spot where a cluster of carts can be found, "we are like a family, very friendly." The other, mostly male, vendors are protective of her, helping her out whenever she's in need of a hand.

Within her successful first year, Doris expanded A-Pou's Taste to another cart on West 72nd Street and Broadway on the Upper West Side, where business is very different from the other two carts. Downtown workers want boxes quickly filled with an assortment of the dumplings—"they want to eat everything" she'll tell you with a laugh—whereas, uptown, they buy in bulk and typically want each kind in its own separate container. But like the other two carts, many of her customers are frequent visitors, including one who has to pick up dumplings for her son on a regular basis as his pre-dinner snack. Doris attributes her base of frequent customers to the fresh ingredients in the daily-made dumplings and her refusal to use MSG or other unnatural ingredients. "We try to give them healthy and good stuff." After all, she, herself, isn't a fan of greasy, processed foods, so why would she sell that to her customers? In a city where ritzy dumplings can cost you well over a dollar apiece, getting a box of ten fresh classic pan-fried Asian dumplings for $8 outside of the confines of Chinatown isn't just a treat—it's a bargain.

"I'm really proud of my own process. I'm really proud of our food, we serve really healthy and great stuff." —DORIS YAU

JAPANESE VEGETABLE DUMPLINGS

Adapted from Doris Yau's recipe

The trick to recreating Doris's dumplings is to roll out the wonton wrappers thinner than you buy them, and don't seal them with too much water. You can pack the dumpling filling in bit to keep them from unwrapping in the pan, but don't move them too much while they're cooking.

YIELD: ABOUT 48 DUMPLINGS

6 ounces dried shitake mushrooms

2 ears of corn, cut in half

3 large carrots, peeled

5 large cabbage leaves

1/3 cup teriyaki ginger sauce

1 teaspoon ground white pepper

1 teaspoon salt

48 circular wonton wrappers

oil

Cover the dried shitake mushrooms with water in a bowl and let sit until fully hydrated adding more water if necessary, approximately 30 minutes. Meanwhile, fill a medium pot with a few inches of water. Bring to a boil, place a steamer basket with the ears of corn inside, cover, and reduce heat to low. Steam the corn for approximately 10 minutes, until tender. Once done, remove and cut off the kernels.

Squeeze the excess water out of the mushrooms and place them, along with the corn kernels, carrots, cabbage, ginger sauce, pepper, and salt into a food processor. Pulse three or four times until finely chopped and well mixed.

Using a rolling pin, flatten a wonton wrapper until it is paper-thin. Place about a tablespoon and a half of the filling on top of the wonton wrapper. Fold the wonton wrapper over the filling lengthwise and seal with a finger dipped in water.

Warm a nonstick skillet on medium-high heat, allowing two tablespoons of oil to heat inside. Place dumplings into the pan, being sure not to overcrowd. Pan fry on both sides just to the point of golden, about 30 seconds each side. Once both sides are done, add about 1/4 cup water to the pan, cover and remove from heat. Allow the dumplings to steam until tender and cooked through, about 5 minutes. Add additional oil for each batch of dumplings. Remove from pan and serve with your favorite dipping sauce.

TAIWANESE PORK DUMPLINGS

Adapted from Doris Yau's recipe

Taipei, Taiwan has some of the best street food available in the entire world, with numerous vendors serving up delicious, juicy pork dumplings, the addition of ginger root, garlic, and scallions may sound like the dumplings served up at your favorite Asian restaurant. We recommend seeking out Chinkiang black rice vinegar for dipping sauce.

....

YIELD: ABOUT 48 DUMPLINGS

4 stalks celery, roughly chopped

½ medium onion, roughly chopped

3 scallions, roughly chopped

1 ounce ginger root, peeled

½ pound ground pork

3 large cabbage leaves

1 head garlic

1 teaspoon salt

48 circular wonton wrappers

canola Oil

Place the celery, onion, scallions, and ginger into a pot of boiling hot water. Turn heat to low and let simmer until translucent and tender, or about an hour and a half. Strain.

Place ground pork, cabbage leaves, garlic, salt, and tender vegetables into a food processor. Pulse a few times until well mixed.

Using a rolling pin, flatten the wonton wrappers until they are paper-thin. Place about a tablespoon of the mixed filling onto the center of a wonton wrapper. Fold the wrapper over the filling, lengthwise. Seal the edge with a finger dipped in water.

Warm up a nonstick skillet on medium-high heat, dropping about a tablespoon of oil in it. Place wontons into the pan without overcrowding. Pan fry on both sides just to the point of golden, about 30 seconds each side. Once both sides are done, add about ¼ cup of water to the pan, place the heat on low and cover. Allow the dumplings to steam until cooked through, about 5 minutes. Add additional oil for each batch of dumplings. Remove from pan and serve with your favorite dipping sauce.

DONATELLA'S MEATBALL WAGON

One of the dishes famous TV celebrity cooking judge and successful restaurateur Donatella Arpaia has become well known for are her meatballs. They've won accolades from some of the industry greatest critics, though it wasn't her eighth restaurant, Mia Dona that her version of meatballs—modeled after her Puglian mother's meatball recipe—was featured on the menu. What makes Donatella's meatballs exceptionally delicious is her twist of utilizing a slow braise in a rib ragu. "My mother used all beef, but I switched it to veal," though of course her mother had to approve of the final result before they hit the menu. Donatella learned a fair amount of her cooking skills from her mother and aunts, during Sunday dinners and childhood summers in the Puglia region of Italy, home of hearty pasta meals tossed with sautéed green vegetables and tomatoes, or slathered with rich meaty ragus, and also from the successful restaurant her father, Lello, ran in Woodmere, Long Island. It was at his insistence that she originally chose the career track of a lawyer. But soon after joining a firm, she found herself convincing her father to open a restaurant with her. In 1998, the two opened Bellini, and Donatella would go on to open seven more. Mia Dona first opened as a collaboration with chef Michael Psilakis in 2008, but after he bowed out in the spring of 2010, Donatella reimagined the restaurant as an ode to her family's Puglian roots.

One day, one of her chefs sandwiched the savory meatballs between two slices of fresh focaccia topped with a few spoonfuls of the ragu and fresh argula, starting a back-of-the-house trend. "Every time someone had it, they'd freak out over it," Donatella explains, "but no one knew about it."

But it didn't take long for the idea of setting up a meatball sandwich cart in front of Mia Dona to emerge. Donatella procured a little hot dog cart from a big box store—"I didn't want to spend the money unless I knew it was going to really work"—gave it a new awning, and out onto the front sidewalk it went in April 2010. Then "it just took off. It became like a cult following." The cart soon became a gathering place for area office workers in a part of Midtown full of generic delis and high-end restaurants. Even in the height of summer, the workers lined up for piping hot sandwiches with their choice of either spicy or sweet sauce. "God forbid we closed one day—people would complain!" In addition to the meatball cart, a second cart appeared in July offering gelato sandwiches on fresh Sicilian-style brioche rolls for sale during the late afternoon for a much-needed summer sugar rush. Both carts managed to last two summers before Donatella finally made the decision to shut down Mia Dona in the fall of 2011, partly to focus more of her time on her newborn son. The good news for meatball fans is that that cart does make appearances at her Chelsea restaurant Donatella during the summer. "We can open the doors and put it right inside." For days it doesn't, you can simply get a dish of her meatballs at the restaurant, maybe even finding Donatella sitting in the back or being the ever gracious host and greeting her customers. Except on Sundays, when she hopes "to continue that tradition of the Sunday meal and slow cooking" with her new husband and baby.

"My biggest compliment is when people say [the meatballs] taste better than their grandmother's." —DONATELLA ARPAIA

MAMA'S MEATBALLS AND RIB RAGU

Adapted from Donatella Arpaia's recipe

These famous meatballs can be served up in a sandwich or over pasta—it's really up to you. Switching in ground beef for the ground veal used at Donatella's restaurant yields a meatier flavor. If you want things a little spicy, add in some red pepper flakes while making the ragu. If you like your meatballs lighter, trade out some of the ground beef for ground pork.

YIELD: ABOUT 20 MEDIUM-SIZED MEATBALLS

FOR THE RAGU:

2 tablespoons extra-virgin olive oil

1 celery stalk, with leaves, roughly chopped

1/2 medium onion, roughly chopped

Kosher salt and freshly ground black pepper

3/4 pound (about 4) meaty, bone-in pork spareribs, rinsed

3/4 pound (3 to 4 links) sweet Italian sausage with fennel seeds, pierced all over with a fork

1 garlic clove, peeled and finely chopped

1/2 cup red cooking wine

2 (28-ounce) cans tomato purée

handful of fresh basil leaves

FOR THE MEATBALLS:

1/2 small loaf stale Italian bread (about 4 thick slices), torn into 2½-inch chunks

1 pound 80% lean ground beef chuck, broken up

3 garlic cloves, peeled and coarsely chopped

1/4 cup flat-leaf parsley finely chopped

1 large egg, lightly beaten

3/4 cups Parmigiano-Reggiano or Grana Padano grated

Kosher salt and freshly ground black pepper

canola oil for frying

TO MAKE THE SAUCE:

Warm the olive oil in a large, heavy-bottomed pot over medium heat. Add the celery and onion, generously season with salt and pepper, and sauté, partially covered, about 5 minutes, until golden and soft.

Add the ribs and sausage in a single layer, raise the heat to medium-high, and sauté, again partially covered, turning occasionally until the meat is nicely browned all over, about 7 to 10 minutes.

Add the garlic and cook until fragrant, about 1 minute. Add the wine and cook until it evaporates, about 5 minutes.

Add the tomato purée and the basil, and season generously with salt and pepper. Partially cover, bring to a boil, then reduce the heat to medium-low and let the sauce simmer quietly for 1½ to 2 hours, adjusting the heat as necessary to prevent it from boiling.

TO MAKE THE MEATBALLS:

Put the bread in a bowl and add enough warm water to cover the bread. Let stand for 5 minutes, turning to moisten evenly. Squeeze gently to remove as much water as possible from the bread chunks (they will fall apart, which is okay) and place in a large bowl.

Add the beef, garlic, parsley, egg, and ½ cup of the Parmigiano-Reggiano to the bread and combine. Season generously with salt and pepper. Knead the mixture with your hands—rinsing your hands under warm water occasionally to keep the meat from sticking to them—until it is uniformly combined and smooth. This will take at least 5 minutes.

Pinch a rounded tablespoon of the meat from the mound and shape it into a ball between the palms of your hands. Place on a baking sheet or tray and repeat with the remaining meat mixture. You should have about 20 meatballs.

Fill a 10-inch skillet halfway with canola oil and heat over high heat. Allow the oil to heat to about 325°F, you should see strands forming along the bottom of the pan when it is hot enough to add the meatballs. Working in batches, gently slide 8 to 10 meatballs into the skillet without overcrowding the pan. The meatballs should be only three-quarters submerged in the oil. Reduce the heat to medium and fry, turning once, until they are firm and golden, 12 to 14 minutes total. Use a slotted spoon to transfer the meatballs to a bowl lined with paper towels. Raise the heat to high between batches to ensure that the oil is hot when you slide the meatballs into it. Twenty minutes before serving, add the meatballs to the simmering tomato sauce; you don't want them to soak up too much of the liquid and become soggy.

Remove the meatballs and pork ribs from the ragu and transfer to a rimmed serving platter. Place the platter of meatballs and ribs and a large bowl of sauce on the table and serve either as sandwiches with fresh focaccia bread or with individual plates of pasta, each topped with a ladleful of sauce.

When Sri Lankan Thiru "Dosa Man" Kumar set up his dosa cart on Washington Square South in 2001, it was because he "wanted to do something different." Thiru was a vegetarian then (now a vegan), who had almost immediately noticed the lack of food carts with great vegetarian options upon immigrating in 1995. It took three and a half years after applying for his license for him to finally receive it, and the first location he chose was right outside of Washington Square Park, smack in the middle of the New York University campus. "This way, people can eat good food while sitting in the park." Within the first few weeks of being open, journalists from both the *New York Daily News* and *New York* magazine stopped by to interview this former restaurant manager and motorcycle racer. It was during his motorcycle racing tours back home in Sri Lanka that he had partly learned how to cook while having cookouts on the beach. He also learned "from the best, my grandmother," whose influence inspired Thiru's favorite menu item, the Jaffna Lunch: four small pancakes topped with a dried coconut chutney that comes with a samosa on the side.

Walk up to N.Y. Dosa any day, and you'll find Thiru smiling and chatting with customers, especially his regulars. "You can see their faces—they're so happy," he says of his customers. It's this interaction with his customers that makes Thiru happy, himself.—"I don't want to be inside the kitchen." Some have been stopping by his cart regularly since the very beginning. Now all they have to do is pop their head in his window, and he knows exactly what to give them, if he has it. Ask him "what's the

best thing on your menu?" and he'll set you up with a crisp dosa filled with roasted vegetables, lentils, and potatoes, along with some samosas. To make dosas, Thiru first ladles his batter onto the flat hot grill, letting it bubble and puff up from steam before turning a golden brown on the bottom. Once that happens, it's time to place the filling inside and quickly fold the dosa similar to a burrito. A flick of his wrist, and your dosa has landed into its container and is ready to be eaten by hand or with a fork and knife.

"It's always busy—4:00 to 4:30 is a dangerous time to come," because everything has usually run out by then. Even during the massive, multiyear remodeling of Washington Square Park by the New York City Parks Department, who actually controls Thiru's vending license, the cart's lines only grew. Waits for lunch today can easily stretch into a half hour. Thiru was nominated for a Vendy three years in a row but had to watch fellow NYU-area cart Sammy's Halal and the meat-riffic Hallo Berlin win the cup before it was finally his turn in 2007, which helped with his popularity. "I was very excited when I won," he says. It was also a win for New York's oft-overlooked vegan community.

"The customers are happy when they see the food on the grill right here, everything's cooked right in front of them, it makes everyone so happy." —THIRU KUMAR

PONDICHERRY DOSA
Adapted from Thiru Kumar's recipe

Dosas are a pancake dish made from fermented rice and lentils popular throughout south Asia. Thiru makes his on the spicy side with the addition of dried chiles and chili powder, but feel free to cut back on both if you can't handle the heat. Soaking and blending the rice and lentils separately leads to a thinner batter—the consistency should end up similar to pancake batter. Thiru's trick to spreading out the batter is to use a metal measuring cup to pour the batter onto your griddle or pan, and then use the bottom of the cup to spread it out in concentric circles, ultimately forming a paper thin circle. Due to the heat of the pan setting the batter, try to do the spreading within the first thirty seconds. Traditionally dosa are served with a vegetable stew called *sambar* and coconut chutney. You can buy pre-made *sambar* and chutney at Indian specialty shops like Patel Grocery (see page 277).

YIELD: SERVES 6

1 cup uncooked rice (any type, according to your preference)

1 cup Urad Dal (lentils), split and shelled

Kosher salt

3 whole medium potatoes

2 carrots

2 large whole green lettuce leaves

2 bell peppers (mixture of red, green, yellow, orange), seeded

1 two ounce piece of ginger, peeled

2 tablespoons turmeric powder

2 medium onions (any type), finely chopped

1 tablespoon of olive oil

Indian spices:

1 tablespoon turmeric powder

2 teaspoons ajwain seeds

2 teaspoons mustard seeds

2 teaspoons chili powder

1 teaspoon black pepper

3 to 4 curry leaves

1 tablespoon fenugreek seeds

3 red dried chiles

Cooking spray

3 cups *sambar*, for serving

2 cups coconut chutney, for serving

Place the rice and lentils in separate large bowls and cover generously with water. Cover the bowls to encourage fermenting and soak the rice and lentils in water for at least 6 hours, until hydrated.

Drain the rice and lentils separately reserving their soaking liquid. Add the rice to a blender or food processor with approximately ¼ to ½ cup of the soaking water, blend until smooth, about a minute. Return the rice mixture to its bowl, then repeat with the lentils. Once the lentils are smooth combine the rice and lentils then blend together, adding salt to taste. As you're blending, add additional soaking water in order produce a batter about the consistency of pancake batter—not too watery or too thick. Transfer the batter to a large bowl, cover and let it rest at room temperature or in a warm spot in your kitchen for at least 6 hours so that it can ferment naturally.

Meanwhile, to make the curry, peel and cut the potatoes into bite-sized pieces. Boil them until fork-tender. Roughly chop the carrots, lettuce, and peppers mixing them together, like you would for a salad, and set aside.

Sauté the onions with olive oil over low heat. Once the onions are translucent and tender, about three minutes, mix the Indian spices in with them and continue sautéing. Once the onions are fully coated and the spices have become aromatic, remove from heat and mix the cooled potatoes in to make the curry.

After the batter has finished fermenting—it will double in size and begin to give off a sour aroma—you are ready to make the dosa. Using a long-handled metal ladle, pour a ladleful of batter onto a heated grill or large non-stick pan prepared with cooking spray, trying to make circle. Working quickly use the back of your ladle to spread out the batter to create a large circle. Cook the dosa until the bottom is golden brown, and the top is dry. Once golden brown spots begin to appear on the top, add a heaping serving of the potato curry and the fresh veggies on top, roll up the dosa and put it on a plate. Serve with coconut chutney and *sambar* to dip the dosa in.

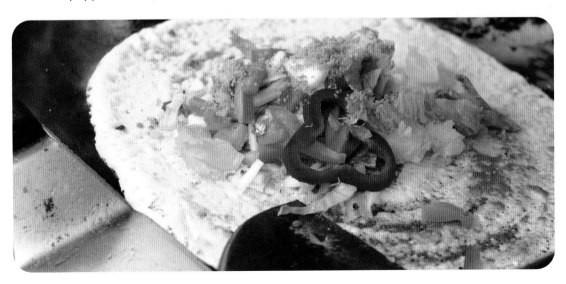

(M) | (GF) (V)

JAFFNA DOSA

Thiru's Jaffna Dosa is named after his hometown in Sri Lanka and the recipe is inspired by his grandmother. The Jaffna Dosas are softer and spongier than the paper-thin Pondicherry Dosa (page 48) and are served with a homemade dried coconut chutney.

....

YIELD: SERVES 6

1 cup uncooked rice (any type, according to
    your preference)

1 cup Urad Dal (lentils)

Kosher Salt

1 medium red onion, finely chopped

1 tablespoon olive oil, plus oil to coat cooking
    surface

Indian spices

1 tablespoon turmeric powder

2 teaspoons ajwain seeds

2 teaspoons mustard seeds

2 teaspoons chili powder

1 teaspoon black pepper

handful of curry leaves

1 tablespoon fenugreek seeds

1 teaspoon fennel seeds

3 red dried chiles

FOR THE DRIED COCONUT CHUTNEY:

½ cup of frozen, fresh grated coconut

1 teaspoon chili powder

3 cups *sambar*, for serving

2 cups coconut chutney, for serving

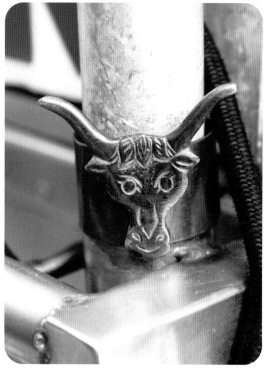

Place the rice and lentils in separate large bowls and cover generously with water. Cover the bowls to encourage fermenting and soak the rice and lentils for at least 6 hours, until hydrated.

Sauté the onion with 1 tablespoon olive oil on low heat, for about five minutes. Once the onion is translucent and tender, mix the Indian spices in and continue sautéing until the onion is fully coated and the spices become aromatic. Set aside to cool to room temperature.

To prepare the dried coconut chutney: Defrost fresh grated coconut, then mix with 1 teaspoon chili powder. In a medium skillet or frying pan, toast mixture over medium heat, stirring frequently for a few minutes until lightly browned. Set aside.

Drain the rice and lentils separately reserving their soaking liquid. Add the rice to a blender or food processor with approximately ¼ to ½ cup of the soaking water, blend until smooth, about a minute. Return the rice mixture to its bowl, then repeat with the lentils. Once the lentils are smooth combine the rice and lentils then blend together, adding salt to taste.

As you're blending, add additional soaking water in order produce a batter about the consistency of pancake batter—not too watery or too thick. Add cooled onion mixture and blend until smooth. Transfer the batter to a large bowl, cover and let it rest at room temperature or in a warm spot in your kitchen for at least 4 hours so that it can ferment naturally. The batter has finished fermenting when it's doubled in volume and gives off a sour aroma.

When the batter is ready, heat the grill and spread olive oil all over a flat-top grill or large non-stick pan. Then, using a long-handled ladle, mix the batter well and take a ladleful of the batter and spread on the grill into a circle, using the back of the ladle to smooth out and distribute the batter. Drizzle some olive oil onto the dosa. After 2 minutes, flip the dosa so the other side can cook. Cook until the surface of both sides of the dosa are dry and lightly golden brown. Carefully recoat your cooking surface with oil before each dosa. Top with dried coconut chutney and serve warm *sambar* and coconut chutney for dipping.

Trindadian native Veronica Julien had an entire previous career in municipal government before opening Veronica's Kitchen in 2004, a career that came to an end when she was laid off during the slight recession that occurred in New York City after the 9/11 attacks. She thought, *Oh God, I'm finished. How am I going to pay my mortgage?* the typical questions every laid-off worker faces. Instead of sitting around waiting for a position to open up in her field, she followed her sister's advice and began exploring the option of running a food cart. "I walked all around Manhattan looking for a spot, and God led me here," to downtown's Front Street. At first, it appeared her instincts to look elsewhere were correct. "The first day, I sold $20, and it stayed like that for three months," at which point she finally gave herself an ultimatum. One more month with the cart, and if business didn't take off, she was going to give up. Plenty of downtown office workers who line up regularly for her juicy, spicy

jerk chicken should be thankful that during that month, "business started building."

One of twelve children who are all amazingly still close, Veronica immigrated to New York City in 1983, leaving the small village outside of Port of Spain, Trinidad, where she grew up. "We had a lot of land there; we could run and play." After a few years in the fast-food industry, Veronica decided to pursue a different path, ultimately ending up as a microfilm consultant to the New York City Department of Buildings. These days she can be found serving up her signature West Indian food to near-constant lunch lines. A typical days in her life begin in the middle of the night, around 3:00 a.m., when she awakens to finish prepping the day's food, which consistently sells out sometime between 2:00 and 2:30 every afternoon. One of her nephews helps out throughout the day, though she's tried to teach all of her family's younger generation how to cook. "They don't realize it takes time to cook."

"I'm walking the streets, praying, and then the Lord tell me to come here, and I said, 'What? Why would I go there?' It turned out to be good, right?"

—VERONICA JULIEN

FRY BAKE & CODFISH

Adapted from Veronica Julian's recipe

Trinidadian street food includes the popular "Shark & Bake" dish, a shark sandwich made with fried bread. Here in the States, shark isn't as easy to find or affordable, so Veronica substitutes salt codfish. You can usually find the well-preserved fish at your local fishmonger, sometimes referred to as clipfish. Be sure to boil the fish twice to get all the salt out, possibly adding a couple of cut limes to the second boil if you feel inclined.

YIELD: 4 SERVINGS

FOR THE FRY BAKE:

1 cup bread flour

2 teaspoons baking powder

1 teaspoon salt

½ teaspoon sugar

2 cups oil

½ cup of water

Combine the flour, baking powder, salt and sugar, in a large mixing bowl. Slowly add the water to the dry ingredients while continuously kneading the entire mixture until a smooth dough is formed, about 2 to 3 minutes. Cover dough with plastic wrap, and let rest for 30 minutes. Make dough into small palm size balls then flatten. In a medium skillet, heat 2 cups of oil on high heat for around five minutes. Add one disc of dough once the oil is hot, and fry on both sides until brown. The dough will expand while frying into a golden round bake loaf. Place on a paper-toweled plate once done.

FOR THE SAUTÉ:

½ pound salted cod fish fillet

1 medium tomato, diced

½ medium onion, diced

½ of a medium head of cabbage, finely chopped

3 tablespoons oil

Place the codfish fillet in a large pot of boiling water, and boil for 30 minutes. Meanwhile, boil more water in a kettle. Drain the water from the pot, and refill the pot with the kettle water, with the codfish in the pot. Bring to a boil again, leaving it to boil for 30 more minutes. When done, the fish should be flaky and not too salty. Strain.

In a large heated skillet, add the oil. When it is heated, add the onion and tomato and saute until the onions are translucent and tender.

Flake the codfish into smaller pieces and add to the onion and tomatoes. Then slowly add the cabbage to the sauté. Cover to simmer until tender, about 10 minutes

Serve hot in between pieces of fry bake.

CHINATOWN STREET EATS TOUR

The winding streets and blind alleys of Manhattan's Chinatown hold much promise for adventurous and bargain-conscious eaters. But for a neighborhood widely considered as an epicenter for cheap eats, the street food options in Chinatown aren't as bountiful as one might expect. Narrow side streets with tiny sidewalks are off-limits to vendors, leaving carts to congregate on stretches of the larger thoroughfares like Canal, Grand, or Centre Street. In addition to the limited space for vending, carts have to compete with bargain-priced meals—think under $5—at local brick-and-mortar joints. Carts in Chinatown distinguish themselves from their tonier uptown counterparts by offering super cheap snacks like fried fish balls, plates of noodles, and egg rolls priced from $1 and up. Here's a guide to some of our favorite street foods in Chinatown and where to find them.

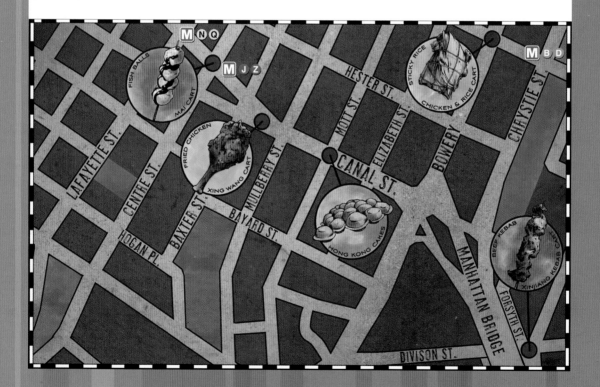

Chinese-Style Kebabs: At the intersection of Forsyth and Division Street, directly under the Manhattan Bridge ramp, you'll find the 2012 Vendy Finalist, Xin Jiang Prosperity Kebabs, serving up tender $1 kebabs grilled over hot coals. Choose from tender chicken and beef, fish balls, fish tofu, or deliciously fatty lamb, and say yes to a brushing of their spicy chili paste concoction. But buyer beware: the "pork sausage" is of the Oscar Mayer variety, so unless you're craving a grilled hot dog on a stick, you'll want to go for the other kebab options.

Tripe and Zongzi: A short walk up Forsyth past the handball games and tai chi sessions in Sara D. Roosevelt Park will take you to Grand Street, where two blocks to the west you'll find the "Chicken & Rice Cart." There is no chicken or rice, and "Tripe & Noodles" would be a more apt title. The owners of this cart speak very little English, and the menu is only written in Chinese, but the vendors will gladly show you their offerings, which include fish balls, rice noodles, lo mein, *har cheung/cheong fan* (rice noodle rolls), tripe, and sticky rice. At $1.50, the *zongzi* (sticky rice) is quite the bargain. The glutinous rice is mixed with roasted peanuts and wrapped around a center filling of pork, then encased in bamboo leaves, tied, and steamed. You could make a meal out of a single *zongzi*.

Hong Kong Mini Cakes: There are several Hong Kong Mini Cake carts around Chinatown, including one on the south side of Canal at Mott Street. Since it takes all of five minutes to make a batch, it's entirely possible to get a bag of 15 for $1 still warm. Hong Kong cakes are so delicious plain that there's really no need for any toppings, and they are ideal for the more timid eaters.

Fried Foods on a Stick: Across the street between Mulberry and Baxter is the Xing Wang cart, a must-hit destination for fried food lovers. Unlike other carts in Chinatown, the breading on the fried chicken here is thick and stays put during the frying. You can't beat the $1-a-drumstick price at any food chain. But it's in the "food on a stick" category that the cart really stands out. For the less adventurous, there's banana, tofu, even a hot dog that can be thrown in the hot oil for your afternoon snack. Courageous eaters can try the seafood and meats like octopus on a stick. Crispy and not-too-fishy, anyone who's a big fan of calamari would definitely be pleased with this.

Rice Noodles and Fish Balls: If it's rice noodles and fish balls you're after, look no farther than the "Mai Cart" directly outside the JMZ subway exit on Centre Street at Canal. There are two carts on this block, both of which serve fish balls, but the slightly more northernly located "Mai cart" also specializes in congee, tea eggs, tripe, and fresh steamed rice noodles topped with a mixture of peanut sauce, hoisin, and soy sauce, and sprinkled with sesame seeds. The cart's owner is friendly and engaging, and has operated her cart in that spot for more than fifteen years. The curried fish balls, in a slightly thick and spicy sauce are a standout. For $2.75 you can get a pint of rice noodles topped with eight fish balls, a satisfying meal that demands a return visit.

THE CULTURE OF TASTE

TEN QUESTIONS WITH THE GODFATHER OF LUNCH, ZACH BROOKS OF MIDTOWNLUNCH.COM

mid • town lunch n. (mid-toun luhnch) **1.** an inexpensive (under $10), authentic, unique, and interesting quick-service lunch, preferably near where you work; **2.** an adventure in urban lunching.

When Zach Brooks launched his site MidtownLunch.com on June 8, 2006, he unwittingly started a movement for workers in the heart of Manhattan to take back their lunch hour. Saying no to generic delis and boring, overpriced salad joints, Zach tirelessly pounded the pavement seeking out good food and good deals wherever they could be found within the bounds of Midtown (roughly the area from 30th Street to 59th Street between Third and Eighth Avenues). No restaurant was too divey, no food was off-limits. In the years since, Midtown Lunch has expanded to include Downtown Lunch, Midtown Lunch Philadelphia, and Midtown Lunch Los Angeles, where Zach is currently based with his family.

. . . .

1. What's the story behind starting Midtown Lunch?

It's actually a very complex, intriguing tale involving many twists and unexpected turns. It involved many acts of surprising courage and unmistakable valor. I was a fat guy, searching for the best lunches near my office in the food wasteland of Midtown Manhattan. After finding a few gems, I thought to myself, "Gee, I'll bet other people would be interested in this stuff." On week two of the site, I ate at a different falafel place every single day. Gawker made fun of me, and the rest is history.

2. Did you have any favorite carts or trucks in Midtown prior to the blog?

To be completely honest, I don't remember lunching in Midtown before the blog. It's all a haze of cheap Chinese food and street meat.

3. What was your favorite street food discovery?

There are so many that have a special place in my heart, but if you pushed me to pick a favorite it would have to be the Biryani Cart (page 80). I can't take full credit for Meru and all his success, because he would have eventually been discovered with or without me. But I was there the first day he added kati rolls to his menu, and having watched him grow from a standard Midtown halal cart into one of the more famous street food purveyors in all of New York brings me much happiness.

4. As the founder of Street Meat Palooza, how do you define "street meat"?

Chicken and/or lamb/gyro over rice with white sauce and hot sauce!

5. How has the street food scene changed since you started blogging?

Well, the whole gourmet food truck trend didn't start until a few years into Midtown Lunch's existence, and that has certainly changed the street food scene enormously. Not just in New York, but around the country.

6. Now that you're L.A.-based, what do you see as the main differences between the East Coast and West Coast street food scenes?

I've actually been more surprised by the similarities between the two coasts more than the differences. Despite L.A. being an entirely food truck–based scene and New York being primarily carts, the stories and struggles of the old-school Mexican taco trucks in California and the old-school halal carts in New York City are so similar. The main difference is that California street food became popular as a late-night food option in communities that needed late-night food options, while much of the modern NYC street vendor scene is more geared toward tourists and office worker lunches. That being said, halal food started as a late-night option for Muslim cab drivers . . . so, there's another similarity.

7. L.A.'s Kogi BBQ launched the Korean taco craze, what other fusion street foods have you seen that have been successful?

I don't think that there will ever be another Kogi, or another "fusion" street food that will see a similar amount of success. There's a reason why taco trucks and halal trucks are able to last while other more gourmet trucks struggle to turn a profit. Tacos and street meat is cheap food that can be served up quickly, in high volume. Cheap, quick, volume. Lose any one of those three things, and you're not going to be suc-

cessful. The reason Kogi was so huge is because they're just a taco truck, making burritos and tacos and quesadillas. They didn't change the model, just the salsas.

8. Are there any New York trucks or carts that you especially miss?

STREET MEAT! I'd give just about anything for a decent chicken and lamb over rice plate with white sauce and hot sauce.

9. Years ago you wished for a Thai food cart and it came true! What other street food would you love to see in Midtown?

You know . . . I'm not sure there's anything left to wish for. Midtown seems to have everything at this point!

10. Where do you see street food in New York going?

Street food has always been cyclical, and history would say that we're at the tail end of one of the cycles. But on the other hand, there seems to have been a breakthrough recently that would be tough to reverse. I think that hot dogs and halal carts will always be moneymakers for many of the vendors in New York City. But as lines grow at places like the Biryani Cart (page 80) or Eggstravaganza (page 75) or Uncle Gussy's (page 69), you'll see more and more vendors take a chance on more and more interesting fare.

Some of the best hot dogs in New York are really the wurst. More than a century after Charles Feltman first served sausages on buns in Coney Island in 1867, it's hardly surprising that it would take a fellow German immigrant to cultivate the city's taste for a superior sausage. At the northwest corner of 5th Avenue and 54th Street, lunchers line up down the block to get their "German Soul Food" fix at Hallo Berlin. Founded by the late Rolf Babiel, the Hallo Berlin cart specializes in a hearty and extensive menu that includes your choice of nine types of wursts, ranging from your standard better-than-a-hot-dog Knockfrank to pork Bratwurst, chicken Alpenwurst, veal Weisswurst, and beef Currywurst. While Germans may lay claim to thousands of varieties of sausages, rest assured that the best of the best are covered here.

Born in Hoyerswerda, East Germany, in 1952—the very year that they closed the inner German border—Rolf was allowed to emmigrate from East Berlin to West Berlin in 1975. When he came to the United States six years later, he brought little with him, but he had big plans. "When he came here it wasn't about food," says his wife and business partner, Bernadette. "Rolf had ideas. He had a tremendous amount of ideas." A former machinist back in East Germany, Rolf found construction work when he first arrived. "He was working on a building doing Sheetrock for $3.50 an hour, and he saved every penny. He did not go out to lavish parties. He was as simple as he could be."

While German pushcart vendors had been a vibrant part of the Lower East Side during the late nineteenth century, by the early 1980s most Germans had left the pushcart trade to newer immigrant groups like the Greeks and Egyptians, and Rolf saw an opportunity. As Bernadette explains, "There were no European pushcarts at that time in the streets, so he walked around the whole city. Brooklyn, Bronx, Queens, Long Island, he went all over. An associate of ours used to work at the University Club—that was before Fifth Avenue looked the way it looks—he figured okay, that was it. He stood around hours and hours to observe the traffic of the people." Rolf told Jesse Baker of NPR's *Weekend Edition* in 2005, "I had a couple of times these hot dogs, and I said, *New York deserves something better*."

The cart itself is compact and efficient—clearly a product of German engineering. Sausages sizzle

"New York would never have another vendor like this character. You have all the new vendors coming along . . . I see so many vendors copy his ideas . . . I love to see other people embrace his ideas." —BERNADETTE BABIEL

on little pans alongside German fried potatoes and sautéed onions before getting placed in a crusty roll with cabbage, onions, and a sinus-clearing home-made mustard. As the winner of the inaugural Vendy Awards in 2005, the quality of Hallo Berlin's food is indisputable, but beyond the sausages and sauerkraut, it was Rolf's way with people that made him so special to everyone who knew him. "He was always very funny with the customers," says eldest son, Peter Babiel. "He always gave them a reason to come back. Not just because of his food, but because of his personality. He made friends with everybody."

Charming and engaging with a wicked sense of humor that still permeates every aspect of the cart from the way the sausages were all named after German automobiles (the Bratwurst is the Mercedes, while the chicken Alpenwurst is the East German

Trabant) to the popular Joseph Stalin Dictator Special and Winston Churchill Democracy Special. With Stalin, you pay less, but you get no choice. With Churchill, you pay more but you get to choose your own sausages and sides and get a couple extra meatballs thrown in. How do Americans vote? Surprisingly pro-dictator. As Rolf explained to *Weekend Edition*, "And so strange as it sounds, this is the hit in New York. They want this special."

Rolf grew his pushcart business into a Hallo Berlin empire that today includes a full-service restaurant and beer garden on 10th Avenue between 44th and 45th Streets and a tavern upstate in Conklin, New York. But success was not without years of hard work and personal sacrifice. "He did everything. From stocking the cart with food, cleaning it every night, bookkeeping," says Peter. "You see them out there only for a couple of hours

JOHN F KENNEDY
DEMOCRACY SPECIAL
ANY CHOICE OF 2 WURST
#One Through Eight
TOPPED WITH GERMAN FRIES
or Potatoe Salat + The Works
REDWINE CABBAGE, SAUTEED ONION
BONUS Bavarian Meatball
12 00

JOSEPH STALIN DICTATOR
SPECIAL
NO CHOICE
ONE BERLINER KNOCKFRANK (VOLKSWAGEN)
ONE BRATWURST (MERCEDES)
Sliced in a Dish, topped with
German Fries, Red & White Cabbage,
Sauteed Onion & a Small Soup
10 00

but the job goes from early in the morning to late at night. There's actually more to it behind the scenes than people realize." With all the demands on his time and attention, Rolf still found the time to engage with each and every customer even as his line stretched down the block and around the corner. "The cart was the first wife; I was the second wife," says Bernadette with a smile. She'd tell Rolf, "When you finish with your first wife, you can come home to your second wife."

When Mayor Koch was cracking down on street vendors in the late '80s, Rolf's vending license and cart were confiscated by the city. Rolf fought back and collected signatures of support. At the time he told David Handelman in a *New York* magazine interview "I came out of East Germany by fighting that government. I have the guts to fight the city. That cart is my life." Rolf was unyielding in his efforts. "He went all over the streets," says Bernadette. "He was there at nighttime. He was there at lunchtime. He would get up early in the morning. . . . I still have all of the signatures. I still have them. From actors, you name them, government people. . . ." Mayor Koch relented and gave Rolf back his permit, but to this day Bernadette has no idea what happened to the original cart. "I don't think anybody had the soul, the pain that he went through to build this legacy . . . as long as I have breath, I'm going to try to keep that legacy."

Though Rolf was the face of Hallo Berlin, he and Bernadette built the business side by side. In the beginning, they worked together at the cart, but while Rolf thrived off street life, he hated to see its effect on his wife. "The people used to come in the cart, and they didn't know who I was. They thought I was just, whatever, she's just a worker, you know."

As much as New York is known for being cosmopolitan and progressive, as a biracial couple in the '80s the Babiels still faced prejudice from both customers and strangers. It was Bernadette who came up with the concept of German soul food, a story she's never shared until now. "One day we were cooking and I said, *You know what honey, I got an idea. You know how we're going to get people to love us? To accept us for who we are? German man, Haitian woman together? Let's call it German Soul Food.*" Rolf added it to the menu, and it's been there ever since. According to Bernadette, that will never change. "We get a lot of questions, *what is German Soul Food?* German Soul Food is black and white. Because whenever you go to the South you hear, soul food, soul food, soul food. Germany never had any soul food. There's no such thing as soul food in Germany, so we figure, us as a couple, as a black woman and a European man, we make soul food. *German Soul Food.*" The concept resonated with customers immediately. Sales skyrocketed. To this day the German Soul Food combos are still among the most popular orders with regulars and newbies alike.

These days the Hallo Berlin tradition is carried at the cart by Rolf's younger brother, Wolfgang Babiel. The brothers operated the cart together from 2004 until Rolf's passing in 2009 and Wolfgang's devotion is palpable. He works long hours to maintain the cart to Rolf's high standard of excellence. "This was made with his *heart*," Wolfgang says. "Not only for making money. This came from his inside. I'm here and as long as I can do this, I do it in his name." After Rolf's passing, the cart was sidelined for over a year while the family dealt with paperwork and permitting issues. These days, fans are overjoyed to have their favorite lunch-on-wheels back in its regular spot, though Bernadette admits there's the occasional complaint from customers missing Rolf's larger than life presence. "Look, if I could, I'd be the first one to bring my husband back. I'd be the first one in that line, boy, I'd give my life for it. I would sell everything just to get him back, but at least you've got part of him in the street. You see—that's it. That was him. Without the cart, there wouldn't be this," she says, gesturing to the bustling beer garden around her. "Without the cart, there wouldn't be anything." As for the future, that will one day be in the hands of their sons Peter and Alex. "My husband and I, we always say, you can build a dream and what your children do with the dream, it's up to them, you know. It's not easy to build up dreams today. So this is not a dream. This is a legacy."

KÖNIGSBERGER KLOPSE
(GERMAN MEATBALLS WITH LEMON CAPER SAUCE)
Adapted from Rolf Babiel's recipe

In addition to the Hallo Berlin cart, Rolf Babiel's legacy lives on at what he referred to as "New York's Wurst Restaurants" Hallo Berlin Beer Garden on 10th avenue and 44th street in Manhattan and Hallo Berlin North Tavern just off of I-81 in Conklin, New York. At the restaurants you can enjoy a stein (or two) of German beer along with an extensive menu of German delicacies that aren't practical to prepare in the confines of the cart. The *Königsberger Klopse*, an epic boiled meatball platter with lemon caper sauce served over Garlic Mashed Potatoes (page 68) is especially popular.

YIELD: SERVES 4

5 ounces stale baguette or other crusty bread

⅔ pound ground beef

⅓ pound ground pork

2 egg yolks

2 cloves garlic, mashed

¼ teaspoon marjoram

¼ teaspoon caraway seeds

¼ teaspoon salt, plus more for salting

¼ teaspoon ground white pepper

4 egg whites

½ cup lemon juice (about 2 lemons)

1 teaspoon lemon zest

½ teaspoon all-purpose flour

4 tablespoons drained capers

FOR THE MEATBALLS:

Break baguette in half and place it in a large bowl. Cover with water then use a plate to weigh down the bread. Soak about 5 minutes or until fully saturated.

In a large bowl, mix together beef, pork, egg yolks, garlic, marjoram, caraway, salt, and pepper. Squeeze out as much water as possible from the bread. Break bread into pieces and work into meat mixture. Roll meatballs into golf ball–sized balls.

Bring 1½ quarts of salted water to boil in a large and deep sauté pan. Turn the heat down to low and add the meatballs. Cover and simmer for 20 minutes.

Move oven rack to center position and preheat the oven to 225°F. Using a slotted spoon, remove meatballs from simmering liquid and transfer to an oven-safe baking dish then keep in warm oven while you prepare the lemon caper sauce.

FOR THE LEMON CAPER SAUCE:

In a medium bowl whisk together egg whites, lemon juice, zest, and flour until flour is thoroughly incorporated. Transfer mixture to a small saucepan and heat over very low heat, whisking constantly until mixture thickens to a silky white gravy, about 5 minutes. Remove from heat, stir in capers then transfer to a gravy boat or bowl for serving.

Portion meatballs on top of Garlic Mashed Potatoes (page 68) and top with lemon caper sauce. Serve immediately.

GARLIC MASHED POTATOES
Adapted from Rolf Babiel's recipe

Warm and comforting, these garlicky mashed potatoes are a popular side dish at Hallo Berlin Tavern in Conkin, New York, as well as their Hell's Kitchen beer garden. Pair these with Rolf Babiel's *Königsberger Klopse* (page 66) or serve them with your favorite roasted chicken or meat loaf.

YIELD: SERVES 4

8 medium red potatoes, peeled and quartered
1 teaspoon salt
2 cloves garlic, peeled and mashed
4 tablespoons salted butter

Add potatoes and 2 quarts of water to a stockpot, season with salt and boil until potatoes are fork-tender, about 10 minutes. When potatoes are close to done, add garlic and butter to a small saucepan. Heat over medium-high until butter is melted and the garlic is fragrant, about 2 to 3 minutes. Remove from heat and set aside. Drain potatoes and transfer to a large bowl. Pour butter mixture over potatoes and mash potatoes. Serve with *Königsberger Klopse* (page 66).

I got one double pork pita, extra white, no hot," Nick Karagiorgos shouts above the sizzle of the onions and the hum of the engine. With his younger brother, Franky, running the grill, Nick keeps the long line moving, remembering his regulars' orders and chatting with the patrons as they wait for their food. He got his start at a tender age working his uncle's souvlaki cart. "I was getting sodas for my Uncle George at age nine or ten." It wasn't long before his uncle built him a kid-sized metal cart, from which he began selling frozen fruit pops at $1.50 each. "Everyone gave me $2 and told me to keep the change. This was in the mid-1980s, so I was making bank."

These days as co-owner of Uncle Gussy's Truck, Nick works the same spot in the shadow of St. Bart's on East 51st and Park that his Uncle Gus cultivated years earlier. "My uncle was one of the first vendors to sell on Park Avenue. There was no one here when he started," says Nick.

When Uncle Gus retired in 2008, Nick and Franky were already running a breakfast cart

"I come from a line of vendors. My cousin's a vendor; my uncle's a vendor. My other cousin and my other uncle are vendors. And my mom gives it all the love." —NICK KARAGIORGOS

nearby. They bought the lunch business, but taking over their uncle's cart wasn't an easy transition. A rival halal vendor several blocks away was furious when they started offering chicken over rice and threatened to set up a cart right next to them. "I said to them, *My man, this is America. You can do whatever you want. But I tell you what, I guarantee you people will come to me and not you, because* you don't care."

It's not hard to find a gyro in Midtown. What sets the 2012 Vendy Award finalist apart is their rotating array of authentic Greek specialties prepared by their mom, Ekaterini Karagiorgos. Lines queue early for tender grilled lamb chops, steaming cups of *avgolemono,* lemony chicken soup with orzo, and *pastichio,* a "Greek lasagna" made with beef, macaroni, and cheese topped with béchamel sauce.

Besides preparing everything from the *tzatziki,* a thick, garlicky yogurt sauce to the lemon-intensive *souvlaki* marinade from scratch, Mrs. Karagiogos oversees the purchase of all meat that hits the grill. "When she lived in Greece, she lived in the countryside," says Nick. "She knows when there's a piece of old meat and when it's a piece of new meat." If the order doesn't look up to "Mom's" standards, she's not shy about saying, "No, no, give me the good stuff." The tireless commitment to quality—from shopping to prep work to cooking—is time consuming. Her friends tell her, "you're going to die faster," but Mrs. Karagiogos is nonplussed: "That's OK. I don't care. I like it nice and perfect. You eat; I'm honored you eat."

As the business grows, Nick finds himself in a quandary. "Sometimes I don't know how people like me and my mom do it. It's a lot of work." Turf wars continue to be an ongoing struggle. As new vendors hit the streets in shiny trucks with PR backing and big dreams, there's a lack of respect for the order of things. Nick's biggest fear is having someone "pull up on his spot" and sour the delicate relationship with the buildings in the area and the NYPD Alpha Unit, the squad that monitors vendors in Midtown that his family has cultivated since the 70s. "One comes, then the next one comes, then the next comes, then the cops come, and everybody goes. I try to tell everyone, have a little common courtesy. There's a corner for everyone."

In 2012, Nick went back to his ice pop roots opening Pägō, a gourmet ice cream cart featuring tangy frozen yogurt along with a line of sorbets and ice creams developed with the help of a master gelato maker. Like the truck, Pägō is full-throttle Greek. The frozen yogurt is made from real Greek yogurt, and their flavors—like a rich coffee frappe—take their inspiration from Greece. Dreams of further expansion are tempered by concerns regarding quality. Nick's hope is to someday open a restaurant where he can set his mother up in a big kitchen so she can really shine. "When I wake up, I love to go to work. So does my mom. I think I got it from her."

GREEK-STYLE PORK CHOPS

Adapted from Ekaterini Karagiorgos' recipe

Mom's pork chops and lemon potatoes special always sells-out on the truck. Rocking the Twitter hashtag #grillinlikeavillian when the chops are on, regulars know to hurry over to the truck to get their fix. If you don't have access to a monster grill like the one on board the Uncle Gussy's truck, you can make it an indoor meal with ease using a cast-iron skillet and a broiler.

YIELD: SERVES 6

6 center-cut pork chops

¼ cup red cooking wine

¼ cup extra-virgin olive oil

1 tablespoon Greek oregano

1 tablespoon salt

1 tablespoon ground black pepper

Rinse the pork chops and pat dry then place them in 13 x 9–inch baking dish or pan.

In a large measuring cup add the cooking wine, olive oil, oregano, salt, and pepper. Whisk together until thoroughly combined.

Pour marinade over pork chops and rub it in. Marinate for 30 minutes.

Move rack in broiler to highest position.

Warm a large cast-iron skillet over high heat for about 5 minutes. Pan should be very hot but not smoking. Working in batches, add pork chops to pan in a single layer so they fit without overlapping. Sear pork chops about 1½ minutes per side, then transfer the cast iron pan to the broiler. Broil on high for 5 minutes without turning, until pork chops reach an internal temperature of 135 to 140°F. Remove from broiler and tent with aluminum foil for 5 minutes to let meat rest, then serve with Tzatizki (page 73) and Lemon Potatoes (page 74).

> **TIP:** To avoid dry pork chops it's best to let the meat rest for a few minutes before serving so it doesn't release all of its juices upon cutting. To keep the meat from getting cold take a large sheet of aluminum foil, fold it in half like a tent and use it to loosely cover the meat while it rests.

TZATZIKI (GREEK YOGURT SAUCE)

Adapted from Ekaterini Karagiorgos's recipe

There are few things in life that aren't made better by a healthy slathering of Mrs. Karagiorgos's killer *tzatziki*. Her secret? Use both Greek whole milk yogurt and sour cream for a super smooth and creamy sauce.

YIELD: SERVES 6

1 medium cucumber, peeled

8 ounces Greek whole-milk yogurt

8 ounces sour cream

2 garlic cloves, peeled

3 teaspoons white vinegar

½ teaspoon salt

⅛ teaspoon dried dill

dash of white pepper

Slice the cucumber lengthwise, use a spoon or melon baller to scoop out the seeds, then coarsely chop and add to the bowl of a food processor or blender with remaining ingredients. Pulse several times to break up the cucumber pieces, then blend on high until smooth. Serve with Greek-Style Pork Chops (page 71) and refrigerate leftovers in an airtight container for up to 2 days.

ROASTED LEMON POTATOES

Adapted from Ekaterini Karagiorgos's recipe

Mrs. Karagiorgos's kitchen runs on olive oil, lemon juice, and Greek oregano. These simple ingredients find their way into her meat marinades and her famous roasted potatoes. Covering the pan with aluminum foil allows the lemon flavor to steam into the potatoes as they cook. One bite will have you forsaking all other tubers.

....

YIELD: SERVES 6

1 tablespoon Kosher salt

½ tablespoon dried Greek oregano

3 teaspoons freshly ground black pepper

7 medium-sized white or yellow potatoes, washed, dried, and cut into wedges

¾ cup, plus 2 tablespoons extra-virgin olive oil

⅓ cup freshly squeezed lemon juice

Move oven rack to center position and preheat the oven to 450°F. In a ramekin mix together the salt, oregano, and pepper. Set aside.

Add the potatoes to a 13 x 9–inch baking dish. Drizzle two tablespoons of olive oil over the potatoes and rub in. Add the spice mix to the potatoes and toss to coat.

Whisk together the remaining olive oil and lemon juice with ½ cup water, and pour the mixture in between the gaps created by the potatoes.

TIP: Be careful not to pour the mixture directly onto the potatoes, to avoid washing off the spices.

Cover the pan with aluminum foil and cook for 45 minutes. Remove the foil, stir potatoes and continue cooking, stirring occasionally for 10 to 15 minutes, or until the potatoes are crispy and golden outside and fork-tender on the inside.

On any given weekday morning, generic coffee and doughnut carts dot the corners of Midtown's busiest thoroughfares. But at the intersection of East 52nd Street and Park Avenue, Eggstravaganza Cart stands apart from the rest. Simple egg-and-cheese sandwiches are the bedrock of the breakfast trade, but the Eggstravaganza Cart doesn't make your typical egg and cheese. Homemade chorizo prepared by owner Arturo Macedo's butcher father sizzles on the grill until it reaches crisped perfection for an unparalleled breakfast sandwich trifecta. And forget McGriddles—a fluffy stack of Arturo's from-scratch pancakes with bacon will only set you back five bucks.

Monday through Saturday, Arturo and his younger sister, Maribel Tellez, rise at 4:00 a.m. to get ready for early breakfast service, and lunch doesn't wrap until 2:00 or 2:30 p.m. Maribel manages a streaming line of construction workers and investment bankers ordering breakfasts that would cost upward of three times as much at any of the surrounding white-tablecloth joints. "I see them, and I serve them. They don't even have to say anything," Maribel says. Despite the long days, Arturo and Maribel never fail to greet their customers with a smile. "A smile for everybody, all the time," says Maribel.

In the tight confines of their cart, the siblings have their rhythm down. They've been cooking together for years. Arturo and Maribel's father left Puebla, Mexico, to work in America when they were young, and their mother had to work long hours while filling the role of mother and father. "As children, my sister and I would cook for the family. We started cooking simple foods: eggs, pancakes," Arturo says. His earliest memories growing up in Mexico were in the kitchen watching his grandmother Maria cook. "My grandmother was one of five ladies hired to cook for weddings—big ones—two-day-long events. Three or four hundred people would come. In the courtyard they would line up tables and tables with *atole*, *tamales*, and *mole*. She could take even the simplest ingredients and make something crazy delicious," he says.

on East 57th Street and Lexington Avenue. He waited tables, ran the counter, prepared food, and picked up the nickname "The Chopper." But after ten years struck out on his own and in 2008 he opened a mini breakfast cart with his sister, initially only selling the standard bagels, doughnuts, and coffee. Business was fine, but Arturo wanted more. Working in the neighborhood for a decade had given him a good sense of the customer base; many of his patrons were finance guys looking for power breakfasts. He expanded their menu to include egg whites, multigrain bread, and breakfast wraps—adding the chorizo was Maribel's idea. They've since made the spicy pork sausage a signature, adding it to wraps, breakfast sandwiches, and tacos. Their chorizo, egg, and cheese caught the attention of SeriousEats.com head honcho, Ed Levine, in July 2009. His glowing review proclaimed that it "deserves a place in the pantheon of New York breakfast sandwiches" and put the cart on the map. A profile on the Cooking Channel's *Food(ography)* with Mo Rocca followed, and in 2011, they were named Vendy Award finalists.

When Arturo came to this country in 1991, his first job was as a dishwasher for a restaurant in Chinatown. "I would watch the cooks there chopping the ingredients. They were so fast with their knives. I thought, *I could do that, too.*" He soon took on the task of prep for the menu mainstay, chicken and broccoli, chopping three cases of broccoli a day. "In my free time I would practice with the broccoli scraps."

Arturo's knife skills came in handy in his next job as a jack-of-all-trades at a Greek/Italian dinner

"It's not easy," says Arturo. "You have to compete with vendors that have been here for years. You have to come up with tastes to convince the customers to try you." Arturo dreams of expanding to a truck and possibly a restaurant one day if he can raise the capital. "We're like a flower with roots. Now we need the fertilizer and water so we can grow."

"Honestly, I didn't like to sell just doughnuts and coffee. It's simple—it's easy. But I don't want to catch the money. I want to catch the opportunity. If you catch the opportunity, the money will follow." —ARTURO MACEDO

MEXICAN GRILLED CHEESE

Adapted from Arturo Macedo's recipe

Chorizo is well represented across Eggstravaganza's menu on wraps, breakfast sandwiches, and tacos, but it is possibly best showcased in their Mexican Grilled Cheese. This decadent sandwich—made with American cheese, plenty of chopped bacon and chorizo, and topped with grilled tomatoes and pickled jalapeños—easily ranks among the city's tastiest sandwiches. Perfectly crisp chorizo and bacon are crucial to this recipe. "Time makes the difference," says Arturo. "Just wait. Good food takes time."

....

YIELD: SERVES 2

¼ pound Mexican chorizo, casings removed

¼ pound bacon

4 slices tomato

1 tablespoon butter

4 slices multigrain bread

6 slices American cheese

2 smoked jalapeño peppers (*Chiles jalapeño en escabeche*), sliced

Coarsely chop the chorizo and bacon, and mix together. In a large skillet, fry the chorizo and bacon over medium-high heat, stirring occasionally for 5 minutes or until brown and crispy. Remove the meat from the pan and set aside. Drain off all but one tablespoon of grease.

Return the skillet to the stove and fry the tomato slices in the reserved grease about 1 to 2 minutes or until lightly brown on each side. Set aside.

Add the butter to the skillet, and heat over medium until melted and beginning to bubble. Add slices of bread. Place 1½ slice of cheese on each slice of bread. Grill open-faced for about 5 minutes or until cheese is melted and bread is golden brown, about 5 minutes.

Add chorizo and bacon mix to two of the bread slices, top with tomato, jalapeño peppers, and other two slices of bread. Cut and serve.

STEAK AND EGG TACOS

Adapted from Arturo Macedo's recipe

Texan refugees will be the first to lament the paucity of breakfast tacos in the Big Apple. While you might not be able to score a breakfast taco on every corner, Arturo's has Midtownites covered with his signature steak and egg tacos, the perfect hungry man's breakfast or hangover helper. Either way, Arturo's not judging. There are a number of different Adobo seasoning mixes you can use for marinading the meat. Arturo recommends the Goya® version with pepper.

YIELD: SERVES 2

½ pound skirt steak or flank steak

¼ teaspoon Kosher salt

1 teaspoon Adobo seasoning

½ tablespoon butter

½ medium white onion, finely chopped

6 large eggs

1 tablespoon whole milk

1 tablespoon vegetable oil

12 small corn tortillas

¼ cup salsa, for serving

¼ cup *cotija* cheese, for serving

¼ cup guacamole, for serving

Sprinkle both sides of the meat with salt, cover and refrigerate overnight.

In the morning, rinse off the salt and pat dry. Cut the steak into small chunks and sprinkle the meat with Adobo. Set aside.

Add butter to a large cast-iron skillet and heat on medium-high. Once the butter begins to melt and bubble, add the onions and sauté, stirring occasionally, until onions are translucent and beginning to brown, about 5 minutes. Add the steak and cook 2 to 3 minutes per side, until meat is browned.

While steak is cooking, in a medium bowl, lightly whisk eggs with milk. Heat the oil in a frying pan or skillet on medium-high for about a minute. Add the eggs, wait a few moments for the eggs to begin to set then remove from heat and stir with a spatula to move eggs toward the center while tilting the pan to allow the raw and runny parts of the eggs contact with the hot surface. Return the eggs to the heat and repeat, taking the pan off the stove and stirring when the eggs begin to come together. Continue cooking until the eggs are nearly dry or close to the desired degree of doneness,

Transfer the eggs to the pan with the cooked steak. Turn the heat to low to keep warm, the low heat will finish cooking the eggs. Rinse the egg pan and return it to the stove to warm tortillas. Working in batches, if necessary, add tortillas to the pan in a single layer and heat 30 seconds per side over medium-high heat. If your tortillas are stiff or old, brush each side with water before warming.

Top warmed tortillas with steak, onions, and eggs. Add the salsa, the guacamole, and sprinkle with *cotija* cheese.

NOTE: Like in most *taquerias*, Arturo serves his tacos atop two stacked tortillas to preserve the structural integrity. If you prefer fewer carbs and don't mind risking a mess, you can portion each taco atop a single tortilla.

TIP: Try these tacos with Salsa Fresca (page 240) or Ají (page 220)

When he left Bangladesh in 1992 at the age of 22, Meru Sikder wasn't heading to New Jersey with the intention of opening two food carts in Midtown Manhattan. He was simply seeking a better life. But after settling in New Jersey, getting an associate's degree, and honing his culinary skills for eight years as the banquet chef at a Hilton first as a part-time sushi chef for New Jersey's then largest Japanese restaurant, he longed to run his own establishment. As he was searching for a small restaurant space in Midtown, he got the notion of running a cart. "I saw all these shish kebab, hot dog, pretzel vendors, and there were no Indian carts." Offering a full lunch menu off of a cart wasn't something the other vendors were focused on. So he procured the vendor license for

the southwest corner of West 46th Street and 6th Avenue, and opened the Biryani Cart in 2004.

Meru's menu has evolved from the typical halal cart meat over rice to being full Indian take-away with the introduction of his namesake biryani. The chicken biryani—spiced basmati rice mixed with chicken pieces and topped with a golden hard-boiled egg—quickly became a fan favorite. Regulars also gravitate to his chicken tikka—tender pieces of chicken thighs that have been marinated in yogurt and spices before hitting the hot grill. Anything served by a man whose favorite ingredients are habanero sauce and Sriracha is guaranteed to have a spicy kick to it, and it wasn't long before Meru found a following among office workers looking for a flavorful and reasonably priced Indian dishes being

served up. Midtown is flush with pricey, mediocre Indian buffets, and Meru filled a niche for them it is one step away from a sit-down Indian joint, without the Bollywood music.

One of the most popular items on the menu, the kati roll, wasn't offered until the late spring of 2007. Originating in Kolkata, kati rolls are now a ubiquitous street food in India, where anything you want can be folded into the *paratha*, an unleavened flatbread made by alternating several layers of thin dough with clarified butter or *ghee*. Kati Roll Company, an Indian take-out shop on 46th Street had popularized the dish with the neighborhood lunch crowd. Meru says, "I wanted to offer the same thing." But instead of using the traditional *parantha* roll, he opted to make his rolls with slightly thinner *chapati* bread, also an unleavened disc made with ghee, but one that uses a whole-wheat flour and fewer costsists of layers. The *chapati* swaddles fillings made with a base of either spicy meat, potatoes, or eggs before being topped with cooling lettuce and onion.

On May 30, 2007, Biryani Cart, Meru, and his "Indian burritos" were profiled on MidtownLunch.com, causing a flood of publicity to the cart, which sold out of 300 kati rolls before 1p.m. "As soon as Mr. Zach wrote about me, I exploded," he says. When Kati Roll Company moved into a new restaurant space seven blocks south, Biryani Cart filled the void and its popularity increased exponentially. In 2008, the cart was named the People's Choice winner at the annual Vendy Awards. "Winning was very good," says Meru. The following morning he appeared on the CBS's *The Early Show*. 2009 brought another People's Choice Vendy win and an article in the *New York Times*'s "$25 and Under" column. Now Meru is the one being imitated. "Everyone around me has biryani now," he says with a chuckle.

CHICKEN TIKKA

Adapted from Meru Sikder's recipe

Though Biryani Cart didn't originally offer kati rolls, they've since become famous for them. Meru's chicken tikka recipe can be served as a main dish over rice or with other sides or rolled into chapati bread (page 83) with grilled onions and lettuce for homemade kati rolls. Either way is delicious when drizzled with a creamy

YIELD: SERVES 4

2½ pounds boneless skinless chicken breast or
   dark meat, cut in to 1½-inch cubes
½ teaspoon salt
1 teaspoon toasted cumin seeds
1 teaspoon toasted coriander seeds
1 teaspoon red chili powder
1 teaspoon cornstarch
½ teaspoon ground cloves
½ teaspoon ground celery seeds
¾ cup fresh ginger, garlic, and onion paste
¾ cup plain yogurt
fresh cilantro, chopped (for garnish)

Mix all ingredients together in a large bowl, coating the chicken. Marinate covered in the refrigerator for at least one hour letting all the spices soak in.

Place a flat-top grill or large nonstick pan on high heat. Place a generous amount of chicken cubes into the pan, being sure to not overcrowd, pan searing for 15 minutes total until the meat is charred.

CHAPATI RECIPE

Adapted from Meru Sikder's recipe

Chapati is India's whole-wheat equivalent of the Latin tortilla, an unleavened flat bread easily made fresh in your own kitchen. Though they can be made a few hours ahead of time, with a quick reheat before serving, they are much better and more pliable when made to order.

YIELD: 8 CHAPATI

½ cup all-purpose flour

1 ½ cup whole wheat flour

⅛ teaspoon salt

3 tablespoons unsalted butter, melted

¾ cup warm water

Butter for frying

In a large mixing bowl, combine all the dry ingredients together. Make a well in the middle, pouring in both the melted butter and water. With your hands, mix the dough together until it is well combined. If you find your dough needs more water, add a bit at a time until it is moist. Once ready, knead the dough for about 5 minutes, either in the mixing bowl or on a lightly floured surface, until smooth. Divide into 8 equal parts and let them rest, covered with a damp paper towel, for 15 minutes.

Lightly flour a flat surface and roll out each ball of dough to about an 8-inch disc. Stack the discs on top of one another on a plate in preparation for frying. Place a large flat pan or griddle on high heat, allowing the pan to warm first before greasing with butter. Once hot and greased, place a disc into the pan, allowing the dough to fry. It should start puffing up with air within the first 2 minutes. That is the sign to flip the chapati. Allow the second side to fry for a couple of more minutes before removing from the pan. Be sure to grease the pan in between the chapatis.

If there's a street cart that you've sworn you've heard about, it's most likely Midtown's Kwik Meal. For Mohammed Rahman the idea to open a halal cart came after tasting a chicken and rice platter down by the former World Trade Center in early 2000. At the time he was a sous chef at the famous Russian Tea Room and was entirely underwhelmed by the platter he bought. *I'm a chef. I can serve better food*, he thought. The Bangladeshi Canadian relied on his years of restaurant and home-cooking experience—as well as a stint in culinary school—to make his cart a success. He procured his license and cart, ultimately setting up shop where he can still be found most days, on West 45th Street and Sixth Avenue by August of that year. He still shows up every day to serve in a chef's toque and ascot, a nod to his professional training and a bit of marketing appeal.

When Mohammed originally set up his cart, hot dog carts were still the most common offering on the street, but New York was facing an influx of Egyptians and Middle Easterners. This rising immigrant community gravitated toward the few halal meat carts, forming lines of parked taxis as they caught a quick bite to eat while on their shifts. Mohammed noticed that most carts offered only chicken and falafel, so he went out on a limb and added lamb to his menu. He marinates it overnight in a spice-filled yogurt sauce, complete with papaya purée, and uses a bit of papaya in his sauce to tie the flavors together. The succulent lamb can be served in a puffy pita or over a heaping mound of Jasmine rice. It wasn't long before office workers and cab drivers began realizing that though it was lamb coming off a cart, it was one of the most tender and delicious lamb dishes to be found in Midtown. "Everybody loves it."

Mohammed quickly garnered fame for his menu—which also uniquely has daily fish specials—and was written about in numerous articles including a few mentions in the *New York Times*. It was no surprise when he was nominated into the Vendy Awards in 2007. He went home with the honor of being the People's Choice Winner and was nominated in again the following year. His success has allowed him to branch out with a few other carts in Midtown, though he doesn't have any plans to open a restaurant version of the cart. He'd rather be on the cart, enjoying the interactions with customers and getting home to his family at night.

KWIK MEAL'S LAMB

Adapted from Mohammed Rohman's recipe

A unique aspect of Mohammed's lamb is the marinade where the addition of papaya, whose main enzyme, papain, works to tenderize the meat. Lamb shoulder, a relatively inexpensive cut is fattier than the leg or ribs, but excellent for roasting. If you can find it as a roast—ask your butcher for blade or arm chops. Serve the chunks of lamb over jasmine rice cooked in broth or rolled into a pita with slices of lettuce and tomato, and the famous white sauce/hot sauce (page 86) on the side.

....

YIELD: SERVES 4

1 pound boneless lamb shoulder roast, trimmed
    and cubed

1 teaspoon garlic powder

1 teaspoon onion powder

1 teaspoon ground cumin

1 teaspoon toasted and ground coriander

1/2 cup plain yogurt

1/4 cup green papaya, mashed

1 teaspoon canola oil

1 teaspoon salt

1 teaspoon pepper

In a large nonreactive bowl mix everything together, coating the lamb well. Place in a plastic bag or cover the bowl with plastic wrap, and let marinate overnight in the fridge.

When you're ready to cook the lamb, preheat your oven to 325°F. Place all of the lamb onto a foil-covered baking sheet and place in the oven for about 15 minutes. While the lamb is roasting, heat a skillet or cast iron pan over high heat. Once the lamb has released its juices, and the internal temperature reaches 135°F, take out the lamb and place in the hot pan for a quick sear, about 5 minutes on each side. When finished, the lamb will have a good char, yet still be tender.

WHITE SAUCE

"White sauce, hot sauce" is the ubiquitous condiment option at every halal street food cart in New York. And any cart worth their salt has their own unique recipe for their sauces, a recipe that few are willing to ever part with. This recipe is one inspired by many trips to Kwik Meal—a cart with one of the best white sauces—and is a surefire addition to any meal involving lamb. Using Greek yogurt is essential since it provides you with a thicker, richer sauce. For your hot sauce, cook down your favorite spicy salsa verde, similar to how you would in Mexicue's "Green Chile Mac 'n' Cheese" (page 198).

YIELD: 1 CUP

½ of a medium-sized cucumber, peeled
½ cup Greek yogurt
¼ cup sour cream
¼ cup cottage cheese
1 teaspoon sugar
1 tablespoon fresh lemon juice
1 tablespoon white vinegar
2 tablespoons water

Place the cucumber in a food processor until puréed. Place in a medium bowl along with the rest of your ingredients. Whisk everything together until combined. If you find your sauce is too thick, add a bit more water to thin it out.

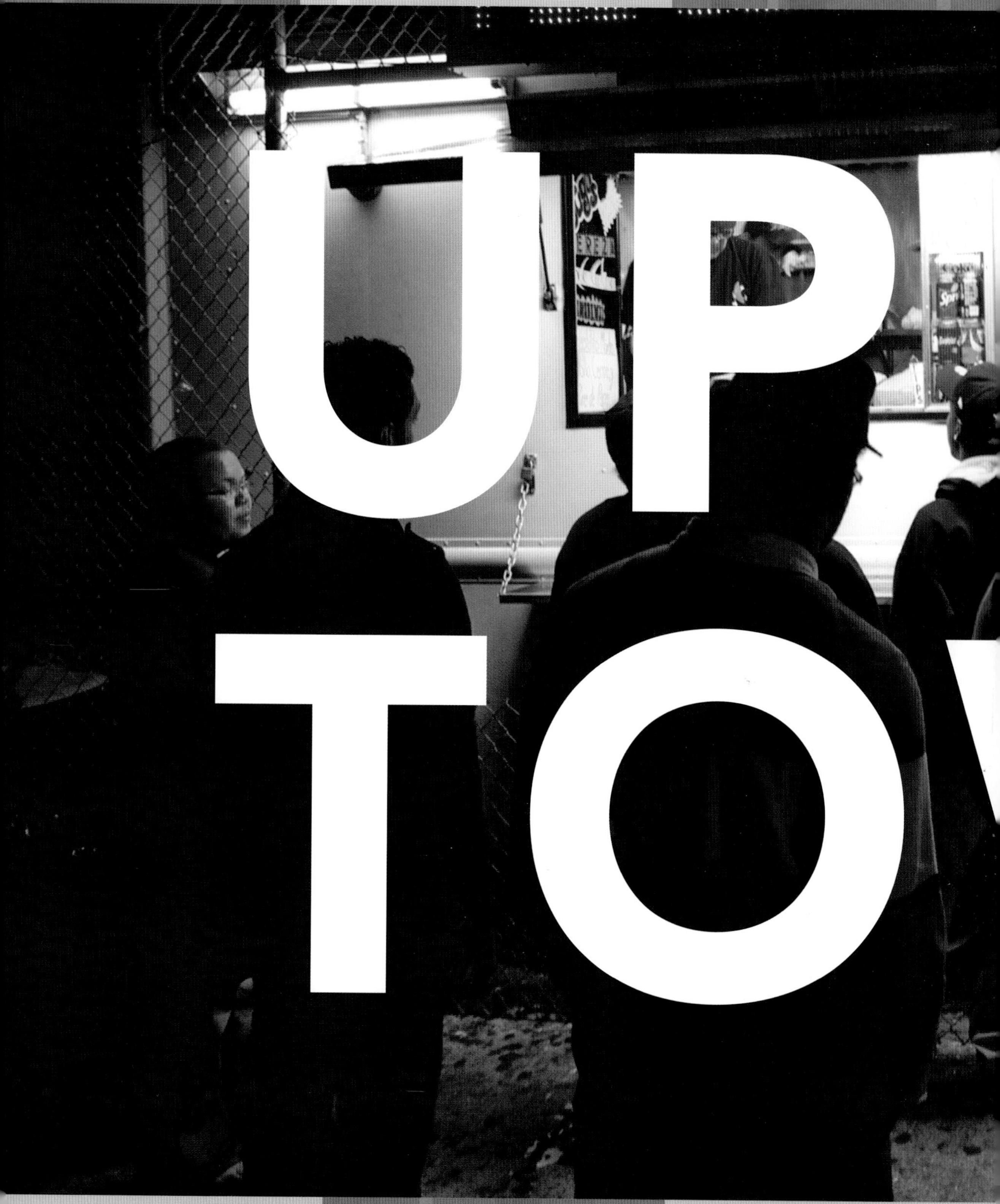
UP
TO

After a night of drinking and dancing, the first thing almost everyone wants is some deliciously unhealthy fried food. Consider yourself lucky if your night takes place in Manhattan's Washington Heights, home to a Dominican enclave, doing the merengue at Umbrella Lounge, one of the largest Dominican clubs in New York City. Right outside every night from 7:00 p.m. to 6:00 a.m. is the only Venezuelan food truck in the entire city, Patacon Pisao. More than twenty years ago, Liliana Velasquez, with her infant son Jonathan in tow, immigrated to America from Maracaibo, Venezuela. She left behind a life of working for a sewing company to work in the restaurants and cafés of Manhattan. As the manager at a well-known Fifth Avenue café, she honed her skills in the kitchen and learned the ways of the New York restaurant business. Through her hard work she persevered, achieving the American dream right down to creating a home for her and her two boys in Elmhurst, Queens.

But by the mid-2000s, Liliana "wanted to branch out and had saved up some money," to go in a new direction with her career. The few Venezuelan restaurants around served only simple food from the Caracas region, like regular cheese arepas. Back in Maracaibo, the region's signature sandwich is the *patacóen*, made with pounded and fried plantains holding together a sandwich filled with roasted and shredded meat, along with fried cheese, ketchup, and mayonnaise. Despite the fact that plantains are a beloved ingredient throughout the Caribbean and in neighboring Latin America, no food truck in New York was serving patacones or any of Maracaibo's famous dishes. Liliana spotted this hole in the market, but it wasn't until she met Adolfo Gonzales "that one thing led to another" and they conceived the idea to start a truck with Adolfo as manager and Liliana doing the cooking. Though there wasn't a large Venezuelan community in New York, they knew that the well-established community of plantain-loving Dominicans in Washington Heights would provide just the right audience for a Venezuelan menu, and the Patacon truck opened there in 2005. The name morphed into Patacon Pisao or "flattened plantain," the nickname granted to the truck from the regular customers.

It wasn't just the *patacónes* on the menu that would attract the starving club-goers. A cornmeal equivalent can be found in their fried arepa sandwich. If customers are in the mood for something sweeter, there is also a *cachapa,* a sweet corn cake, sandwich. Liliana made sure to include another Maracaibo specialty, the *tequeño,* a strip of fried cheese encased in fried dough. One crunchy bite yields the gooey, salty cheese inside. One item on

"Plantains [to Dominicans] are like white rice." —JONATHAN VELASQUEZ

the menu is a Liliana original though, the *tachucho*. Seeing that Americans like wrap sandwiches, she decided to make one up for her customers. It has all the same fillings as the other sandwiches, but instead of fried cheese, she used classic American cheese. She came up with the name by "putting taco and Maracucho together," Maracucho being a person from Maracaibo.

As the truck's popularity increased, Liliana found that she needed more cooking space than her home kitchen allowed. She made do for a while cooking out of a rented restaurant kitchen, but when a kitchen space opened up around the corner from their Elmhurst home, she had finally found enough space to cook for the masses appearing at the truck every day.

The first recognition of success by mainstream New York media came in the form of a Zagat rating. Then they were asked to participate in the *Village Voice*'s exclusive Choice Eats tasting event in 2010, which was topped later that year when they received a Vendy Awards nomination. Despite not winning, they finally got the chance to meet and try food from other vendors. All of the success has meant that Liliana can finally rest on her laurels and allow recent college graduate Jonathan to take over some of the operations, yet she still chooses to be heavily involved. They've even been fortunate enough to the Elmhurst kitchen space into the sister restaurant to the truck, the perfect spot for those who don't find themselves in Washington Heights very often.

CARNE MECHADA (SHREDDED BEEF)

Adapted from Liliana Velasquez's recipe

Patacon Pisao's carne mechada is the perfect filling for two of their popular sandwiches: the tacucho and the signature patacón. If you find you have extra left over, it's also an authentic filling for tacos. Liliana recommends using skirt or flank steak, two long, flat cuts from the underside of a cow—skirt from the diaphragm muscle or flank from the abdominals—both of which are excellent choices for braising.

....

YIELD: ENOUGH FILLING FOR 5 SANDWICHES

¼ cup canola oil

1 pound skirt or flank steak

½ large onion, roughly chopped

1 teaspoon salt, plus more to taste

1 teaspoon pepper, plus more to taste

½ large onion, finely chopped

½ red bell pepper, seeded and finely chopped

2 cloves garlic, peeled and minced

1 cup tomatoes, peeled, seeded, and chopped

Heat the oil in a skillet over medium-high. Sear the meat on both sides to brown well, about 4 to 5 minutes per side.

Remove the steak from heat and place it in a large pot with the roughly chopped onion, salt, 1 teaspoon pepper, and enough water to cover. Bring to a boil, then reduce heat to low, cover, and simmer 1 to 1½ hours, or until meat is very tender.

Remove the meat from the pot and set aside to cool, reserving the broth in a separate bowl. When cool, shred the meat with your fingers or two forks.

Reheat the skillet, adding more oil if necessary. Add the finely chopped onion, pepper, and garlic, and sauté until the onions are translucent, about 10 minutes.

Stir in the shredded meat, chopped tomatoes, and salt and pepper to taste. Add a ½ cup of the reserved broth to moisten, and simmer for about 15 to 20 minutes. Once the meat is tender, remove from heat. Serve as filling for the Tacucho (page 94) or Patacón (page 95).

(M) | (V)

TACUCHO (TACO-MARACUCHO)

The tacucho is a classic taco, quesadilla, burrito, and wrap all in one. Be sure to hold the ends to avoid losing any of the delicious carne mechada filling.

YIELD: 1 SERVING

2 slices white American cheese

1 (12-inch) flour tortilla

½ cup carne mechada (page 93)

½ teaspoon ketchup

2 large tomato slices

½ cup chopped romaine lettuce

1 teaspoon mayonnaise

Place the two slices of cheese in the center of the tortilla. Place carne mechada on top of cheese and spread the ketchup on top of that.

Layer the tomatoes and lettuce on top of the beef. Spread the mayonnaise on top the of lettuce.

Fold the tortilla tightly, like you would a burrito or wrap. Heat a flat-top grill or large pan on high heat, placing the tacucho inside when hot. Grill for about 2 minutes on each side or until tortilla is golden and crisp on both sides.

PATACÓNES (GREEN PLANTAIN SANDWICH)

Crispy, salty, and intensely satisfying, it's no wonder that Liliana's signature patacónes are a favorite late-night snack for club-goers. For these you want to use starchy, un-ripe green plantains. To peel off their hard, thick skins, cut off both ends and make cuts length-wise along the plantain.

....

YIELD: 1 SERVING

¼ cup canola oil

1 green plantain, peeled and halved

½ cup carne mechada (page 93)

2-ounce slice of queso blanco

1 large lettuce leaf

2 large slices of tomato

2 tablespoons ketchup

In a large skillet, heat oil over medium-high. Add plantain halves and cook until edges begin to brown, about 5 minutes. Remove from oil and open the plantain by splitting halves length-wise, being careful not to cut all the way through. Flatten plantain halves into discs with a meat tenderizer or mallet. Return plantain discs to the hot oil and fry until they are crispy and golden on the outside, about another five minutes.

Once discs are finished frying, remove the discs from the oil, placing them on a few paper towels. Add the carne mechada to the top of one disc.

Lightly fry the slice of queso blanco about 30 seconds on each side until it slightly bubbles and turns golden. Remove and place the slice on top of the meat.

Top the cheese with lettuce, tomato, and ketchup, and close sandwich with other fried plantain disc.

Despite being eighty years old, Manuel Cruz is still an important part of the food truck he opened in 1987, Chimichury el Malecón. "He grinds the meat every day—it's his thing!" says daughter Monica Cruz, who now runs the truck along with her brother David. Escaping the Trujillo dictatorship in the Dominican Republic, Manuel immigrated to New York City in 1957, originally settling in the Bronx before moving to Inwood in 1978. The neighborhood had yet to face the influx of Dominicans who would immigrate during the mid to late-1980s, a period that would ultimately overhaul the demographics of northern Manhattan. In 1987, as the numbers of Dominicans were picking up, Manuel—then a worker in a neighborhood factory—thought to start selling the national street food of chimichurris from a food kiosk on the corner of Sherman Avenue and 207th Street. He originally wanted something more along the lines of a food kiosk, but soon realized the kitchen space limitations of such a small enclosure. Regardless, at the time, "there really wasn't anything like it in the neighborhood," explains Monica.

Feeding the new population proved to be a success for Manuel, even though his first week out held a minor catastrophe when the ventilation caught fire. Open now for more than twenty years, Chimichury el Malecón has become a neighborhood institution and a required stop for anyone visiting, including former residents. "There's a family from Boston. Every time they come here to visit, they have to get chimis." About two years ago, Manuel had an idea to build a new cart replacing the truck he previously had. In his son's New Jersey backyard, they made an entirely custom-made cart, designed to have enough kitchen space for at least two people, a sliding door, and a huge take-out window at just the right height for the street. The only time this cart has moved from its home on

Sherman Avenue was on a trip downtown and across New York Harbor to Governors Island for the 2011 Vendy Awards. Being nominated and appearing at the Vendys was "really awesome" and "a surprise" for the entire family even though "everyone knew a month before [we] did" due to an e-mail snafu. While there, the truck received numerous compliments, and a few vendors checked it out for their own purposes. With the business slowly moving hands to the younger generation of Cruzes, they do hope to keep Manuel's dream alive. They've been thinking of opening a brick-and-mortar location in the neighborhood, where Monica still lives a few blocks away from her parents. But for now, you can still sit outside the truck, eating the best chimis in Inwood every evening.

"We've been here the longest. People might try another food truck and come back to us."

—MONICA CRUZ

CHIMICHURRI
Adabted from Monica Cruz's recipe

The main differences between the American hamburger and the Dominican chimichurri lie with the spices blended into the meat and the toppings added to the finished sandwich. Yet, similar to the American cousin, you can add in more toppings to your liking; the Cruzes recommend trying out hot sauce. If your local bakery doesn't sell Portuguese rolls, you can substitute Kaiser rolls for the chimichurri.

YIELD: SERVES 5

½ large head of cabbage, thinly sliced

1 large carrot, finely chopped

¼ cup vinegar

1 clove garlic, peeled and chopped

1 tablespoon Worcestershire sauce

¼ cup ketchup

¼ cup mayonnaise, plus more for the sandwiches

5 large Portugese Rolls

1 large tomato, thinly sliced

Salt

2 pounds fresh ground beef

2 tablespoon oregano

1 medium onion, thinly sliced

Combine the cabbage and carrot in a medium bowl with the vinegar and salt. Set aside.

Prepare the chimi sauce by combining the Worcesterhsire sauce, ketchup, and mayonnaise in a small bowl. Set aside.

Hand mix the ground beef with the oregano and a pinch of salt. Separate the beef into five patties, thinning each into an oblong shape. Warm a flat pan on medium-high heat, placing the patties inside without overcrowding. Cook on each side for approximately four minutes or until your preferred doneness.

Toast a Portugese roll until lightly brown, brushing on mayonnaise onto both sides

Place a generous amount of the cabbage slaw, a slice of tomato, and a few slices of onion on the bottom bun. Over this, drizzle two tablespoons of the sauce.

Add one beef patty, and close with the top bun. Cut in half and serve.

LONGANIZA FRITA

Adabted from Monica Cruz's recipe

Longaniza is one of the sausage styles brought to Latin America from Spain that now has many different varieties depending on which country you're in. For this recipe, you'll want to seek out Dominican *longaniza*, a pork sausage spiced with sofrito—a tomato-based spice paste filled with bell peppers, onion, garlic, annatto, oregano, and cilantro—before its curing.

YIELD: SERVES 4

2 pounds, about 6 to 8 links, longaniza pork sausage

1 cup lime juice, freshly squeezed

¼ cup sour orange juice

4 tablespoons soy sauce

2 tablespoons brown sugar

2 tablespoons Worcestershire sauce

1 tablespoon dried oregano

4 cloves garlic, minced

2 quarts oil for frying

lime slices, for serving

ketchup, for serving

Cut the sausage links into small bite-sized pieces, and set aside. Combine the rest of the ingredients in one large bowl to create a marinade. Marinate the sausage pieces for at least an hour, preferably overnight.

Heat the oil in a deep-fryer or large pot to 375°F. Once hot, carefully place your sausage pieces into the oil, and fry until extra crispy, about 5 minutes. When done, place them on a plate covered with paper towels for a few minutes to soak up the oil. Serve hot with slices of lime and ketchup.

If the Good Humor Man and Betty Grable had a daughter, she would be Chrissy Michaels. Known as Miss Softee, with her vintage aprons and sassy charm, she harkens back to a kinder, gentler time when ice-cream men remembered their regulars' cones and doled out smiles like sprinkles.

In her few short years on the streets, Chrissy developed a cult following in Midtown for her specialty cones. Her whimsical-yet-simple creations include the American Cone, vanilla soft serve rolled in crushed chocolate chip cookies and rainbow sprinkles, and the Cherry Dream, cherry dip and vanilla meringue, "which together tastes like a giant Lucky Charm marshmallow." But Chrissy's favorite of the dozen plus specials is the Potato Chip Chocolate Dip. A vanilla or chocolate ice-cream cone dipped in chocolate and rolled in crushed potato chips, it's a perfect treat for sweet and salty fiends and "tastes like dipping your French fries in a milkshake!"

Chrissy's success as an ice cream queen traces back to her previous life in advertising. After the economy bottomed out in 2008, she decided to pursue a long-suppressed desire to drive an ice cream truck and signed up with Mister Softee, one of the country's oldest soft ice cream vending operations. Once Chrissy got behind the wheel, she discovered that the streets of Manhattan were far less cushy that her former Madison Avenue gig. "As odd as that sounds in this day and age, one of the biggest obstacles about this job is being a woman," says Chrissy. With long hours, physical labor, and intimidating rival vendors jockeying for prime spots, the work tends to skew male, and "it takes time to prove that you can do the same job as well as (or better than) the guys."

It wasn't long before Chrissy began baking homemade cookies, brownies, pies, and more for "à la mode" specials that kept her regulars coming

"Everyone is happy to see you every day. You get to share in celebrations, cheer someone up when they're having a rough day, and help bring back fond childhood memories dripping with chocolate and rolled in sprinkles."

—CHRISSY MICHAELS, AKA MISS SOFTEE

back. "I run things a little differently than a lot of the other 'new school' vendors. First off, I'm a one-woman show! I stock, clean, maintain, park, drive, bake, tweet, and serve for my truck." The higher-ups at the depot took notice of her success. In 2011, Chrissy was promoted to manage a small fleet of Softees in the city, with a charge to revamp their whole operation: from training and overseeing new workers to rolling out her signature specials on all the trucks in their franchise group. The end of that summer was capped with a dessert Vendy nod and the bittersweet announcement that Miss Softee was going off road, Chrissy was officially hanging up her apron to pursue new ventures.

Even if Chrissy's no longer dipping cones, her heart has never strayed far from the kitchen. "As a single parent, my mom worked really hard to raise me and my younger brother with a solid foundation in the kitchen. No matter what was going on, she would cook dinner every single night at home, from scratch." Lately those skills learned at her mother's side are being put into use as the executive chef and manager of a small farm-to-table CSA (community supported agriculture). "I create the menu daily and also work with the farmers to curate the packages for CSA members." Chrissy is also channeling her energy into Chrissy's Cooking Club, a Brooklyn-based, community-focused nonprofit that she founded in 2011. In her spare time you can find her holed up in a supersecret test kitchen set up in the back of an ice cream truck, where she's working on developing her own all-natural soft serve.

APPLE CRUMBLE PIE
Adapted from Chrissy Michaels's recipe

"I'm a renegade, so to the dismay of hardcore apple pie enthusiasts in the Northeast, I like to use Granny Smith apples in my pie," says Chrissy. The tartness balances well with the sweetness of the crumble, and the apples hold up well to cooking. Not surprisingly, this dessert is best when served warm and topped with vanilla ice cream.

YIELD: SERVES 8

1 cup quick-cook oats

1 cup all-purpose flour

1 cup light brown sugar, firmly packed

¼ teaspoon salt

1 teaspoon cinnamon

4 tablespoons unsalted butter

1 tablespoon lemon juice

7 medium-sized Granny Smith apples, peeled and cored

2 tablespoons cornstarch or arrowroot powder

1 cup granulated sugar

2 teaspoons vanilla extract

1 quart vanilla ice cream, for serving

Move oven rack to the center position and preheat the oven to 350°F. In a large bowl, mix together the oats, flour, brown sugar, salt, and cinnamon. Melt the butter in a small saucepan and add to the dry mixture. Toss together until the mixture forms into loose clumps in your hand. Set the mixture aside.

In a large bowl, mix together two cups of cold water and the lemon juice. Thinly slice the apples lengthwise and add to a bowl of water and lemon juice as you finish slicing them, to keep them from browning. Once all of the apples are sliced, drain the water, reserving about a cup for the cooking. Dust the apple slices with the cornstarch or arrowroot powder (a thickening agent), and toss to mix until apples are just barely coated.

Pour the reserved water and white sugar in a large saucepan, and slowly heat mixture over medium heat until sugar is dissolved and it becomes a syrup, about 3 to 5 minutes. Add the apples and vanilla. Stir the mixture with a wooden spoon occasionally until it comes to a boil and a thick syrup forms. Remove from heat and set aside to cool.

In a pie tin, press half of the crumble mixture along the bottom and sides of the pan to form a crust. Parbake crust for about 5 minutes or until firm. Add the apple filling and top with the remaining crumble. Bake until it is golden brown and the crumble is firm, about 30 to 40 minutes. Let cool before slicing so that the apples can set. Serve à la mode with vanilla ice cream.

MAKE-YOUR-MARK COFFEE-CAKE ICE CREAM SUNDAE
Adapted from Chrissy Michaels's recipe

At the 2011 Vendy Awards Chrissy Michaels, aka Miss Softee, wowed the crowds with her Maker's Mark®-infused-crumb cake ice cream sundae. Booze soaked raisins and an alcoholic glaze make this dessert one strictly for the 21 and over crowd. Don't like raisins? You can substitute cranberries, dried apples, or figs. Just make sure that when you're choosing a dried fruit, you find one that doesn't have added sugar or preservatives. To optimize the flavor, the fruit needs to be soaked in alcohol for at least 2 days, but the good news is that alcohol-soaked fruit lasts for up to a month stored in the refrigerator. Pressed for time? Chrissy suggests subbing you favorite store-bought crumb cake. After a few bourbon soaked raisins, your guests won't notice (or care) that it's not homemade.

YIELD: SERVES 8

FOR THE RAISINS:
1 cup raisins
1 cup bourbon

FOR THE CRUMB TOPPING:
1¼ cup all-purpose flour
½ cup quick-cook oats
½ cup light brown sugar, firmly packed
¼ cup granulated sugar
1 teaspoon cinnamon
¼ teaspoon salt
8 tablespoons unsalted butter, melted

FOR THE CAKE:
1½ cup all-purpose
1½ teaspoons baking powder
¼ teaspoon salt
8 tablespoons unsalted butter, plus more for
    greasing the pan
1 cup granulated sugar
6 large egg yolks
½ cup buttermilk
2 teaspoons vanilla extract

FOR THE GLAZE:
5 tablespoons unsalted butter
½ cup confectioners' sugar
2 tablespoons light brown sugar
2 tablespoons bourbon
2 tablespoons whole milk
1 quart vanilla ice cream, for serving

Add raisins to a large sterilized canning jar and top with bourbon. Cap the jar, then shake lightly to distribute the alcohol. Store in the refrigerator for at least 2 days or up to a month.

Move oven rack to the center position and preheat the oven to 350°F. Grease and flour an 8 x 8–inch glass baking dish. In a large bowl, mix together the flour, oats, sugars, cinnamon, and salt. Stir melted butter into the dry mixture. Toss together until the mixture forms into loose clumps in your hand. Set the mixture aside.

In a medium bowl whisk together flour, baking powder, and salt and set aside. In a large bowl or an electric stand mixer beat together butter and sugar on medium speed until light and creamy, about 3 to 5 minutes. Add egg yolks and beat on medium until just incorporated, scraping down the sides of the bowl as necessary, about 2 minutes. Add flour mixture and beat on medium until just incorporated. Add buttermilk and vanilla extract and beat on medium until fully incorporated, about 2 to 3 minutes. Scrape batter into prepared baking dish spreading with a spatula to distribute. Sprinkle evenly with crumb topping and bake for 55 to 60 minutes or until top is golden brown and a cake tester comes out clean. Cool cake in the pan on a wire rack for 15 to 20 minutes.

TO PREPARE THE GLAZE:

When cake is near cool, begin preparing the glaze. In a medium stainless-steel saucepan, melt butter over medium heat, stirring constantly. Timing will vary according to your stove and cookware, so watch butter closely as it begins to foam. It will change in color from yellow to a golden brown that's flecked with browned bits. Remove from heat and transfer butter to a medium bowl. Whisk in sugars, bourbon, and milk until smooth.

TO SERVE:

Slice cake into equal portions, top with a scoop of ice cream, sprinkle with raisins, and drizzle with glaze.

If Phil Lee has his way, one day, perhaps one day soon, there will be a jar of kimchi in every refrigerator across America. Some fifteen years ago, when the Kimchi Taco Truck owner wrote his final paper for Cornell's Hospitality Management program, he pledged to put kimchi, the national dish of Korea, on the map in the United States. Most people associate kimchi with the spicy, pungent, red chili-infused variety of the fermented cabbage, but as Phil explains, "there's over a couple hundred kinds of kimchi." And kimchi finds its way into every single dish on the Kimchi Taco Truck, in exciting and inventive ways.

Phil's path to opening the Kimchi Taco Truck was a long and winding one. Despite his early enthusiasm for kimchi, his postgraduate career track found him in front-of-house roles at fine dining establishments around New York City. After more than a decade working as a general manager for prominent restaurateurs, including Jeffrey Chodorow and Steve Hanson of the BR Guest

Hospitality, Phil was ready to make a change. "I went to BR Guest thinking I was just going to be there a few years, but then I had a family and kids and all that. The next thing you know it's nine years. And you're like, *it's time to do this*. The kids are a little bit older. You've got to take a chance at this point or else you're going to end up dying regretting it."

Phil grew up on Long Island, where American foods and kimchi existed side by side on the Lees' table. If Phil's mom packed him a turkey sandwich, it had a few pieces of kimchi on top. For Thanksgiving, the family enjoyed a turkey with all the trimmings, but his dad "would still need Korean food."

Pairing American classics with a Korean twist came naturally to Phil. He wanted to make Korean food accessible to people who might never think of stepping into a traditional Korean restaurant. But with the economy still in a slump in 2010, gathering the capital to open a storefront was a challenge.

"For me it's about my personal goal of trying to get Korean food to as many people as possible, especially kimchi. It's something that I grew up with, something that I'm proud of. It's part of my heritage and culture, and I want to share it with as many people as possible. Hopefully I've done that. . . . That's what it's all about." —PHIL LEE

From a business standpoint, the more that Phil looked into opening a truck, the more sense it seemed to make. The Kimchi Taco Truck not only had to build a following, but they also had to create a market for kimchi. With that in mind, the lower investment and mobility of a food truck proved to be an advantage. "I think New Yorkers definitely get bored very easily because there's always new things happening all the time. Just understanding that mentality, I think the truck is the perfect concept because you don't have to go to one place seven days a week. You go to different places and keep them wanting more."

As the food truck landscape has grown, so have the number of Korean taco trucks in New York, with many patterning themselves after Kogi BBQ, the Los Angeles-based truck that first popularized Korean-style barbecue tacos in late 2008. While no fewer than four other trucks serve Korean tacos in the New York City, the Kimchi Taco Truck takes that concept one step further, melding traditional street foods and Korean traditions to come up with dishes like "Kim-Cheesesteaks" served Philly style ("wit'" or "wit'out Whiz") and BBQ nachos topped with *bulgogi*, a marinated barbecued beef, as well as spicy seared pork decked out with kimchi, queso blanco, cheddar, pico de gallo, green onion, and a miso crema. Their falafel is milder than its Middle Eastern cousin. Made from tofu, edamame and chickpeas, it's flavored with perilla seed and cilantro, and is served up with kimchi-infused refried beans alongside a light and refreshing summer cucumber and pickled daikon kimchi.

Still, cultivating a following wasn't easy. "Even though kimchi was really good to me and went well with everything. It didn't go well with everything for everyone," Phil admits. Over the first year, their menu underwent several extensive overhauls.

Their kimchi recipes have changed to better balance the flavors. "It terms of the traditional kimchi, the red kimchi, we're only using it in the pork because it can stand up to it. With the beef, which is a very delicate meat, along with the chicken and the falafel, we use different types of kimchi." Chicken and falafel are paired with the summer kimchi, which pickles for a just a few days so that it retains a bright crispness. The barbecued beef is matched up with a house blend of the red kimchi and the summer kimchi.

The kimchi pickling and prep work for the truck is all done at The Kimchi Grill, their take-out shop in Prospect Heights, where they are able to offer a more extensive menu that includes include soups, pork belly, and Korean fried chicken tacos, items that are hard to serve on the truck due to constraints in space and equipment limitations. "The biggest issue is the equipment itself. You're dealing with propane as opposed to natural gas, so your BTU is not as powerful. When you're trying to do x amount of volume at a certain BTU, the meats don't get seared properly. Things don't get hot as quickly as you want them to." The truck supported the eventual opening of the store, and now the store supports the truck, by allowing Phil's team to experiment more with their menu, constantly tweaking and improving it.

As a seasoned restaurateur, Phil has long enjoyed street food in the New York City and frequents a number of the food trucks. A food lover, first and foremost, Phil enjoys seeking out new dishes and flavors. With regard to other trucks, he says, "For me personally, I think the more the merrier. That's what New York's all about. You're able to have different variety, different options. I think that's what makes New York special."

BBQ BEEF KIM-CHEESESTEAK

Adapted from Phil Lee's recipe

Many halal carts offer Philly cheesesteaks, but the Kimchi Taco Truck takes that concept one step further, replacing the thin pieces of chopped steak with *bulgogi*, Korean barbecue beef. This recipe calls for sirloin steak—the tender cuts of meat from a cow's hips—but if you want to go all out, use rib-eye, the delicious well-marbled cuts from the meaty top of the ribs. For ease of preparation, ask your butcher to thinly slice either of these cuts for you. A sesame oil and soy sauce fruit marinade is enhanced with white wine and *mirin*, a sweet Japanese rice wine makes the *bulgogi* meat super tender. The sugars from the marinade caramelize when the meat hits the grill giving it a nice char. At the truck you can get it true Philly-style with Cheeze Whiz or provolone cheese.

YIELD: 6 SANDWICHES

½ medium-sized white onion, puréed

4 cloves garlic, peeled and pressed

1 Asian pear, peeled and grated (about ¾ cup)

1 apple, peeled and grated (about ¾ cup)

1 kiwi, peeled and grated

2 scallions, white and green parts julienned

⅓ cup soy sauce

2 tablespoons granulated sugar

2 tablespoons sesame oil

2 tablespoons *mirin*

2 tablespoons sauvignon blanc or chardonnay

1 teaspoon garlic powder

½ teaspoon black pepper

1½ pounds sliced sirloin or rib-eye, thinly sliced (about ¼-inch thick)

1½ cup red kimchi

6 (6-inch) hoagie rolls, split

12 slices of provolone cheese, halved

In a large bowl, combine onion, garlic, pear, apple, kiwi, and scallions. Stir in soy sauce, sugar, sesame oil, *mirin*, white wine, garlic powder, and black pepper. Add beef and toss to combine and completely coat meat.

Cover and marinate meat in refrigerator for at least 4 to 5 hours or overnight.

Heat a large cast-iron skillet over high heat for 5 minutes. Working in batches, add 4 or 5 slices of beef to the pan and cook on high heat for about 2 minutes to get a nice sear. Add 3 or 4 pieces of kimchi to the pan and stir to let the juices release. Turn the meat and cook for another 1 to 2 minutes, being careful not to overcook the meat. Transfer cooked meat and kimchi to a cutting board and coarsely chop.

Cover both sides of each roll with chopped beef. Add two provolone slice halves to each side of the hoagie. Place under the broiler for 1 minute, or until the cheese is completely melted, keeping a close eye on the sandwich so as not to burn the cheese. Join the two halves to form the sandwich and serve.

Note: If you're a huge kimchi fan, coarsely chop ½ cup kimchi and add several table-spoons to the top of each hoagie before closing the sandwich.

KOREAN BBQ PORK

Adapted from Phil Lee's recipe

Daeji bulgogi or Korean barbecue pork is marinated in *gochujang*, a spicy Korean fermented red pepper paste that can be found at Asian specialty shops. American pork tends to be ultra-lean and can dry out quickly upon cooking. Because of this, Phil Lee recommends using pork butt, the marbled cut of meat front the top of a pig's shoulder. The word "butt" derives from an Old English term, and don't confuse this cut of meat with pork shoulder roast. You want the pieces of pork to be very thinly sliced against the grain. You can ask your butcher to prepare the pork for you to ensure that it's cut properly. The pork can be substituted for beef in the BBQ Beef Kim-Cheesesteak (page 111).

....

½ medium-sized white onion, puréed

4 cloves garlic, peeled and pressed

1 apple, grated (about ¾ cup)

⅓ cup soy sauce

2 tablespoons granulated sugar

2 tablespoons sesame oil

4 tablespoons *gochujang* (Korean red pepper paste)

1 teaspoon garlic powder

½ teaspoon black pepper

1½ pounds pork butt, thinly sliced

In a large bowl combine onion, garlic, and apple. Stir in soy sauce, sugar, sesame oil, *gochujang*, garlic powder, and black pepper. Add pork and toss to combine and completely coat meat.

Cover bowl and marinate meat in refrigerator for at least 4 to 5 hours, or overnight.

Heat a large cast-iron skillet over high heat for 5 minutes. Working in batches, add 4 or 5 slices of pork to the pan and cook on high heat for about 2 minutes to get a nice sear. Add 2 tablespoons of marinade and stir to coat pieces. Turn the meat and cook for another 1 to 2 minutes, being careful not to overcook the meat. Transfer cooked meat to a cutting board and coarsely chop. Store covered for up to 2 days.

To Make the Korean Tacos:

....

Top warmed double stacked small corn tortillas with ¼ pound of either Korean BBQ Pork or Korean BBQ Beef (see page 111) finish with Korean Style Pico de Gallo (page 114), Miso Crema (page 114), and shredded kimchi.

KOREAN-STYLE PICO DE GALLO

This fusion *pico de gallo* gets its pucker from rice vinegar and lime juice and makes for a great topping for Korean style tacos with Korean BBQ Pork (page 113) or Korean BBQ Nachos (page 115).

YIELD: ABOUT 1 CUP

1½ large tomatoes, diced

1 small red onion, finely chopped

1 jalapeño pepper, deveined, seeded, and finely chopped

1 tablespoon rice vinegar

2 tablespoons fresh lime juice (about 1 lime)

In a medium bowl, combine diced tomatoes, red onion, jalapeño, rice vinegar, and lime juice. Store covered in the refrigerator for up to 2 days.

MISO CREMA

Ordinary sour cream gets a new identity with a touch of miso paste.

YIELD: ¼ CUP

¼ cup sour cream

½ teaspoon mild miso paste

In a small bowl, whisk together sour cream and miso paste. Serve immediately or store in the refrigerator for up to 1 day.

KOREAN BBQ NACHOS

Adapted from Phil Lee's recipe

Perfect for game time or anytime, these Korean BBQ nachos pack a pungent punch and will last you through overtime.

YIELD: SERVES 8

1 (16-ounce) bag yellow corn tortilla chips

12 ounces cheddar cheese, shredded
   (about 3 cups)

½ pound Korean BBQ beef (page 111)

½ pound Korean BBQ pork (page 113)

1 cup kimchi, coarsely chopped

1 cup Korean-Style Pico de Gallo (page 114)

¼ cup Miso Crema (page 114)

½ cup grape tomatoes, sliced

Move the oven rack to the top position. Preheat oven to 350°F. On a large oven-safe plate or platter spread ⅔ of the tortilla chips in a single layer. Sprinkle with about half of the cheese and top with half of the beef, half of the pork, and half of the kimchi. Cover with remaining tortilla chips; sprinkle with remaining cheese; and then cover with remaining meats.

Place the nachos in the oven and heat for 10 minutes or until the cheese is melted. Remove from oven, top with *pico de gallo*, miso crema, and tomatoes, and serve.

New Yorkers first met the Belgian waffle at the 1964 World's Fair in Flushing. Lighter and crispier than its flat American counterpart, the attraction was instant. In the forty years since, waffles have strayed from their roots, so much so that the Belgian King Albert II directed the Ministry of Culinary Affairs to send a Special Wafel Envoy to lead a movement to restore Belgian waffle credibility—or so the story goes according to the cheeky blog counterpart to the award-winning, internationally recognized, Wafels & Dinges truck.

While King Albert may not have had a direct hand in the inception of Wafels & Dinges, Brussels-born Thomas DeGeest did find the American version of his country's national snack to be "very upsetting." A former IBM consultant, Thomas left a jet-set, six-figure job to roam the streets in a temperamental 1968 Chevy box truck, changing culinary perceptions one waffle at a time. One of the first dessert trucks in the city, Wafels & Dinges was also a pioneer in social media connectivity. "In those days nobody really had Twitter. I would call my wife, and she would update our location on the blog.

Finally she got fed up—rightfully so—and that's how I became the first truck to have a Twitter."

Most customers are surprised to discover that Wafels & Dinges packs not one, but two different Belgian waffles. There's the Brussels waffle—what most Americans think of as a Belgian waffle—and the Liège waffle—a denser yeast-dough waffle made with pearl sugar, which gives it a caramelized exterior and crunchy bursts of sweetness throughout. Though Belgians tend to be purists, adding minimal toppings, Thomas recognized the demand for customization and created an extensive menu of toppings known as *dinges* (ding-us), the Flemish word for "whatchamacallits." Dinges range from Texas-style pulled pork with slaw to Kool-Aid–soaked pickles to real Belgian chocolate sauce, nuts, and seasonal fruit. For an extra two bucks you can turn your waffle into a WMD (aka "waffle of massive deliciousness"), adding as many toppings as you want. On Saturday mornings, the wide leafy sidewalks of Park Slope are packed with parents steering their Bugaboos with one hand and balancing their WMDs with the other, all smiles.

These days Thomas commands a waffle fleet

"My life was ten days in New York, ten days in L.A., ten days in Paris, and ten days in Tokyo. Then repeat. I loved my job, but are you really going to do that for the rest of your life?" —THOMAS DEGEEST

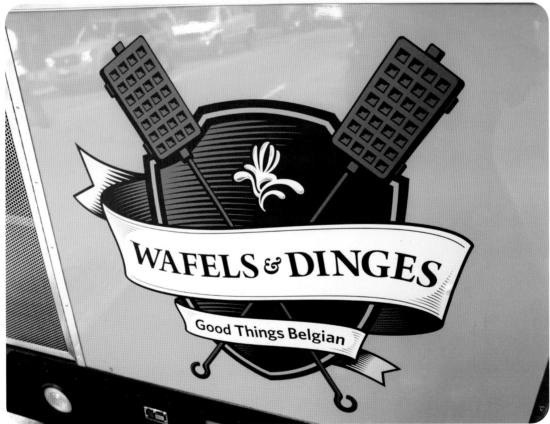

that includes two trucks and five carts that turn up anywhere from Williamsburg to the Upper East Side. But he'll never forget his humble beginnings aboard the original waffle truck. Within a few months of opening the business, the nearly forty-year-old Chevy stopped starting on its own. Since the truck had a manual transmission, Thomas would throw it into second gear and tow it each morning with his car—but that was only a temporary fix. "Because we were tow-starting it every day, the timing of the engine got out of whack. We started getting a tremendous amount of backfire." One day the bottom of the truck caught fire somewhere on Park Avenue South. "I was a little more scared," Thomas says, "so we decided instead of tow-starting it, we would just tow it." For a couple of months they attached a big rope to the waffle truck and then coupled it to Thomas's old Mercedes station wagon. "It was really scary when we had to make left and right turns. Pedestrians didn't know the two were attached."

After a few months, Thomas and his team were getting good at their covert towing operation, and everything was fine—until they got caught. One day as they were returning from a catering event, Thomas had a feeling that they were going to get caught. Within half a block, they heard the sirens. "They were like, *What are you doing boys? It's illegal to tow a truck in Manhattan*," Thomas says. Thomas and his employee were summoned to court. They put on their best suits and found themselves in front of a grumpy, old judge. When he saw their files, he brightened. "The judge goes, *So boys, you guys sell waffles. So what do you put on these waffles?*" Thomas told him about the various dinges, and the judge proceeded to cross-examine them with *You put whipped cream on them, too?* Case dismissed.

With towing the truck off the table and a new truck being built, Thomas roughed out a few months selling from a spot near his apartment, moving the truck only for street cleaning. Business was very slow. "My workers would give me the revenue from the day, and I would basically give it back to them as a salary." Things finally turned around when they got the shiny new truck, but Thomas misses his old ride. "I so regret sending that old truck to the junkyard. I'm so upset with myself that I didn't have the vision to keep the truck. I think one day I will buy a similar model on eBay."

In 2009, with the new truck in place, they took home the Dessert Vendy Award. The win was especially sweet because the previous year they had been unexpectedly scratched from the competition after the old truck broke down the night before. Thomas still can't believe that they won. "Big Gay Ice Cream (page 184) had a phenomenal product and a very strong following. I think what we did well was we had a very good operation going that could pull it off to serve a lot of people that day. It was great—it really put us on the map. It was a very big boost. The aftershocks are still being felt now."

Next to the Vendys, one of the biggest moments for Wafels & Dinges came in 2011 when Belgium's Prince Philippe and Princess Mathilde made a surprise visit to the cart. "I had no idea that was actually coming. They were on a trade mission to New York, the prince and princess. That day I was on a trip to China with my wife. I suddenly saw it on the blogs." The prince and princess had planned a tour through Central Park. "At the end of Central Park at 60th Street and Sixth Avenue, they saw the Belgian flag, and it was kind of hard for them not to stop and get a waffle. I'm still waiting for the king and the queen to come. They're invited."

CLASSIC BRUSSELS WAFFLES

Adapted from Thomas DeGeest's recipe

Thomas DeGeest likens the *Liège* waffle to the Belgian equivalent of the hot dog. "It's street food. You get it in a little kiosk. Belgians eat it with no toppings. It's soft. It's sweet. It's chewy." While the Brussels waffle is "the Belgian equivalent of a bratwurst. It's eaten inside in tearooms, a little more formal. It has to be very light and crispy. Very airy." With this recipe, you can make authentic Brussels waffles at home that would even impress King Albert.

YIELD: 8 (5 x 4–INCH) WAFFLES

1½ teaspoons instant yeast

1 cup warm water (between 105°F and 115°F)

1 tablespoon sugar

3 cups all-purpose flour

½ teaspoon salt

1 cup whole milk

8 tablespoons unsalted butter, melted

2 large eggs, whites and yolks separated

1 teaspoon vanilla extract

confectioners' sugar, for dusting, if desired

Belgian Chocolate Fudge Sauce (page 121), for serving

In a small bowl, dissolve the yeast in the water. Add sugar and stir to dissolve. Cover bowl with plastic wrap and set aside for 5 minutes to activate.

In a large bowl, whisk the flour with the salt. Whisk in the activated yeast mixture, milk, butter, egg yolks, and vanilla until smooth.

In a medium bowl, beat the egg whites until soft peaks form. Fold them into the batter, cover and let stand for 20 minutes.

Move oven rack to center position and preheat the oven to 225°F. Prepare the waffles according to your manufacturer's instructions, cooking them until golden brown. Transfer each waffle to a pan in the oven to keep warm until serving. Repeat with the remaining batter. Dust the waffles with confectioners' sugar, if desired, and drizzle with the Belgian Chocolate Fudge Sauce, and serve.

TIP: For an epic dessert (or true breakfast of champions) try these waffles topped with Coolhaus's Browned Butter Bacon Ice Cream (page 156).

BELGIAN CHOCOLATE FUDGE SAUCE

Adapted from Thomas DeGeest's recipe

This decadent chocolate sauce recipe demands real Belgian chocolate.

YIELD: MAKES 2 CUPS

10 ounces 70% cacao Belgian chocolate

1 cup heavy cream

2 tablespoons confectioners' sugar

Chop chocolate into small pieces and add to a medium bowl. Set aside.

In a small saucepan, bring the cream to just a boil over medium-high heat. Remove from the heat and slowly pour the cream into the bowl of chocolate. Let stand for 2 minutes, then whisk until the chocolate is melted. Add the confectioners' sugar and whisk until smooth. Drizzle over waffles before serving. Refrigerate any remaining sauce in an airtight container for up to 2 days.

CORN WAFFLES
Adapted from Thomas DeGeest's recipe

Though Wafels & Dinges may be on an international culinary mission, the Special Wafel Envoy is not afraid to buck tradition with nouveau waffle concoctions, like their popular corn waffles. Slightly salty, slightly sweet, these make for a lighter riff on cornbread when served up with your favorite chili recipe. Thomas suggests topping with vegetarian or beef chili, grated cheese, sour cream, and fresh cilantro.

....

YIELD: 8 (5 x 4–INCH) WAFFLES

1¼ cups all-purpose flour

1½ cups yellow cornmeal

½ cup granulated sugar

1 teaspoon baking powder

½ teaspoon salt

2 cups milk

2 large eggs

¼ cup canola oil

1 cup canned corn kernels, drained

Move oven rack to center position and preheat the oven to 225°F.

In a large bowl, combine the flour, cornmeal, sugar, baking powder, and salt.

In a separate bowl whisk together the milk, eggs, and oil until just combined. Whisk wet ingredients into dry ingredients just until combined, then stir in corn.

Prepare the waffles according to your manufacturer's instructions, cooking them until golden brown. Transfer each waffle to a pan in the oven to keep warm until serving

TIP: For a sweet, breakfast take, pair these Corn Waffles with the Cinnamon Snail's Pine Nut Butter (page 164) and fresh maple syrup.

What do you get when you combine butter, flour, sugar, and five tons of steel? Why, The Treats Truck, of course! The idea was so simple that it came to owner/baker/driver Kim Ima fully formed: outfit a truck to sell comfort desserts, then drive it to different neighborhoods, spreading treats (and joy) around the city. The menu wouldn't be too fancy, just little tastes of childhood—fudgy brownies, whimsical sugar cookies, and tricked-out Rice Krispies Treats— simple homemade desserts just like Mom's (maybe even better than Mom's . . .). "I've always wanted to try my hand at being an entrepreneur, and if ever there was something I could get behind, this is the thing I really want to do. I just really wanted to see it happen."

The petite proprietress didn't own a car and had never driven a truck, but that wasn't going to stop her. And neither would a few baking blunders. Six months before The Treats Truck hit the road, Kim holed up in a commercial kitchen, perfecting her recipes. After some trial-and-error scaling disasters—"I was like a grown-up Girl Scout in the kitchen"—Kim transformed from a small-scale baking enthusiast to a full-fledged professional baker.

Ice cream carts—and later trucks—have been a mainstay for sugar-rush seekers on the go since the nineteenth century, but The Treats Truck was the start of an entirely new phenomenon: the gourmet dessert truck. It was the beginning of New York's mobile foodaissance when "Sugar," Kim's retro-chic, silver, red, white, and blue truck, hit the streets in June of 2007. It was new. It was novel. And most of all, it was fun.

Whether you're treating yourself or others, Kim makes the experience delightful. There's always a tray out to entice passersby with samples like

"I have a lot of room in my heart for all treats." —KIM IMA

intensely cinnamon-laced Mexican Chocolate Brownies and buttery Caramel Crème "Truckers," one of Kim's signature sandwich cookies. These bite-size nibbles have been known to convert more than just a few sales since one taste is never enough. If you have a particular cookie in mind, don't hesitate to let Kim know. "I love when people point to the one that they want," she says with a laugh. Order a brownie or slice of cake, and she'll ask you which type of piece you prefer—corner, center, or side.

When the truck hits the Upper West Side, Kim is always sure to pack plenty of sparkly sugar cookies—jolly-looking snowmen during the winter and brightly hued flowers in the spring and summer. Park Slopers are partial to the cran-almond Rice Krispies treats and oatmeal jammies, while Midtowners tend to favor the PB&J sandwich cookies. But plenty of treats have unexpected crossover appeal—think corporate suits ordering ice-cream-cone cupcakes.

While the truck seems like a natural fit in stroller-centric nabes, Midtown Manhattan has proven to be one of Kim's favorite places to visit. Stop by the truck when it's parked in the mid-40s and you'll find gray-haired captains of industry queued with well-dressed publishing junior staffers. On sunny days the lunchtime line often stretches down the block. "Whatever you're doing in Midtown whether you work in an office or you're making deliveries, I feel like people are looking for something that they can enjoy or that's a break from what they're doing."

Most of all Kim cherishes the interactions with her customers. "Daily there are these little moments that are special. For me, not just for them. It's an opportunity for them to make my day better, for me to make their day better." As "The Treats Truck lady," Kim exudes a certain approachability that she occasionally dips into the confidante zone typically reserved for priests and bartenders. "I had a woman tell me, *I'm going to get a cupcake—I'm cancer free.* That same afternoon a young couple came by and said, *We were just thinking we needed something sweet,* so I started helping them out, and the woman says, *We just found out we're having a baby.* Then she turns to her husband and says, *Does everything look different to you?* And he says, *Yeah, everything does look different.*" It's moments like these that make all the work worthwhile. "I so fell in love with the idea for this business that I love it. And it's *so hard* that you've got to love it."

The food truck scene has changed drastically from when The Treats Truck first launched. "In the past there was this informal code of honor. You knew the landscape of where people were and who people were, so you could respect that, but now, it's very hard to do that." Citywide crackdowns on mobile vendors have made it more difficult to do business. "Being able to have good spots and reliable spots are the biggest challenge," but Kim keeps on trucking. In 2011 she published a collection of her recipes called *The Treats Truck Baking Book,* and 2012 brought about the long-anticipated opening of The Treats Truck Stop, a brick-and-mortar extension of the truck, in picturesque Carroll Gardens, where visitors can check out the treats' production through a giant window or sit a spell to enjoy a frost-your-own cookie plate. With all of the expansions and new ventures, Kim still treasures her time on Sugar interacting with the customers. "I've always loved the regulars. It just becomes this lovely little moment. You don't know each other's names, but you have these little exchanges. Whether you have a food truck or you're driving a bus, we all have the opportunity to make the city better."

COFFEE ICEBOX CAKE

Adapted from Kim Ima's recipe

Icebox cakes are a quick and easy dessert that are fun to customize. They can be as basic as homemade whipped cream with vanilla or chocolate wafer cookies, or you can doll them up, like this coffee version. The Treats Truck owner Kim Ima always says, "It's fun to name your creations."

....

YIELD: SERVES 12

3 cups whipping cream

½ cup granulated sugar

4 tablespoons instant espresso powder

2 teaspoons vanilla extract

1 (9-ounce) package of chocolate wafer cookies

In a medium saucepan add the cream and sugar. Heat over medium, whisking until the sugar has dissolved and the mixture is warm (do not let it boil), about 2 to 3 minutes. Remove the pan from the heat and pour the cream into a large bowl. Whisk in instant espresso powder, cover, and refrigerate mixture until completely chilled, about 1 to 2 hours.

Chill the bowl of an electric stand mixer or a large mixing bowl and whisk beater attachments in the freezer for 10 minutes. Combine cream mixture and vanilla extract in the chilled mixing bowl. Using the chilled beaters, beat on high until soft peaks form.

On a large plate or platter, place a single cookie in the center and six cookies around it to form a hexagon-like shape. Cover with about a ½ cup cream spreading the cream in a circle leaving just a ¼ of an inch of cookie exposed around the edges, then repeat, staggering the cookies, to create a basket weave-like pattern, finishing with cream on top. The cake will have five layers of cookies and five layers of cream. Refrigerate covered with a cake dome at least 3 to 4 hours before serving or overnight.

> **TIP:** If you don't have a cake dome, make your own by inverting a glass bowl large enough to cover the entire cake and plate without marring the cream. Alternately you can store uncovered, but you may risk the cream taking on undesired flavors from odors in the refrigerator.

SPICED ZUCCHINI CAKE

The Treats Truck owner Kim Ima is famous for her übermoist cakes and muffins, and this spiced zucchini cake is no exception. Make it your own by stirring in a cup of chopped nuts or semi-sweet chocolate chips just before baking. Frost with your favorite cream cheese or chocolate frosting.

2 ½ cups all-purpose flour

1 ¼ teaspoons baking powder

1 teaspoon baking soda

½ teaspoon ground nutmeg

½ teaspoon salt

1 ½ cups confectioners' sugar

½ cup dark brown sugar, firmly packed

1 cup vegetable oil

4 eggs, lightly beaten

1 pound of zucchini, ends trimmed

Move oven rack to the center position and preheat the oven to 350°F. Butter and flour a 13 x 9 inch pan and set aside.

Fit food processor with a fine grater disk– and grate zucchini. Set aside.

In a large bowl, whisk together the flour, baking powder, baking soda, nutmeg, salt, confectioners' sugar, and brown sugar. Stir in the oil until flour is moistened then add eggs, stirring until thick batter forms. Stir in zucchini until just combined.

Pour batter into pan and bake until top is golden brown and a toothpick comes out clean, about 30 to 40 minutes.

Cool completely before serving.

When chef Samir Afrit came to the United States from Casablanca in 1999, he didn't know how to cook. At all. It's said you can get anything in New York, but Moroccan food prepared just like Mom's proved elusive. So Samir did the next best thing. He set out to learn the staple recipes one by one, with his mom teaching him centuries-old techniques via decidedly modern technology: Skype. Samir streamed his mother into his own kitchen so they could cook side by side, even if thousands of miles apart. Their first challenge? Couscous, a fine-grained pasta made of semolina and the national dish of Morocco.

Once Samir mastered couscous, he moved onto *harira*, a hearty tomato, lentil, and chickpea soup typically eaten for dinner during the holy month of Ramadan. After harira, Samir progressed to *tagines*, slow-cooked Moroccan stews prepared in a conical earthenware pot. With each recipe, his confidence increased, as did his love of cooking.

Soon Samir and his now-wife, began hosting dinner parties, at which he was known for his use of bold and unique flavors like sharp Moroccan green olives and preserved lemons. "Our house had become like Mecca for the group," he says. One night a friend asked Samir to cater a rehearsal dinner. "Listen, I know how to cook for you guys, but I don't know how to do catering," he recounts. Samir's friend wore down his resistance, and he pulled together a successful meal for thirty people. From that first party came more catering requests. "From the third party, I really enjoy it. I really had fun. You go—you do the shopping. You spend the whole day just cooking this and that. So I start thinking to take it to the next step as a business."

With a small budget, opening a restaurant "was impossible . . . it was not a plan." In 2009, food trucks were booming in the city, and Samir liked the concept. "You cook and you see people. It's not like a restaurant where you're in the kitchen and nobody knows who is cooking and whatever. And I like to talk to people. So the food truck was going to be the best option for me." Samir quit his job managing a souvenir shop and devoted all of his attention to get the food truck up and running.

The Department of Health capped the number of food vending licenses at 3,100 in 1983 and the waiting list to get a license from the city is years long. While the city officially issues two-year permits to vendors for $200, the black market value of the permits is upward of $20,000. Just locating a license can be a challenge. "The license was the most difficult thing to find . . . there is no one who is going to give you that answer." Samir paid $2,000 just to get an introduction to someone with an available permit and who was willing to enter into a partnership so he could vend. While it took three to four months to find the license, getting a truck was much easier. Samir got his on the first try on eBay. "I was not fan of eBay. I never get anything on eBay. The first thing I get on eBay was a truck," he says.

Months of work went into preparing the Comme Ci Comme Ça truck. Like Samir, the design is bold, colorful, and, most of all, playful. Still some of Samir's Moroccan friends were skeptical. When he told them, "I would like to do the couscous and bring it to the street," they said he was crazy, that it wasn't possible. And maybe they were

"My first recipe was the couscous because I missed it so much."

—SAMIR AFRIT

right. With traditional couscous, the meat is cooked in the broth. With limited space on a truck, how could Samir offer more than just a few things on his menu? But Samir was not deterred. "I live in New York City. I feel myself New Yorker. I say, let's do a little switch to convert it for the truck." By cooking the couscous on the side in vegetable broth and the meats on the grill, he could use the same couscous base for vegetarians as for carnivores.

Though couscous makes up a big portion of the menu, the vibe of the truck is decidedly pan-Mediterranean. Crusty ciabatta bread from a family-run Italian bakery near Samir's home in Astoria forms the base for inventive sandwich combos like fire-roasted veggies with feta or *merguez*, a spicy North African lamb sausage, which Samir pairs with roasted tomatoes, caramelized onions, and green olives. Whatever the dish, Samir's quartet of house-made sauces are a must-try. With his lemon-and-olive-oil-infused Spicy Andalusian Sauce and Casablanca Sauce, Samir puts his own stamp on the

white and hot sauces that are typical of halal street meat carts. The inventive Spicy Mint Sauce and Green Olive Sauce are entirely his own creations. Once the menu was in place, hopes were high when the truck hit the road. But trouble lay ahead.

"For the first day it was really great. We were, like, sold out. I was so happy coming back home . . . I was so excited. That's when I had my accident. The first day going back home." Peddling home and going fast down a hill, his bag strap got caught in the wheel of his bike. The bike flipped; Samir was thrown; and his arm was torn open. "It was the best day of my life and one of the worst." Several surgeries and months of rehabilitation time were needed. The Comme Ci Comme Ça truck was off the road for the entire summer, the most profitable season for food trucks. "My scar is my first day of my business," he says with a smile, looking down at the inches-long scar extending from his bicep to his forearm.

When the truck relaunched that fall, they were

a little more cautious. "We were taking it easy. We decided not to start going everywhere. Just to learn. It was not a good idea to be in the same spot five days, but we said, *okay, let's stay here just to see.* Also, the first day I had an accident, so I lost, you know, this confidence, you know." They stayed on 55th near Lexington for a couple of months and learned their business. They figured out how to streamline the process from the shopping to the preparation to managing the orders. Their hard work soon started to pay off, as the buzz started to build and blog recommendations began to pile up. "Midtown Lunch is number one. People trust it so much. I have people come to my truck just because of Midtown

Lunch. Every time I have an article, I get new people at the truck."

After such a rocky beginning, Samir was humbled to be named a Vendy finalist in the new vendor category in 2011. By chance, the ceremony coincided with his mother's visit from Morocco to see Samir's newborn son, and she looked on with pride as he served three types of couscous to thousands of hungry attendees. Looking forward, Samir would like to open a shop. "I hope we can have a small business. Something small so you can have more things . . . I'm not thinking about restaurants. I would never have a restaurant. Even if I win the lottery tomorrow."

KOFTA (MOROCCAN SPICED MEATBALLS)

Adapted from Samir Afrit's recipe

Kofta is a catchall term for spiced ground meat that can be shaped into meatballs or formed into sausage-like cylinders and cooked on skewers. On the Comme Ci Comme Ça truck, Samir serves the kofta sandwich-style in a crusty Italian bread topped with *Charmoula* (page 132) and Green Olive Sauce (page 132). He recommends washing it down with a hot or iced mint tea.

....

YIELD: SERVES 8

1 medium-size white onion, very finely chopped

¼ cup fresh parsley, finely chopped

¼ cup fresh cilantro, finely chopped

2 cloves garlic, peeled and minced

1 tablespoon cumin

1 teaspoon salt

1 teaspoon sweet paprika

1 teaspoon cinnamon

¼ teaspoon cayenne pepper

1 tablespoon dried mint leaves

¼ teaspoon white pepper

¼ teaspoon ground cloves

1½ pounds ground lamb or ground beef

In a large bowl, combine the onion, parsley, cilantro, and garlic with all of the spices. Add ground meat and mix well. Cover and refrigerate for at least an hour but no more than 2 hours. Note: Refrigeration is necessary to properly chill the meat so it can easily be formed on skewers.

Preheat gas grill to 400°F or prepare charcoal grill.

TO PREPARE AS BROCHETTES (KEBABS):

Form ground meat mixture into little cylinders about the thickness of two fingers. Place meat on skewers, squeezing it around the skewer to secure it. Place skewers on grill and cook approximately 5 minutes per side or until nicely browned. Serve with *Charmoula* (page 132) and Green Olive Sauce (page 132).

Note: If you use wooden skewers be sure to soak them in water for 30 minutes prior to using to avoid burning.

TO PREPARE AS MEATBALLS:

If you don't have easy access to a grill you can prepare the kofta as meatballs. Shape ground meat mixture into approximately 1-inch meatballs. Place oven rack in the center position and preheat the oven to 400°F. Place meatballs in a 13 x 9–inch or larger baking dish or pan lined with aluminum foil. Bake for 10 minutes and then turn the meatballs. Continue baking for another 10 minutes or until meatballs are lightly browned and cooked through.

CHARMOULA
(MOROCCAN CARAMELIZED ONION AND TOMATO SAUCE)
Adapted from Samir Afrit's recipe

This versatile Moroccan condiment combines caramelized onions and tomatoes, and is used as both a marinade and a topping. Samir adds *Charmoula* to all of his sandwiches and burgers.

YIELD: ABOUT 2 CUPS

3 tablespoons extra-virgin olive oil
3 large white or yellow onions, julienned
pinch of salt
½ teaspoon ground black pepper
½ teaspoon cumin
¼ teaspoon paprika
½ cup tomatoes, finely chopped
1 green bell pepper, seeded and finely
  chopped

In a large skillet, heat the olive oil over medium-high heat for one minute. Add the onions and stir to coat with olive oil. Sprinkle onions with salt. Sauté onions, stirring occasionally until they are tender and beginning to brown, about 3 minutes. Add remaining ingredients, reduce heat to medium-low, and continue to sauté, stirring occasionally, until onions are fully caramelized and a deep golden brown, about 20 to 30 minutes. Serve warm with *Kofta* (page 131). Refrigerate leftovers in an airtight container for up to 2 days.

GREEN OLIVE SAUCE
Adapted from Samir Afrit's recipe

While green olives are popular in Moroccan cuisine, this sauce is entirely Samir's invention. It goes well on both his Moroccan-Style Lemon Chicken (page 136) and the *Kofta* (page 131).

YIELD: ABOUT 2 CUPS

1 cup green olives, pitted
¼ cup fresh Italian parsley, chopped
¼ cup fresh cilantro, chopped
½ cup mayonnaise
2 tablespoons lemon juice
½ teaspoon dried oregano
½ teaspoon pepper

Add all ingredients to a food processor or blender, and blend until smooth. Cover and refrigerate for an hour before serving. Store covered in the refrigerator for up to 1 day (though it might not last, it's that good!).

(M) | (V)

VEGETABLE COUSCOUS
Adapted from Samir Afrit's recipe

In Morocco, traditionally the meat is slow, cooked with the couscous. For ease of preparation on the truck, Samir cooks the meat separate from the couscous and sauce so vegetarians and carnivores can both enjoy this dish. Because the different vegetables in the sauce require different cooking times, they are added in stages to ensure that none of the veggies get overcooked.

YIELD: SERVES 6

FOR THE SAUCE:
¼ cup extra-virgin olive oil

1 large white onion, coarsely chopped (about 1¼ cups)

2 large tomatoes, peeled and coarsely chopped (about 2 cups)

2 tablespoons fresh parsley, finely chopped

2 tablespoons fresh cilantro, finely chopped

1½ tablespoons salt

½ tablespoon pepper

1 teaspoon ground ginger

½ teaspoon turmeric

6 carrots, peeled and quartered

2 small sweet potatoes, peeled and quartered

4 small zucchini, quartered (about 2 cups)

1 small acorn squash, stem and seeds removed and cut into 1-inch wedges

1 cup canned chickpeas

FOR THE COUSCOUS:
1 tablespoon salted butter

¼ teaspoon salt

½ tablespoon cinnamon

½ tablespoon ground turmeric

1 tablespoon extra-virgin olive oil

3 cups couscous

TO PREPARE THE SAUCE:

In a large saucepan, heat oil over medium-high for 1 minute. Add the onion, tomatoes, parsley, cilantro, and spices and stir to coat. Reduce heat to medium and cook uncovered, stirring occasionally until the onions and tomatoes form a thick sauce, about 15 to 20 minutes.

Add 8 cups water, cover, and bring to a boil over high heat. Reduce the heat to medium, then simmer for 25 to 30 minutes.

Add the carrots and sweet potatoes, and cook for about 15 minutes. Then add the zucchini, the butternut squash, and the chickpeas and cook for another 25 minutes, or until all vegetables are fully cooked and tender.

TO PREPARE THE COUSCOUS:

In a large saucepan, combine 3 cups water, butter, salt, cinnamon, turmeric, and olive oil. Bring to a boil over medium-high heat. Remove from heat. Add couscous and stir. Cover and let stand for 10 minutes. Before serving, fluff couscous with a fork to break up clumps.

TO SERVE THE COUSCOUS:

Portion out couscous on each plate, forming it into a mound with a well in the center. Place vegetables and sauce in well and top with Moroccan-Style Lemon Chicken (page 136), if desired. Serve with Green Olive Sauce (page 132)

MOROCCAN-STYLE LEMON CHICKEN

Adapted from Samir Afrit's recipe

Preserved or pickled lemons, a common ingredient in Moroccan cuisine, are key to giving this grilled chicken dish its intense lemon flavor. Once pickled in salt and water you can use the entire lemon, peel, pith and all. Preserved lemons can be found at Middle Eastern markets, Whole Foods, or online spice and ethnic food purveyors like Kalustyan's (kalustyans.com). Samir serves this grilled chicken both over couscous or basmati rice topped with Green Olive Sauce (page xxx). For this recipe chef Samir suggests using the best quality extra-virgin olive oil.

YIELD: SERVES 6

½ cup lemon juice

¼ cup extra-virgin olive oil

1 tablespoon ground black pepper

1 tablespoon oregano

1 tablespoon thyme

½ tablespoon salt

½ cup preserved whole lemon, finely chopped

4 boneless chicken breasts, cut into bite-sized pieces

In a large bowl, whisk together the lemon juice, olive oil, black pepper, oregano, thyme, and salt. Stir in the preserved lemon pieces, then add the chicken and mix well to coat. Cover and refrigerate for 2 hours. Place chicken on skewers.

On a very hot grill , cook chicken skewers, basting frequently and turning occasionally, for 7 to 10 minutes.

Remove chicken from skewers and serve with Vegetable Couscous (page 132) and Green Olive Sauce (page 132).

Note: If you use wooden skewers, be sure to soak them in water for 30 minutes prior to using to avoid burning.

Maine native Luke Holden has spent his whole life around lobsters. The son of Jeffrey Holden, a former lobsterman and owner of a large Maine-based lobster and shellfish processing operation, Luke was born and raised in Cape Elizabeth, a charming coastal town south of Portland. He got his start working with his dad as a kid. "When I was eight or ten years old, I started working in the processing plants, and then fourteen, fifteen, I started being a sternman, learning the tricks."

Lobstermen are a salty lot. It's a rough, physical business and not one you can easily jump into. As a sternman—the lobstering equivalent of a deck-hand—Luke baited and emptied traps and learned the ropes of the business—the spoken and unspoken rules of the water. A few years later, he built his own skiff and started lobstering himself, with his youngest brother as his sternman. But it wasn't until he found himself working in New York City post-college and craving a lobster roll that the idea of building his own lobster business took root.

"I was at my desk, doing investment banking in Midtown, and I was looking for a lobster roll. Jumped online and found there was nothing out there that was served at an affordable price in a Down East-style environment. The average price was $30, and it was all white-tablecloth." Luke embarked on a lobster mission, tasting rolls across the city and trying to figure out why the price was so high and why you simply couldn't find a roll likes the ones back home.

It wasn't long before he noticed a trend. In order to keep food costs down, restaurants were diluting the lobster meat with fillers like celery and bell pepper, while dressing up the roll with frills like tarragon, avocado, and kaffir lime leaf mayonnaise—fancy menu marketing to justify the extra-fancy price tag. "There were just all of these really great restaurants who were screwing it up . . . it was a bunch of really high-end chefs who were adding their own interpretation of what a lobster roll was, but not necessarily what a traditional Maine lobster roll was." By specializing in a few menu items and sourcing direct from his

"When anybody looks at our margins, nobody really ever thinks it makes any sense because traditional food costs are much lower than the average ticket price. But for us, this is the tolerable price point. This is where it needs to be from our prospective for quality, and we've been able to match the level of demand with a lower margin to make it work." —LUKE HOLDEN

father, Luke was able to break traditional food cost models by moving volume.

Up north, the rolls are simple: lobster, mayo, split-top bun. Uncomplicated. Unfooled around with. You can get a decent lobster roll at your corner deli or mom-and-pop diner. Ask Mainers to name their favorite lobster roll, and they are bound to have a favorite shack. Luke realized that New York was ripe for an introduction to a real Maine lobster roll. "It was more than just missing a lobster roll. I was missing Maine. I was missing something that I was very proud about; this was an opportunity to bring my passions, work with my father."

While Luke did all of the early legwork to build the business, his partner, co-owner, Ben Conniff, a fellow Yankee from Connecticut, got the operations off the ground. Ben had been working as a freelancer writing for *Smithsonian, Saveur, Playboy*, and *Yankee* when he responded Luke's ad on Craigslist. Ben immediately got Luke's vision for the business and was eager and willing to work hard to make it happen. As they set about opening their flagship shop in the East Village in October of 2009, they imagined a spot where people could go for a breather and get a taste of that Vacationland atmosphere in Manhattan. "It's kind of a way to escape when the city is bearing down on you, as it tends to do," Ben explains. "Giving people that kind of outlet where they can relax and still be eating lobster which historically in New York is thought of as a luxury, white-tablecloth product that's not affordable to regular folks."

Luke's slogan is "From ME to you," with the "ME" set in a little outline of his home state, and that promise is born out both in the shop and on "Nauti," their cheery buttercup and periwinkle painted truck. "We bring all the seafood, the buns, the soda, the soups, the water; the only thing that doesn't come from Maine really is the chips and the paper products. Everything within the restaurant is Maine-based. It's decorated with my old traps, my old buoys, ropes, and nets. That's where the color tone comes from. The blue and yellow is the color of my old buoys."

The menu both at the shop and on the truck is simple: lobster rolls, crab rolls, and shrimp rolls, all sourced and processed by Luke's father. The rolls are prepared the way Luke would eat them at home. Top-split hot dog buns are buttered, toasted, and then filled with chilled claw and knuckle meat, the sweetest most tender lobster meat available. Dressed with only a touch of lemon butter and a dusting of seasoning, customers can get their rolls with a stripe of mayo or go naked. "The top-split bun is important, so you get a good buttery crunch with each bite, but it's really about having fresh Maine lobster."

Lobster sourcing is an important component of Luke's business and a point of pride. "It's relatively easy to source a product for three or four months a year and that's why there's a lot of these shacks that open up in vacation areas up and down the East Coast for three or four months of the year and then they close down," says Luke. "It just becomes very, very difficult if you don't have a direct connection to the source, to be consistent throughout the year. Knowing that and knowing how much time we spend on the ground level to make sure that we're doing things right and we're using the connections we've had for fifty years to do things right, it just becomes a very difficult game to jump in and out of. With lobster it becomes very, very hard to source the product at a fair price and a decent quality from December to June."

Because Luke's seafood is sourced through his dad, they can tell you the catch and the harbor

where each lobster came from. The lobsters are shelled and steamed within hours of being caught. "Once a lobster is actually brought from the ocean it starts to eat the proteins within itself, so it starts to not be nearly as sweet, so it's really important to get from the ocean to your plate," Luke explains.

Spending even just a few minutes with Luke, it's clear the man knows his lobster. He can look at a lobster and tell if it's new shell or old shell, male or female, and fresh or frozen. Quality and flavor depends on several factors: age, season, and time of the lobster year—whether the lobsters are in their old shell or growing into their new one. Lobsters that weigh from a pound to about a pound and three-quarters are the sweetest lobsters. "Once you get above a pound and three-quarters, the meat can get a little fishy and a little bit tougher. The best-quality meat comes from the shedders. Lobsters shed every year, and that meat is always the sweetest; it's the most delicate, the lobster itself is the most delicate," says Luke. When pressed on what kind of lobster is the best, Luke answers without hesitation. "The best possible lobster you can eat is probably a pound and a half, male, shedder. The reason I say male is that you can actually tell whether a lobster is male or female just by looking at its claws. Its claws tend to be a little bit thicker and the pincher claw doesn't tend to be as pointy, so there's just a little more meat in the claws in a male lobster."

With the mission of bringing lobster to the people, it wasn't long before they sought out a more mobile delivery method. "There are so many markets in New York that are high demand for a short period of time, and then that demand goes away," says Ben. "Midtown is the perfect example. There's a real dearth of affordable food here that you can get quickly. Having the truck allows you to serve that need without necessarily paying astronomical rents

on a space that's only going to be working really two to three hours a day. It's also just a great way to move around and see new people all the time and just really expand your audience and get your food in front of more people. It was an exciting thing to do and the fact that we have an existing infrastructure to launch it from was very helpful, as opposed to trying to figure out how to organize all of your products and making a business without any home base." Nauti hit the streets in March of 2011 and has been bringing rolls to on-the-go lunchers around town ever since, converting lunchtime truck customers into neighborhood regulars at their Upper East Side and Upper West Side outposts.

Street vending is not without its challenges. Between the costs of the permits, assembling the right team of workers with all the proper licenses, and the daily drama of battling for parking spots, it's a hard business to grow as successfully as they've grown their brick-and-mortar locations, which number eight and counting, five in the city and three run by Luke's brother in the Washington, DC area. "We're very happy with our current truck," says Ben. "We're happy with how much new attention it's gotten us and obviously the rave reviews. It was Zagat's number one food truck, and that's been awesome, but we're not necessarily looking to expand the truck model." While there might not be a fleet of trucks on the immediate horizon, Ben sees a promising future. Ben continues, "Because of our source through Luke's father and also because of the quality of the team we've been able to build, it's been very scalable to the extent that there's just been zero decline in quality. And as long as we can confidently say that, there's no reason to think we should stop trying to reach new people, new markets, and places that have less exposure to Maine lobster and lobster rolls."

Luke's Lobster Roll Primer

How to Buy Lobsters:

BEN: For age, a lobster becomes mature and we're able to catch in Maine at seven years. It's a little bit bigger than a pound lobster. It's actually a measurement of the shell of the lobster, it corresponds to about seven years and a pound, a little more than a pound. Lobsters from that weight to about a pound and three-quarters are the sweetest lobsters.

LUKE: Once a lobster is actually brought from the ocean, it starts to eat the proteins within itself, so it starts to not be nearly as sweet. So it's really important to get it from the ocean to your plate. One way to tell how long a lobster has been out of the water is that lobsters are carnivorous, so they'll eat each other very quickly, so if they've got the bands on, they'll start to eat their antennae. So a lot of times in grocery stores you'll see that they have short antennae, and that's because they've been eating their antennae.

The Outside:

BEN: We use Country Kitchen buns. They're out of Lewiston, Maine. The really important thing with the split-top and the shaved sides is the way it toasts out. You've got to get butter on the outside of the bun, griddle both sides, and when you do that, it sort of holds in the warmth, even on the inside. You open up the bun and steam comes out. It just becomes this really soft-on-the-inside, crispy-on-the-outside, buttery, kind of cradle for the seafood. You bite into it, and it

kind of melts away in your mouth. It's really the perfect way to serve it. You can't get anything closer with any other type of bread.

The Inside:

LUKE: The claw and knuckle is the sweetest, most tender part of the lobster. The tail is tougher without a doubt, and it can be a little bit fishier. We just take the knuckle and claw meat.

BEN: Straight chilled meat with just the mayo on the inside. First of all, that allows us to serve a roll with no mayo for people who don't like mayo, which is a ton of people actually (including Luke). And second, keeping those components separate just allows you to get a better taste for the lobster. It's not going to be sitting in that mayonnaise over time, which gets kind of gross.

Why Buy Maine?

LUKE: There's so much naiveness in the market, and there's so many folks who can't tell the difference between a fresh lobster and a pounded lobster. A Maine lobster and a Canadian lobster, even more significantly. Same species, similar product, but there's a reason we're using Maine product and not Canadian product and that is because we're trying to support the sustainable industry that Maine's practicing. For so many people it's just about lobster—it's not about where it comes from, what it tastes like, what it looks like, and that's kind of wrong.

LUKE'S SHRIMP ROLL
Adapted from Luke Holden's recipe

Shrimp rolls at Luke's Lobster are prepared in the same manner as the lobster rolls, just chilled whole shrimp with a touch of lemon butter and mayo and a dash of seasonings. "The whole point is to make it really simple, just a tiny bit of an accent to bring out the flavor of the seafood," says co-owner, Ben Conniff. "Unlike your typical shrimp you get anywhere else, the flavor of Maine shrimp is packed into each little one. They're so nice and sweet and tender. Just like good lobster, you don't want to cover that up at all." Even Luke himself admits "The shrimp roll is my favorite. The shrimp are different than shrimp people typically eat. They're little baby shrimp—that's what we catch up in the Gulf of Maine. They're actually not baby shrimp. They're shorter; they're smaller; they're sweeter. The texture is a little better than a cocktail shrimp. For me, those are just as tasty as a lobster."

....

YIELD: SERVES 4

6 tablespoons salted butter

4 split-top hot dog buns

1 pound cooked Maine shrimp, peeled, deveined, and chilled

1 tablespoon fresh lemon juice

4 teaspoons mayonnaise, if desired

pinch of celery salt

salt, to taste

pepper, to taste

Place butter in a medium microwave-safe bowl, cover with waxed paper, and microwave on high for 10 to 15 seconds, stir, re-cover, and repeat in 10-second bursts until butter has completely melted. Brush outsides of buns with butter. Whisk together remaining butter with lemon juice and set aside.

Grill buns in a large skillet over medium-high heat 2 to 3 minutes or until both sides are golden.

If desired, spread a teaspoon of mayonnaise on the inside of each bun, then fill with chilled shrimp. Reheat lemon butter for 10 seconds in the microwave, if it has congealed and drizzle over each roll. Top with a pinch of celery salt as well as salt and pepper to taste and serve immediately.

Note: Sweet Maine shrimp have a short fishery season that starts in January and ends in February. But fear not, flash-frozen shrimp are just as good, if not better to use as Luke says the shrimp is "actually harder to work with when it's fresh—all the proteins from fresh shrimp give it a strange odor."

With its cheerful pink and white flower bedecked sky-blue paint job, there's no mistaking the Biàn Dāng truck. The name translates to "lunch box" in Mandarin, but don't expect your standard Chinese menu. This truck is Taiwanese to the max. "Biàn Dāng has a similar meaning to bento box in Japanese but in Tawainese culture," co-owner Thomas Yang explains, "it's a little weird sounding: *bee-yen dong*. Most people don't get it, they say *be-ann dANG*. We just want to build enough of a reputation that people will recognize it."

Roaming around the city, the Biàn Dāng truck has assumed the role of the city's unofficial Taiwanese culinary ambassador. Their mission? Introducing New Yorkers to Taiwanese comfort food. Their weapons? Fried goodness. While the truck's menu has expanded since their launch in 2009, fried chicken and fried pork chops over rice remain top sellers. The secret is in the family sauce,

a hearty minced pork gravy punctuated by sour notes from bits of pickled mustard greens. The overall effect is meaty, salty, sour, and satisfying. Or, as Thomas says, "crackalicious."

While Biàn Dāng has built its reputation on pork sauce, the origins of the truck trace back to Thomas's undergrad days at Baruch college, when he first noticed the ever-present halal carts near campus. As a budding entrepreneur, the business model intrigued him. He mentioned opening a chicken and broccoli cart to friends. "It started as a joke, and then I started thinking about it more. It's something that stuck in my head." When Thomas realized there weren't any places in the city serving the Taiwanese dishes he loved as a kid, he knew he was onto something.

Partnering with a friend and his sister, Diana, they brought in his uncle, Steven Yang, a highly skilled master chef, to run the kitchen. As with any

"When you hear someone say 'I really love your food,' this makes my week. It's really gratifying." —THOMAS YANG family business the stakes are higher when everyone is invested, and the siblings stick to their competencies. Diana keeps the truck running smoothly while Thomas operates the overall business, which includes stakes in other mobile food ventures, including Fun Buns NYC and the Fishing Shrimp Truck. As a first generation American, Thomas wasn't afraid of hard work on the way to success. "I remember my dad working six days a week out-of-state. I would see him once a week."

Establishing a following was their first challenge. "A big problem is awareness and people's affinity to try new things. People know what pizza is," Thomas laments. Customers can't crave something if they don't know what it is. And in an age saturated with low-carb and low-fat health crazes, eaters need to know that the food is worth breaking their diets for. On their first few outings, "we could not give away a platter of food." Everything changed when MidtownLunch.com guru Zach Brooks alerted his loyal following that the truck—then known as NYC Cravings—had finally made it to Midtown for lunch, and pandemonium ensued.

Thomas and Diana went from zero customers to a hungry hoard. "We were so swamped that day. We couldn't even fulfill most of the demand," Thomas says. Days later when Brooks posted his full review proclaiming "For those of us who wished we worked in Chinatown, this is our new favorite truck," the truck had arrived.

Balancing the crowds and the wait is always a challenge. "People tend to think we're fast-food, but we cook everything fresh on the truck. You can actually see us fry it. . . . Even though we make the food *fast,* we're not *fast-food*." Soon the accolades started to roll in. In their first year on the road, they were named one of the top ten food trucks in the country by *GQ* and received a Vendy nomination in the Rookie of the Year category. Long-term the Yang siblings would like to open the restaurant that their now departed father always dreamed of. But for now as their fan base expands, Thomas hopes to make Taiwanese culture accessible through food. "I think food is a big part of culture. . . . I hope that's what I can give away."

LU ROU FAN (TAIWANESE MINCED PORK OVER RICE)
Adapted from Steven Yang's recipe

Biàn Dāng's minced pork sauce is the stuff of legend, and it's also a closely guarded family secret. The key to a rich gravy with this recipe is using pork belly, the meat from the fatty underside belly of a pig. Most American ground pork is very lean, so be sure to ask your butcher to give you the right type. If pork belly sounds fancy to you, just remember that it's also the fatty end of American bacon. This dish uses a special dark soy sauce that's a bit sweeter and slightly less salty that your standard soy sauce. Look for dark soy sauce and pickled mustard greens at Asian specialty markets.

....

YIELD: SERVES 4

1 pound pork belly, minced

4½ tablespoons dark soy sauce, divided

½ teaspoon granulated sugar

2 cloves garlic, peeled and finely chopped

5 shallots, peeled and finely chopped

½ teaspoon Chinese five-spice powder

2½ tablespoons cornstarch

1 cup pickled mustard greens, for serving

2 cups cooked white or brown rice, for serving

Combine minced pork belly with 2½ tablespoons of soy sauce and sugar. Mix with your hands to thoroughly work the soy sauce and sugar into the meat. Cover and marinate in the refrigerator for 30 minutes.

Heat a large pan or cast-iron skillet on high for 2 minutes. Add the pork belly and use a spatula to break up the pork and stir constantly until the meat is browned, about 5 minutes.

Scoop out the pork belly and put aside, reserve the rendered fat in the pan.

Add the garlic and shallots to the pan, and stir fry over medium-high heat until fragrant, about 3 to 5 minutes.

Add the rest of the soy sauce and the five-spice. Return the pork belly to the pan.

Dissolve 2½ tablespoons cornstarch into cups of water. Add water to pork belly mixture. Cover and simmer for 30 minutes. Serve hot alongside pickled mustard greens over rice.

TEA EGGS

Inspired by Steven Yang's recipe

Tea-soaked eggs are a popular Taiwanese snack. The longer you soak the eggs, the stronger the tea flavor becomes. Any black tea will work here, but feel free to choose your favorite to customize it. For instance Lapsang Souchong will give the eggs a wonderful smoky flavor. This recipe is inspired by the Yang family recipe.

YIELD: SERVES 6

6 large eggs

5 tablespoons soy sauce

2 teaspoons salt

1 teaspoon granulated sugar

2 tablespoons tea leaves

3 star anise

1 small stick cinnamon

Place eggs in a medium saucepan with enough cold water to cover. Bring to a boil over high heat, then simmer over medium-high heat for 2 minutes. Remove pan from heat and use a slotted spoon to remove the eggs. Rinse eggs with cold water so the shells are cool enough to handle, then carefully crack each egg to slightly break the shell. The more places you crack the eggs, the more intricate the pattern will be.

Return the eggs to the pan, then add soy sauce, salt, sugar, tea leaves, star anise, and cinnamon stick, then stir. Cover and bring to a boil over high heat then reduce heat to medium-low and let simmer for 3 hours, adding water as necessary to keep the eggs covered. Remove from heat and refrigerate in a covered pan to steep overnight or up to 12 to 18 hours. Serve cold.

O f all the new-wave food trucks roaming the streets of New York, Coolhaus, an inventive ice cream sandwich truck, is one of the few with roots outside the city. The brainchild of architect Natasha Case and real estate developer Freya Estreller, Coolhaus combines two of their great passions. "Our actual company name is farchitecture: food plus architecture," says Natasha. Architecture lovers can geek out at the triple entendre in Coolhaus—it's a play on the Bauhaus modern design movement; Remment Koolhaas, an influential Dutch architect and theorist; and the actual product. You pick out the cookies ("floor" and "roof") and choose your own ice cream "walls" for a made-to-order ice cream sandwiches.

The concept first came to Natasha her senior year at Berkeley. Her senior project was about extruding land and using the striations of land as different floors. "My professor's criticism was that my building looked like a layer cake, and I remember being like, *he's saying that like it's such a bad thing. What's wrong with layer cakes? Layer cakes are awesome.*" For the next round of the model, she actually baked it as a layer cake. "I could sort of see my peers, they were just paying attention in a different way—when food is involved it brings people together." Natasha began to look for ways to incorporate food into architecture, and she nurtured the idea through grad school, trying to figure out how she could make it into a viable career. It wasn't until she started working at Walt Disney in hotel and master planning, her first job out of school, that she began laying the foundation for Coolhaus. "I was baking cookies and making ice cream and

naming the combinations after architects for friends at work. It was a total hobby thing just to lighten everyone up, and I met Freya around that time." At Disney they had an annual craft fair where employees could bring their homemade products to Disney and sell them. Freya helped Natasha prepare to sell her ice-cream sandwiches. "People liked the architecture niche of it and the product itself—people were reacting in an obsessed way that made you think, *maybe there is something in this project that is worth exploring more.*"

At that point, Natasha was "more of the creative ideas person," while Freya had all the business background as a real estate developer. "We had the common interests of design and architecture and food, but she was able to take what I really thought of as an art project and make it a business," Natasha says. With the recession setting in late 2008, a brick-and-mortar shop wasn't an option. They went on Craigslist and found a postal truck that was so beat up that they had to have it towed to L.A. With no formal cooking background, the roommates started

perfecting the recipes in their apartment kitchen through a process of trial and error. "Actually I think baking is a lot more difficult than ice cream," says Natasha. "If you have a decent machine and you kind of *get* food, you can get pretty good at it, actually. You figure out the basic infrastructure."

They were looking for a way to launch, and Coachella—an annual three-day arts and music festival in Southern California—was coming up. "We thought, *let's go big or go home*." For Coachella, they started out with just a few flavors: vanilla bean; their now classic "Dirty Mint," (page 153) made with brown sugar and flecks of real mint leaves; Meyer Lemon, complete with bits of lemon zest; a homemade strawberry known as "FrankBerry"; and a peanut-butter flavor called "I. M. Peanut Butter"—along with a few different types of cookies: chocolate, chocolate chip, peanut butter, and sugar.

While preparing for Coachella, Natasha realized that there was no way that the two of them could just stay up and make ice-cream sandwiches for 10,000. "We realized we would have to have co-packers, which is still what we do and why we're able to expand. We can give our recipe to a manufacturer to make and buy it back wholesale." With co-packers in place, they towed the truck to the festival and set up a booth next to it. They could only get into the campgrounds to sell, and the buzz built slowly. By the last day, people were starting to get excited. "We really, really started with nothing at all. Coachella led to publicity, mainly viral through blogs. . . . It created a demand. When we came back to L.A., we had clients. People wanted to book us."

Early on, they had New York in their sights. "There's so much connection between L.A. and New York. So many of the brands we had done

"I want to bring food into whatever I do in some fashion, even if it's architecture, because it's a common language." —NATASHA CASE

events for or catering or promotions had an L.A. and New York office." Natasha's mom is originally from New York, and she's spent a lot of time there. Natasha felt that she understood the market and "the sophistication of the typical New Yorker that they would get the puns and the kind of flavors . . . you're in a place where people aren't afraid to say, well, that's maybe a little expensive, but it's probably worth it." As predicted, New Yorkers have embraced Coolhaus, and during the warm months, the lines stretch down the block. Ambitious eaters can attempt to conquer the "Skyscraper"—a tower consisting of seven cookies and six scoops of ice cream. If you finish it in under ten minutes, it's free. Otherwise plan on ponying up $25.

From a rickety postal truck, the 2012 Dessert Vendy finalist has grown to a fleet of nine slick pink and silver trucks: four in L.A., two in New York (plus a cart), two in Austin, and one Dallas, in addition to a storefront in Culver City with a Pasadena location on the way. When Coolhaus expands to a new market, they seek out local businesses to partner with for co-packing. These days, they have an executive pastry chef who helps them develop their seasonal flavors and goes to the co-packers to train them to prepare their recipes.

Natasha and Freya are very much involved with the day-to-day business right down to developing new flavors. While Natasha is glad they started with the baking and making the ice cream, she admits, "I'm more of an entrepreneur. I want to grow a brand. I'm interested in exploring different cities. If I were baking and making ice cream all day, I wouldn't be able to do that—there's no way. I do most of the PR, pretty much all of marketing."

When expanding their menu, they try keep a pulse on the trends and try to stay ahead of the curve. Recent menu additions include: fried chicken and waffles ice cream; red velvet ice cream and cookies; pistachio and black truffle ice cream; a vegan-friendly rice milk and cardamom sorbet; and Peking duck, a sweet plum ice cream with pieces of candied orange and crispy candied duck skin. "At Coolhaus, we want to be more on the cusp of that, set the trends and try to predict the next step."

DIRTY MINT ICE CREAM

Adapted from Natasha Case's recipe

Coolhaus's Dirty Mint Ice Cream was born of a happy mistake. "The reason why it's called 'dirty mint' is because it has brown sugar, which makes it more earthy. Basically we ran out of the sugar, so we had to use half and half. So many recipes through history start as accidents," says co-owner Natasha Case.

YIELD: MAKES ABOUT 1½ QUARTS

1 small bunch fresh mint (about 2 ounces), picked and cleaned
3 cups whipping cream
1 cup half-and-half
¾ cup granulated sugar
⅛ teaspoon Kosher salt
6 egg yolks
½ teaspoon cornstarch
½ cup dark brown sugar, firmly packed
½ cup mini semisweet chocolate chips

Finely chop the mint and place in a large bowl. Set aside.

In a medium saucepan, warm the cream, half-and-half, granulated sugar, and salt over medium heat. In a separate bowl, whisk together the egg yolks, cornstarch, and dark brown sugar.

Once the cream mixture is warm and beginning to bubble around the edges, remove from heat and slowly pour about half of the mixture, a tablespoon at a time, into the yolk mixture, whisking constantly. Once all of the cream mixture has been combined with the yolk mixture, scrape it back into the saucepan, return to medium-low heat, and cook, stirring constantly with a heat-proof utensil, until the custard thickens and coats the spatula. The mixture should register 170°F to 175°F; do not allow mixture to overheat.

Immediately strain the custard into the bowl with the chopped mint.

Rest the bowl of mint custard in an ice bath, and stir until cool. Cover and refrigerate overnight to chill thoroughly and to allow the mint to steep into the base.

Remove custard from refrigerator, then whisk to evenly distribute the mint. Pour into ice-cream maker, then churn according to the manufacturer's instructions. Remove ice cream from the machine, fold in the mini chocolate chips, and freeze at least 3 to 4 additional hours to set. Serve as ice cream sandwiches with Double Chocolate Cookies (page 154).

HOW TO MAKE AN ICE BATH:

Fill a large bowl with 2 trays worth of ice cubes. Add enough water so the ice cubes float, about a cup of water. Fit bowl with custard over ice bath and whisk until custard has cooled—the custard bowl should fit so no water leaks into the custard during whisking.

DOUBLE CHOCOLATE COOKIES

Adapted from Natasha Case's recipe

These dark chocolate cookies were one of Coolhaus's first recipes and remain among their most popular cookies.

YIELD: MAKES 4 DOZEN COOKIES

2 cups all-purpose flour

¼ cup cocoa powder

½ tablespoon salt

1 teaspoon baking soda

½ pound (2 sticks) unsalted butter, room temperature

2 cups light brown sugar, firmly packed

2 large eggs

2 teaspoons vanilla extract

16 ounces semisweet chocolate chips

Set oven rack to middle position and preheat oven to 325°F.

In a medium bowl, whisk together the flour, cocoa powder, salt, and baking soda. Set aside.

In a large bowl or the bowl of an electric stand mixer, beat butter on medium speed until light and smooth. Add the light brown sugar and continue to beat until creamy. Add in eggs, ½ tablespoon water, and vanilla extract, and beat until mixture is thoroughly combined.

Add the flour mixture, and mix until dough comes together. Fold in chocolate chips.

On a large baking sheet or jelly-roll pan lined with parchment paper, drop a heaping tablespoon of dough per cookie, allowing a couple inches space for spreading on all sides. You should be able to fit 9 cookies on a tray.

Bake for 8 minutes, rotate the pan 180°, bake for an additional 6 to 8 minutes, until the edges and tops of cookies are slightly firm and dry. Remove from the oven and cool in the pan for 2 minutes. Then transfer to a wire rack to cool completely. Store in an airtight container for up to 1 week.

BROWNED BUTTER BACON ICE CREAM

Adapted from Natasha Case's recipe

In recent years, bacon has taken the dessert world by storm. The bacon fat lends a smokiness to the browned butter ice cream, and there's plenty of candy bacon pieces here to ensure a little sweet and salty combo with every bite. Adding the maple syrup gives this a distinct breakfast-for-dessert vibe.

YIELD: MAKES ABOUT 1½ QUARTS

FOR THE CANDIED BACON:

½ pound bacon, sliced into ½-inch pieces

½ cup light brown sugar, firmly packed

FOR THE ICE CREAM BASE:

4 tablespoons unsalted butter

2 cups whipping cream

1 cup whole milk

6 egg yolks

⅛ teaspoon kosher salt

½ cup granulated sugar

¼ cup light brown sugar, firmly packed

2 tablespoons maple syrup

2 tablespoons bacon fat (from the candied bacon recipe, above)

½ teaspoon vanilla extract

TO MAKE THE CANDIED BACON:

Place a skillet over medium heat. Add the bacon and begin browning. Once the bacon is about three-quarters crisped, strain off the bacon fat and reserve. Add the brown sugar to the pan, stirring to coat and melt the sugar. Continue cooking bacon until it's fully browned and candied. Remove from heat and allow to cool for 15 minutes.

Once cooled, transfer to a cutting board and finely chop the bacon. Set aside.

TO MAKE BROWNED BUTTER:

Over low heat, in a heavy-bottom, stainless-steel saucepan, melt the butter down and slowly allow it to brown, stirring occasionally. Timing will vary according to your stove and cookware, so watch the butter closely as it begins to foam. It will change in color from yellow to a golden brown that's flecked with browned bits. Remove from heat and set aside to cool for at least 15 minutes.

TO MAKE THE BASE:

Combine the cream and milk in a medium saucepan over medium heat.

Bring the liquid to an almost-boil—you will see tiny bubbles begin to form around the edges of the pot. Remove from heat.

Whisk together the yolks, salt, sugar, and brown sugar in a separate bowl.

Gently add about a cup of the hot liquid, 1 tablespoon at a time, whisking until smooth.

Slowly add the egg mixture to the remaining cream mixture, whisking until smooth. Whisk in the maple syrup, bacon fat, browned butter, and vanilla.

Strain through a fine-mesh strainer.

Cool mixture to room temperature over an ice bath (see page 153), stirring constantly. Add the mixture to an ice cream machine, and prepare according to the machine's instructions. Once the ice cream is complete, fold in the cooled candied bacon pieces, and transfer to a 2-quart bowl or container. Cover with a lid or plastic wrap and freeze overnight to set. Serve as ice cream sandwiches with Butterscotch Potato Chip Cookies (page 158).

BUTTERSCOTCH POTATO CHIP COOKIES

Adapted from Natasha Case's recipe

If you love salty and sweet combos, these cookies will make you swoon. The extra bit of crunch from the potato chips makes for a perfect counterpoint to the soft cookie.

....

YIELD: MAKES 4 DOZEN COOKIES

½ pound (2 sticks) unsalted butter, room temperature

1½ cups brown sugar, firmly packed

1 teaspoon Kosher salt

1 large egg plus 1 egg yolk

1⅓ teaspoons vanilla extract

2 tablespoons whole milk

2⅓ cups all-purpose flour

1 teaspoon baking soda

2 cups butterscotch chips

1 cup lightly crushed kettle-style potato chips

Move oven rack to middle position and preheat oven to 325°F.

In a bowl of a stand mixer, using the paddle attachment, combine the butter, brown sugar, and salt. On low speed, mix until smooth, scraping the sides of the bowl, as necessary, to fully incorporate.

Add in the egg, yolk, vanilla extract, and milk, mixing to combine. The dough will appear a little "broken."

Add in the flour, baking soda, and butterscotch chips, mixing on low to combine, being careful not to overmix.

On a sheet pan, scoop 1 tablespoon of dough for each cookie, spacing them about 1½ inches apart. Lightly smoosh about 1 or 2 teaspoons of crushed potato chips on top of the cookie dough.

Bake 4 minutes, then rotate pans 180°, then continue baking for 4 to 6 more minutes or until cookies are golden brown. Remove from the oven and cool on the pan for 1 to 2 minutes. Then move cookies to a wire rack to cool completely. Store in an airtight container up to 3 days.

Note: Because of the potato chips you'll get the maximum crunch factor when fresh.

No milk, no eggs, no cheese? No problem. With an eclectic menu inspired by Southeast Asian, Central American, African, and Southwestern cuisine, the Cinnamon Snail truck is trying to change perceptions of vegan food one meal at a time. And it seems to be working. Helmed by Chef Adam Sobel, the truck serves up vegan and organic breakfast, lunch, and snacks around the city six days a week to a large and loyal fan base, many of whom are not actually practicing vegans. "It's hard to say exactly, but I would say well over seventy percent of our customers are not vegetarian. Some of them are just open-minded enough to be consciously eating vegetarian food, and some of them really just want something tasty, and we happen to be that. They just see yummy-looking doughnuts, and then they come back, and they're eating a tofu sandwich, and then they're eating raw food. It helps break the stereotypes about vegetarian food."

Though Adam had been a practicing vegetarian for years, it was the birth of his daughter, Idil, eleven years ago that sparked his vegan epiphany. "Both of our kids were born in home births. I just had a major revelation that day about how important it would be for my daughter to be breastfed—how that's important on so many levels, and I wouldn't want to take that away from someone else. I also wanted to raise her vegan with a lot of compassion and respect for living creatures, and I knew that wouldn't be easy to do if I wasn't vegan and my wife was."

Adam had first thought about starting a vegan truck eight years ago, but at the time, he was intimidated by the permitting process and the capital

"Whether or not people go all the way vegan or not, at least for people who are just coming to my truck once a week and otherwise would never go to a vegetarian restaurant, at the very least that's one less animal. I think it's pretty important. I really try to afford other living creatures the same respect that's afforded to me." —ADAM SOBEL

needed to launch a mobile food business. When the vegetarian restaurant he was working at shuttered abruptly, Adam found himself at a crossroads and started his own catering company, Certified Orgasmic. "I inherited a lot of the regular customers and started doing some farmers' markets with a stand. We did that for two and a half or three years. It just was growing really rapidly." With time he was able to save enough to buy a beat up truck on Craigslist, which, through the kindness and support of his friends, was completely gut renovated and decked out with an eye-catching, psychedelic sepia paint job. Taking its name from their puffy cinnamon buns, the Cinnamon Snail hit the road on Valentine's Day in 2010. They began cultivating a following in New York after being named New Vendor finalists at the 2010 Vendy Awards and New Jersey finalists at the 2011 Vendy Awards where their crème brûlée doughnut took home the prize in the Maker's Mark® challenge. When the truck started running afoul of Byzantine food truck regulations in their native New Jersey, they crossed the river and started serving in New York City in the fall of 2011.

Lines queue early and go late for Adam's hyperflavor-packed seasonal menu. His Ancho Chili Seitan Burger isn't your run of the mill frozen veggie patty on a bun. Instead spiced seitan is topped with beer-simmered onions and garlic, arugula, piri-piri pepper sauce, and horseradish cream, and then served up on a grilled herb focaccia. When you see all the elements that go into each dish on the truck, it's not surprising to learn that Adam worked under Tom Valenti at Ouest. "When we started, we had three sandwiches on the menu, and the rest of it was all these super kooky entrées. It's evolved every time we change the menu to be more and more stuff that's kind of more convenient to eat on-the-go. We still try to keep it as complex as the entrées were but they've all become sandwiches; lots of different sauces and marinades and condiments and stuff."

Many an unsuspecting carnivore has been lured in by their massive case of pastries. Their doughnuts are habit-forming, gateway vegan fare and come in inventive and hunger pang–inducing flavors like the Cherry Chocolate Brownie, the Thai Coconut Basil, and an outrageous chocolate-frosted, chocolate-cookie-crumb-covered and chocolate-filled doughnut known as the "Hulk Hogan Transvestite Fudgie Wudgie." Whimsical,

playful, and occasionally downright absurd, Adam and his crew don't take themselves terribly seriously. Rather than proselytizing the virtues of veganism, they show by example how delicious and satisfying vegan food can be. "We try to do a food that's a balance—it's nourishing, it's tasty, it's not super processed, and it's not super boring."

Above all, Adam loves the customer interaction that running a food truck affords. "Working in a restaurant, you're always stuck in the back kitchen. It's not an appropriate setting to really hang out with your customers. Food trucks really provide a nice space for really getting to know the people you make food for and your customers really getting to know each other." With the explosion of social media, the truck is able to connect and stay in touch with its thousands of fans. "It becomes this really open exchange where you're not just forcing your food creations down people's throats, you really hear what people are loving—what people would love for you to make. That's really, really fun. That really brings it alive and stops it from being just a business."

BLUE CORN PANCAKES
Adapted from Adam Sobel's recipe

Inspired by Southwestern cookery, these blue corn pancakes are lighter than your typical whole-grain pancakes and are a favorite of Adam's daughter, Idil. Slather these with cinnamon-laced pine nut butter (page 164) and a generous drizzle of real maple syrup for a healthy and hearty breakfast. Adam favors Vita Spelt® brand spelt flour and Bob's Red Mill® blue cornmeal both of which can typically be found at heath food stores, your local Whole Foods, or online at natureslegacyforlife.com and bobsredmill.com.

. . . .

YIELD: SERVES 4

²/₃ cup blue cornmeal

²/₃ cup spelt flour

1 teaspoon baking powder

½ teaspoon salt

1 cup soy milk

3 tablespoons agave nectar

3 tablespoons canola or safflower oil, plus more
    for greasing the griddle or skillet

2 teaspoons vanilla extract

In a large bowl, add the cornmeal, spelt flour, baking powder, and salt. Whisk ingredients together to combine and remove any lumps.

In a medium bowl or large measuring cup, whisk together soy milk, agave nectar, oil, and vanilla extract.

Create a well in the center of the dry ingredients, and pour the wet ingredients in. Whisk thoroughly to form a smooth, light blue batter.

Heat a griddle or large skillet over medium for 1 to 2 minutes. Ladle ⅓ cup of batter on the heated surface. When small bubbles appear toward the center of the pancakes, flip them and allow them to cook for another minute or two on the other side, or until the pancake is lightly browned on both sides.

Serve with pine nut butter (page 164) and maple syrup.

PINE NUT BUTTER

Adapted from Adam Sobel's recipe

You won't miss dairy with this sweet, salty, and slightly crunchy butter on your breakfast table. Use leftover pine nut butter on muffins, toast, or waffles. If you are preparing this recipe for practicing vegans be sure to look for a dairy-free margarine. Adam recommends the Earth Balance® brand.

....

YIELD: ABOUT 1½ CUPS

½ cup pine nuts, coarsely chopped or pulsed in a food processor

8 tablespoons (1 stick) dairy-free margarine

⅓ cup coconut butter

½ teaspoon salt

3 tablespoons dark brown sugar or panela, firmly packed

1 teaspoon cinnamon

In a small saucepan over a medium flame, toast the chopped pine nuts, stirring frequently to avoid burning.

When the pine nuts are deeply golden, add the remaining ingredients. Once the margarine and coconut butter have melted fully, pour the mixture into a small metal pan (like a 7-inch loaf pan) and chill for two hours or until solidified.

When the butter has solidified, use a spatula to transfer the contents to an airtight container, making sure to distribute the pine nuts throughout the butter, as they settle to the bottom while cooling.

Note: To give the butter a rich hint of molasses, Adam uses Sucanat®, an organic and fair-trade whole cane sugar product made of dehydrated cane juice instead of the dark brown sugar or panela. You can find Sucanat® at Whole Foods and other natural foods stores.

JALAPEÑO LENTIL SOUP WITH CORIANDER AND MINT

Adapted from Adam Sobel's recipe

If you're the slightest bit spice-adverse, beware—this soup packs some serious heat. "There's not really that many places that do really good spicy vegetarian," Adam says. "That's one of the things, I think when you're serving largely non-vegetarians is [spice] kind of gives this food a little bit of balls. They don't want it to be super wimpy, plain food." The Cinnamon Snail offers this spicy lentil soup in the fall. If you like heat as much as they do, reserve the seeds from the jalapeño pepper and use them for garnish, along with your favorite Harissa. Have a milder palate? Reduce both the crushed red pepper and jalapeños.

In a soup pot, heat the olive oil over medium heat. Add the onions and cook, stirring occasionally until translucent, about 5 minutes. Add jalapeños and garlic, along with the spices. Cook, stirring occasionally for 2 minutes, until the spices are evenly distributed but not sticking to the pot.

Add the lentils and stock. Bring the soup to a boil over high heat. Cover and reduce the heat to medium-low for 35 minutes. Add the mint leaves and salt to taste before serving.

....

YIELD: SERVES 6

¼ cup olive oil

1 medium white onion, finely chopped

3 jalapeño peppers, deveined, seeded, and
    finely chopped

6 cloves garlic, peeled and finely chopped

3 tablespoons ground coriander

¼ teaspoon ground cloves

1 tablespoon red pepper flakes, crushed

2 bay leaves

1¼ cup French lentils

6½ cups vegetable stock

3 tablespoons lime juice

¼ cup fresh mint leaves, chopped

salt to taste

When Dennis Kum taught himself to cook at age nine the reason was simple: "I didn't like my mom's cooking," he says. From an early age, Dennis gravitated to Asian cuisine. "We don't have that in my house. My parents are actually from South America—Guyana—so I grew up eating curry, dal soup (which is like a split pea soup), pepper pot (which is like an oxtail stew). When I first went out to a Chinese restaurant, *wow, this tasted really good.*" Dennis went to the library and checked out a stack of Chinese cookbooks. "I went and got the books, and I was cooking my own General Tso's Chicken at home." Soon he was making dinner for the whole family. "I got really fat. Really, really fat," he says with a laugh.

These days, Dennis cooks for a much bigger crowd aboard Big D's Grub Truck, a school bus–yellow food truck that takes its name from Dennis's longtime nickname. When Kogi BBQ hit the streets of Los Angeles in late 2008, offering Korean-Mexican fusion cuisine like short rib tacos and kimchi quesadillas, food lovers across the country took notice. The Kogi phenomenon didn't escape Dennis's attention. He'd long been playing with Asian flavors in unconventional dishes and quickly dreamed up a menu that would feature Korean-esque beef, chicken, and pork tacos that could also be served up pseudo-*banh mi*-style as hefty grinders. Rounding out the menu is a mix of Asian, Latin, and Southern sides ranging from Old Bay– or Sazón- seasoned crinkle cut fries to pork and chive dumplings to fried yucca with a Sriracha-infused dipping sauce. "They didn't have anything in New York at the time. I was actually

scheduled to open in September [2010], and then I had some delays. The truck was actually sitting in the lot all done for three-and-a-half months. And then Korilla came out." Being first to market, Korilla took the bragging rights of introducing Korean tacos in New York, but Dennis doesn't mind. He sees himself as more of a fusion truck than solely a Korean taco truck.

Dennis developed the recipes for the truck in his own kitchen, testing and honing them at dinner parties. Friends were invited to come and eat, but there was a catch—they had to bring a bottle. "I get to cook, you get to enjoy it, and we can all get drunk," Dennis says. As much as Dennis loves the spicy pork and the fries—"I'm always picking at the fries, it's just right there"—he's careful not to indulge all the time. With that in mind, Dennis

developed their ginger chicken recipe as an alternative for customers looking for a healthier street food lunch. The tender grilled chicken is dressed in ginger sauce instead of mayo, then served with plenty of fresh chopped cilantro.

Dennis loves the interaction with regular customers. "I like when they come back—you know their names, you know their orders. It just feels really good. "Big D's fans are loyal and dedicated. "There are a few customers that actually if the weather is nice they'll take the train down. They'll come down to FiDi, they'll come down to Flatiron . . . one time they took a cab." Dennis loves the immediate reaction from the customers. "This guy came down from his office just to tell me how much he enjoyed it."

At times the crowds can be overwhelming. "Certain areas—we've been doing the World Financial Center—they're not used to waiting outside for their food, so they get very impatient. I'm looking at them and I feel bad. Me as an owner at the window, it's like sometimes I don't want to look. I'd rather be in the back because my stress level is through the roof." The lunch rush at the WFC is massive. Just how busy is the truck? Here's what they got through in a typical day: "85 orders of dumplings, 8 bags of fries, 40 pounds of bulgogi, 32 pounds of spicy pork, 60 pounds of chicken thighs, 110 sandwiches, 2 cases of tortillas—that's WFC in two hours. They come in one shot. By 1:30, it's dead."

"I like what I do, except for the whole parking hassle." —DENNIS KUM

JALAPEÑO CHEDDAR CORNCAKES

Adapted from Dennis Kum's recipe

Sweet, salty, and spicy—not to mention crispy from the little fried cheesy bits—these pancakes hit so many satisfaction points, you'll find yourself going in for a second helping. Unlike regular pancakes these don't need any syrup. On the truck Dennis serves them with a side of strawberry jam, but they're perfect on their own. This recipe calls for two types of cornmeal. *Masa harina* is treated with lime and is different from regular yellow cornmeal, it's typically found in the international aisle at grocery stores or grouped in with Latino specialty items. This recipe requires both. You can't substitute one for the other.

YIELD: SERVES 4

³/₄ cup all-purpose flour

¼ cup *masa harina*

¼ cup cornmeal

⅓ cup granulated sugar

1 tablespoon baking powder

pinch of salt

1 cup whole milk

2 large eggs

¼ cup vegetable oil, plus more for oiling the pan

1 cup canned corn, drained

²/₃ cup canned jalapeño peppers, chopped

2 cups cheddar cheese, shredded

In a large bowl, whisk together the flour, *masa harina*, cornmeal, sugar, baking powder, and salt. Set aside. Blend milk, eggs, and oil in a small bowl. Pour the milk mixture into the flour mixture and mix with a large spoon until incorporated, then stir in corn until just incorporated. Heat a large, lightly oiled griddle or cast-iron skillet over medium heat. When the griddle is hot, pour the batter onto the heated surface ⅓ cup at a time. Once pancakes begins to bubble, sprinkle each with jalapeños and ¼ cup cheese. Brown for 1 or 2 minutes on each side. If cakes are browning too fast, turn down the heat a little. Serve immediately.

BIG D'S GRUB MENU

TACOS
Big D serves all of his tacos in a fresh, warm _____ tortilla with a slice of lime. Mix and match for best results!

#1 Bulgogi: (Korean for "Fire Meat"):
Lean beef marinated in soy sauce, garlic, sesame seed oil, served with spicy kimchi puree, zesty scallion relish and cool, rich crema

#2 Spicy Pork:
Juicy pork marinated in Big D's secret spice mix, topped with zesty scallion relish.

#3 Ginger Chicken:
_____ chicken mixed with ginger sauce, served with fresh chopped cilantro

#4 Spicy Chicken: Big D's favorite!
_____ chicken mixed with spicy mayo, served

GBD ON THE SIDE
Big D's rule for sides is GBD, Golden Brown and Delicious!

French Fries
Hot & fresh crinkle cut fries dusted with Old Bay Seasoning and Sazon (optional)

Fried Yuca
Crispy and delicious fried yuca served with your choice of sauce.

Dumplings
Yummy pork & chive dumplings with your choice of dipping sauce: Spicy mayo, Soy garlic, ginger sauce, Sriracha hot sauce or Big D's Secret Sauce

THE SAUCE IS BOSS!
Choose a sauce for your side

Spicy Mayo

_____ with authentic Sriracha sauce for that spicy

While other trucks sport slick paint jobs, the Green Pirate Juice Truck exterior is bedecked with graffiti-style leafy foliage for a look that's decidedly renegade. If ever there was a truck made for roaming the urban jungle, it's the Green Pirate Juice Truck.

Owner Deborah Smith is a holistic health coach and graduate of the Institute for Integrative Nutrition, as well as a longtime home juicer. But even avid juice lovers will admit that the labor-intensive process of completely disassembling a juicer and attacking it with tiny brushes to get rid of all the lingering pulp is a major pain. As Deborah puts it: "My roommate and I were juicing at home on a daily basis and would often wish that there was a juice bar in the neighborhood so at least every once in a while we wouldn't have to clean the juicer." One day they were lying in the park when the ice cream truck rolled by. They thought "it was unfortunate that people had such easy access to food that was not good for them but couldn't get a healthy juice or a salad that easily. Lightbulb."

"It's always helpful to vend in a location where there are a) lots of people, b) good vibes (like the Grand Army farmers' market), and/or in our case, health-minded individuals." —DEBORAH SMITH

The menu on the truck is seasonal and constantly evolving. Juices aren't the single-fruit or veggie affairs you might pick up at your local grocery store, but rather inventive combos with fun names like the McCarrot Park—a zippy blend of carrot, apple, and ginger—or the Pear Essentials—a refreshing mix of pear, cantaloupe, lime, cucumber, and mint. The namesake Green Pirate clocks in with not one, not two, not three, but four green fruits and veggies—spinach, green apple, cucumber, celery, ginger, and lemon.

When it comes to creating new recipes, Deborah says they "start with foods that are packed with vitamins, minerals, antioxidants, and superfood qualities that would have maximum energy and health benefits, then apply knowledge of acid/alkaline foods and try to find a balance." Over the years, the menu has gotten healthier with the addition of more vegetables to the drinks. "When we first got started, there were almost never greens on the truck, and now green juice is the bulk of our business," says Deborah. "After a few years we began selling coconuts and coconut smoothies, adding superfood powders and hemp proteins to smoothies, and growing our own wheatgrass."

Personal relationships with local farmers help keep the truck stocked with fresh veggies. As soon as fruits and vegetables come in season, you can expect to see them make an appearance on the truck. "I love creating specialty drinks out of produce that just popped out of the ground!" Deborah says. While the truck starts up for the year in the spring, fall is actually Deborah's favorite season. "Fall is amazing because the green markets are bursting with colors and flavors, and we can make the best juice! I'd say September and October are our busiest months."

The Green Pirate originated out of Williamsburg and Greenpoint, but recently it's been making regular stops at curated food truck lots around the city. With a couple of lunchtime appearances per week, they've started offering a healthy lunch menu

consisting of vegan wraps and snacks, in addition to juices. During the winter, they make bottled juice deliveries. The business is both health-conscious and ecoconscious. The truck runs on biodiesel fuel. The juices are served in compostable corn plastic cups. Customers who bring their own reusable cups get a fifty-cent discount off their drinks. Organic waste from juicing gets composted and distributed to farmers upstate.

As passionate as Deborah is in her mission to bring juice to the people, the challenges are many. The physical aspects of the job can be draining. It takes a lot of produce to make juice. There are crates to haul and pulp to compost. "Being one of the only women in a male-dominant industry, learning about diesel engines and fuel, dealing with the mechanical aspects of the job, driving a giant step van around that's painted like a peacock, serving a product that's actually good for you, fighting

with ice-cream-truck vendors, having our tires slashed multiple times and our lives threatened, months where it rained every day and we had no business, finding parking, maintaining regular street spots, keeping our product consistent and affordable while navigating the challenges of offering organic vs. local produce, and finding ways to communicate that to our customers, finding and keeping staff . . . shall I go on?"

Still through it all the Green Pirate has enabled Deborah to act as a healthy living ambassador to New Yorkers who might never otherwise seek out her holistic-health coaching services. There's a certain magic in "the look on a person's face when they come to the truck because they think we sell ice cream and I convince them to try a healthy juice—and they discover that they like it! I have personally turned hundreds of New Yorkers onto drinking fresh juice, and that's a good feeling."

THE TROPICOLADA SMOOTHIE
Adapted from Deborah Smith's recipe

This smoothie was inspired partially by Deborah's travels to warmer climes, where it's common to find cooling fruit-based beverages. "It was ushered onto the truck's menu by the demand of our loyal customers in South Brooklyn who hail from the islands Trinidad, West Indies, and other tropical climates, who would come to the truck religiously asking for these items," says Deborah. If you prefer a less pulpy smoothie, you can use just the freeze-squeezed juice from one orange. Deborah recommends peeling and freezing your bananas so they are cold when you blend and you don't need to use ice cubes, which will water your smoothie down.

YIELD: SERVES 2

½ ripe banana, peeled

1 large navel orange, peeled and quartered

1 cup fresh pineapple, diced

¾ cup organic coconut milk

Add all ingredients to a blender and blend until smooth.

TIP: For a lighter version, substitute fresh coconut water for coconut milk.

THE AVOCOLADA
Adapted from Deborah Smith's recipe

For a more decadent and omega-3 rich version of the Tropicolada (page 173), try this variation with avocado.

YEILD: SERVES 2

½ avocado

1 large naval orange, peeled and quartered

1 cup fresh pineapple, diced

¾ cup fresh coconut water or organic coconut milk

Add all ingredients to a blender and blend until smooth.

FRESH COCONUT SMOOTHIE
Adapted from Deborah Smith's recipe

This smoothie is possibly the most piratical of the Green Pirate Juice Truck's beverages. A simple drink consisting entirely of fresh coconut—its juice and its meat, Deborah recommends customizing it to your personal taste. "You can add other flavors to it, such as pineapple, banana—or even throw in some dark leafy greens and blueberries to get your nutrients in there. The basic smoothie is divine, but add your favorite flavor to make it your own!"

YIELD: SERVES 1

1 fresh, young coconut

Open coconut, drain coconut water into a blender, and scrape out as much coconut meat as possible. Blend and serve chilled or over ice.

There are a few concepts in the food truck world that will always be a hard sell, and grilled cheese is definitely toward the top of that list. But this didn't deter Michael Jacober from opening Morris Grilled Cheese, named after his Russian great-grandfather, at the end of June 2011. He first got the idea for starting a truck after he finished touring with his band, Fang Island, in late 2010. He originally wanted to serve up pasta, but surprisingly enough, that quickly appeared to be too complicated. Michael's previous careers at upscale restaurants in Paris and New York, including Per Se, Insieme, and Franny's, gave him superb kitchen skills and means that anything he was going to be cooking on his food truck would have to be of the utmost quality—soggy pasta just wouldn't do. His second choice after pasta ended up being grilled cheese—unbeknownst to him at the time that Morris would be the third gourmet grilled cheese truck in a row to open to the skeptical critics known as New Yorkers.

From the very beginning, Michael definitely wanted Morris Grilled Cheese to be "all about the food." During his time working under famed chef Marco Canora at Insieme, Michael received his "prime culinary education," learning valuable lessons on "cooking, seasoning, and tasting." His days at the seasonally driven Franny's—as well as having a girlfriend who's worked as a farmer at both the Stone Barns Center in Pocantico Hills, New York, and the Queens County Farm—taught him the interesting flavors and value of using local sustainable produce. With these influences in mind, Michael set about preparing his truck and menu for opening.

Their first day open was June 30 on Seventh Avenue and Carroll Street in Park Slope, Brooklyn, where they "hid on the corner and did $70. "They've come a long way since then, even developing a slight cult following. Visit the truck during its days in Murray Hill or Midtown, and expect to hear praise from office workers who can't seem to believe they're buying fancy grilled cheese off a truck. The rotating seasonal menu has to nearly constantly be explained to new customers and regulars alike, but to Michael and his executive chef, Chris Austin, that simply means "we're teaching people about food." Even their best-selling classic grilled cheese sandwich is differentiated by using a mixture of New York cheddar and New Hampshire Landaff. One can expect everything from pastrami to pickled rhubarb to show up in one of their sandwiches, but

Michael adds, "We try to balance every sandwich." Almost all of the ingredients are grown and produced locally, with Michael and Chris making frequent visits to the Union Square and Grand Army Plaza Greenmarkets. Even the duck fat available to have your sandwich grilled in is from the Hudson Valley. This loyalty to local sustainable food eventually led them to become the first food truck to be awarded Slow Food NYC's "Snail of Approval," an exclusive award for quality, authenticity, and sustainability. But the success hasn't gone to their head. The truck still has touches from its early days, including the stick-on vinyl lettering originally used to display their name. Even the addition of an official menu board prompted them to realize "we're becoming more and more like a real food truck." A really, really delicious food truck.

"Our philosophy is using really great ingredients and making really great food that's accessible to the public." —MICHAEL JACOBER

MORRIS'S HOT PASTRAMI SANDWICH

Adapted from Michael Jacober's recipe

YIELD: 1 SANDWICH

2½ ounces Gruyère, shredded

2 slices sourdough bread, both buttered

3 thin slices pastrami

3 ounces papas fritas (page 178)

1½ tablespoons chimichurri (page 178)

Spread the Gruyère on one slice of buttered bread. Place the pastrami atop the shredded cheese, then lay out papas fritas over the pastrami until they cover the sandwich. Spread the chimichurri on the second slice, and lay it on top of the other piece of bread.

Grill the sandwich in a flat pan over medium-high heat until the cheese has melted evenly, about 5 minutes.

PAPAS FRITAS
Adapted from Michael Jacober s recipe

Papas Fritas, or fried potatoes, aren't usually fried in duck fat, but then again, this isn't your usual grilled cheese either. Michael recommends using Russian Banana Fingerlings, but it can be switched up with Russets or new potatoes.

YIELD: ENOUGH FOR 5 SANDWICHES
½ tablespoon butter
½ tablespoon duck fat
1 pounds potatoes, sliced ⅛-inch thick rounds
½ onion

Heat the butter and duck fat in a skillet until the duck fat has melted into the butter. Add the potatoes and cook until they are golden brown. When the potatoes are almost fully cooked through, add the onion into the skillet and toss to incorporate thoroughly.

Set aside to cool.

CHIMICHURRI SAUCE
Adapted from Michael Jacober s recipe

Chimichurri is a Latin American sauce typically used on cooked meats. Michael's use on a grilled cheese, one with pastrami nonetheless, is a truly unique take, and a tasty one.

YIELD: ½ CUP
¼ cup red wine vinegar
½ teaspoon salt
2 cloves garlic, peeled
½ shallot, peeled
½ jalapeño
1 cup fresh cilantro
½ cup fresh parsley
¼ cup fresh oregano
⅓ cup extra-virgin olive oil
Cumin and dried chiles, to taste

Add ingredients to a food processor, and pulse until you have a smooth consistency. Keep leftover sauce in an airtight container in the fridge.

Tips for the BEST grilled cheese EVER:

- Ideal cooking temperature is 490°F on a panini press.
- Best cooking fat is liquid clarified butter (ghee). Use a pastry brush to spread evenly on both sides of bread.
- Duck fat adds a nice meatiness and an extra crisp to the bread.
- Olive oil is better if cooking in a pan because of the higher smoke point.
- When cutting the sandwich, allow it to set for 30 seconds after cooking in order to better preserve the cheese inside.
- For a crispier bread, try ciabatta or focaccia. Multigrain tends to burn quicker. The ideal bread for flavor is sourdough. Pullman has a tendency to become soggy the fastest due to the moisture content of the bread.
- If the pan is too hot and the bread cooks faster then the cheese, put the sandwiches on a cookie sheet in an oven set to a low temperature (250°F) watching closely until the cheese has melted. This also works well when trying to cook several sandwiches at the same time: "set" the bread at a higher heat, set each sandwich aside, and then place them all in the oven together to melt the cheese.
- It's important to think about having an acidic component to help balance the fattiness of the cheese. The best ways to achieve this are with pickles, tomatoes, and fresh lemon juice.
- A nice touch is to rub the outside of the cooked sandwich with garlic to give it a deeper flavor.
- Consider the melting point of the cheese you use when cooking the sandwich. Harder cheeses tend to melt slower, so reduce your cooking temperature to avoid burning the bread.

In 2007, New York City had some great ice cream shops, but no great ice cream trucks. Ben Van Leeuwen wanted to change that. He and his brother, Pete, both former Good Humor truck workers with bona fide sweet teeth, approached Ben's then-girlfriend, now-wife, Laura O'Neill, with an idea: open a truck using super-rich ice cream and the best ingredients they can find. Laura thought, "It sounds crazy enough to be a good idea." They definitely "wanted to do things super simple with all the classic flavors," but also branch out with more adventurous ingredients. But most importantly, they wanted to make their premium ice cream as naturaly as possible—meaning no stabilizers, fillers, or gums. This need for purity ran over into how they sourced their ingredients as

well: "We really wanted people to know where things are coming from." This translates into seeing ingredients like soy lecithin-less Michel Cluizel chocolate; pistachios from Bronte, Sicily; and palm sugar made from Balinese heritage palm sap. With almost no local commercial dairies willing or able to make ice cream how the trio wanted, they turned to their kitchen counter ice-cream makers, making batch after batch of ice cream until they finally had products they could be proud of.

Their signature butter yellow truck—purchased off of eBay for $5,000 and retrofitted to their specifications, including artist Elara Tanguy's hand-painted Victorian-inspired menus—finally hit the road on June 21, 2008, at a small fair in Tribeca. Within the first few hours, they were approached

by a rep from Whole Foods inquiring about selling pints in their stores. "We laughed," reflects Laura. "We'd been in business for like an hour." Though they declined that first time, within a year, you could find their pints in local stores—after they had started to become the next big food truck. The most challenging aspect to the truck—besides securing the initial capital—has been finding good spots. On Bedford Avenue in Williamsburg—a popular spot where a truck can be found almost daily now—actually didn't work out the first time. The first few times, in fact, no one really bought anything, but "then one year later we went back and the spot took." They also all had to work incredibly long, often twelve-hour (or more) days that first summer, though this did mean getting to know their customers and seeing the happiness a cool ice-cream cone can bring on a hot summer day. The hard work, "pushing for what we wanted," and, of course, delicious ice cream paid off, as the trio now run a million-dollar business with six trucks and three stores in Brooklyn and Manhattan. "If you can do a store, do a store. Trucks need to be babied," laughs Laura. Even though it's been five years of ice cream making (and eating) since getting that first idea, all three still get cravings for their ice cream, including Laura's summertime treat: the currants and cream flavor topped with hot fudge.

"We would never compromise the quality of our product. We've fought against people telling us to cut corners." —LAURA O'NEILL

VAN LEEUWEN'S BASE MIX
Adapted from the Van Leewen's recipe

This is Van Leeuwen's standard ice cream base that works for a number of different flavors due to its ultra-high butter fat content, but lower amounts of sugar than many other recipes. By only using milk, cream, sugar, and eggs, the result will be refreshing and rich, instead of cloyingly sweet, allowing the exceptional flavoring ingredients in the ice cream to shine through.

YIELD: 2 PINTS

1½ cups whole milk
2 cups plus 1 tablespoon heavy whipping cream
¾ cup granulated sugar, divided
4 egg yolks

Heat milk, cream and ½ cup plus 1 teaspoon of sugar in a double boiler on medium heat. Using a cooking thermometer, bring the mixture to approximately 145°F.

In a medium bowl, whisk the egg yolks with the remaining sugar.

Slowly add 1 cup of the warm milk/cream mix to the egg yolks while whisking (this tempers the egg yolks and avoids a scramble!), then whisk this mixture into the heated mixture in the double boiler and bring to a medium low heat.

Stir constantly, and as the mixture starts to thicken into a custard, test consistency on the back of a wooden spoon by running your finger through the custard. If the gap on the spoon stays separated, it is ready to be cooled.

Transfer custard to an ice bath and stir for a few minutes to arrest the cooking process.

Refrigerate overnight (or for at least 4 hours).

Pour mixture into a home ice-cream maker and churn, following the manufacturer's instructions, until it reaches soft-serve consistency. At this point you can either enjoy or put into the freezer to harden further.

ADDING FLAVORS:

This base works well with low-moisture and low-fat flavors, for example:

VANILLA BEAN (steep pods in mixture, then split open and add beans before refrigerating)

MINT CHIP (add mint extract after refrigerating, and chips at end of churning)

CITRUS ZEST (steep flaked coconut in mixture, strain, then add fresh shredded coconut before freezing)

COCONUT (steep in mixture, strain, then add fresh zest before freezing)

EARL GREY TEA (steep three teas bag in mixture, then remove before adding eggs)

GREEN TEA (add power to taste before freezing)

CINNAMON (steep quills or powder in mix, allow to infuse, strain before churning)

WORKING WITH FRUIT:

If you would like to add fruit, you will need to increase your fat content to balance out the water in the fruit. For the recipe (on page 182) you would increase the cream to 2¾ cups and decrease the milk to ¾ cup. You will want to up your sugar to 1 cup plus 1 tablespoon, as this will make the ice cream more stable. Use ⅓ cup of the sugar to compote (coat in sugar and allow to sit for 3 hours at least) your fruit before adding to the mixture. The ratio should be ⅓ cup of fresh purée of your chosen fruit to 1¼ cups of base mixture, about 1 cup of purée for 2 pints. Compoting will stop the fruit juices from forming crystals as they freeze. Combine fruit with base just before freezing (no earlier, as fruit will oxidize and lose bright color).

WORKING WITH CHOCOLATE:

We recommend you use a 99% cocoa solid chocolate. As chocolate contains more fat you are going to want to adjust the above recipe to be 1¾ cups of milk and 1½ cups of cream. You will also need to up your sugar to 1 cup to account for the bitter chocolate. You will need 2¾ ounces of 99% chocolate. Carefully melt the chocolate into the custard after it has thickened, before cooling the mixture.

WORKING WITH SPIRITS:

If you want to work you favorite alcohol into the base, add one to two tablespoons while churning. Anymore than that and you might lose the ice creams consistency. Use stronger or spicer liquors to ensure flavors come through after freezing.

If you were an underemployed gregarious bassoonist, what would you do during your summer off? Open an ice cream truck, of course! But not just any old ice cream truck—one that's decorated with large rainbow-swirled cones and that serves up specials like the Salty Pimp and the Bea Arthur. And you would call it the Big Gay Ice Cream Truck, opening your newest adventure in June of 2009 during New York City's Pride Weekend in an experience that can only be classified as a "disaster." As least, this is what Doug Quint did. Oh, and there may or may not have been a magical unicorn involved.

Doug and his partner in life and business, Bryan Petroff, didn't intend for the Big Gay Ice Cream Truck to take over their lives. A friend, Andrea Fisher, had found success with her own ice cream truck usually parked around Times Square when a boss asked her to find more drivers like her. "Her intent was to find pretty girls," but instead she roped Doug in. "We had the crazy idea to actually be good at it. If you're going to get repeat customers, you're going to have to be nice." In addition to utilizing his personality, Doug decided to change up the menu a little bit. New York City ice cream trucks all have the same basic menu, one that's barely changed with the years. But you will find trucks that want to break out of that box and offer off-the-menu specials. "We couldn't change the ice cream, but we could change what was on it." They turned to the desserts they

MOBILE FOOD VEI
TEMPORARY PERMIT
NOT TRANSFERABLE

70541

2009

VALID APRIL 1, 2009 TO OCTO
COMPLAINTS? Cal

BIG GAY
ICE CREAM TRUC

CONES & CUPS $.
(standard toppings included)

SUNDAES & SHAKE!

PREMIUM TOPPINGS

T-SHIRTS $15
MAGNETS $1

had enjoyed over the years, including those found at a pizzeria in Mill Valley, California, and Brooklyn's own Franny's.

After that fateful day during the Brooklyn Pride parade, Big Gay Ice Cream Truck started appearing in Midtown and Chelsea—often at a spot on East 17th Street and Broadway—quickly gaining the attention of the major food blogs. "There was something kind of underground, subversive about it," says Bryan. "It took some finding. You had to seek it out." Fans raved about the premium toppings, such as Trix and curried coconut, but the real turning point came with the debut of the Choinkwich. Bacon was peaking as a trend, and the idea of making an ice-cream sandwich stuffed with bacon and chocolate definitely turned heads. It wasn't long before Doug's nightly line was ten to twenty people deep. But despite gaining success and widespread popularity—including nominations in the 2009 and 2010 Vendy Awards and visits from food critics like *Vogue*'s Jeffrey Steingarten—the Big Gay Ice Cream Truck ultimately ended up taking the winter of 2009–10 off for Doug to tour with an orchestra. Fans rejoiced when the truck reopened for the 2010 season, but it wasn't until the spring of 2011 that rumors began about a brick-and-mortar store. The store finally gave Bryan a reason to leave his corporate day job to take on the (more than) full-time store management. Most days, you can find one or both of the guys there on the truck during the summer season, at the ready with jokes to brighten your day. "The most fun is that it makes it fun for other people."

"To do something really idiotic, to do something fun, that's where the idea came from." —DOUG QUINT

SALTY PIMP SUNDAE

Adapted from Doug Quint's recipe

One of Big Gay Ice Cream's signature cones is the Salty Pimp. When you visit the truck, you'll get a sugar cone lined with dulce de leche before being filled with soft-serve vanilla ice cream. More dulce de leche is pumped into the ice cream that's then dipped into chocolate shell after a sprinkling of sea salt. Since making ice cream truck soft serve is nearly impossible at home, unless you're one of the lucky ones with a machine, Doug and Bryan have come up with an at-home version of their famous treat. This sundae is excellent when using ice cream from Van Leeuwen (page 182).

YIELD: ONE SUNDAE

2 scoops vanilla ice cream
2 tablespoons dulce de leche (page 186)
2 tablespoons dark chocolate shell (page 186)
pinch sea salt

Make sure both the dulce de leche and chocolate shell are cool yet fluid.

Place the ice cream in a bowl and drizzle the dulce de leche on top. Sprinkle with the sea salt. Spoon the chocolate shell over the ice cream and dulce de leche. Let sit for a minute to harden. Enjoy.

DULCE DE LECHE
Adapted from Doug Quint's recipe

Doug and Bryan believe using a Crock Pot® and glass canning jar yield a better dulce de leche than other well-known methods. This recipe may take a long time and need a supervising eye to catch when it hits the right color, but you'll be rewarded with an extra-fancy sauce.

YIELD: ABOUT 1³/₄ CUPS

1 14-ounce can of sweetened condensed milk
french canning jar
2 teaspoons Kosher salt

Empty the sweetened condensed milk into the jar. Add salt and stir. Flip lid closed by don't lock it.

Place jar in a crock pot. Fill crock pot with enough hot water to cover the milk (any higher and the jar will bob up and down).

Turn the crock pot heat on high.

After the first hour, open the jar and stir to ensure the salt is properly combined into the milk.

Periodically check that the water still covers the milk. If it has evaporated down, add more hot water, not cold water to maintain temperature.

Leave the jar in the crock pot for about 4¹/₂ to 5 hours, cooking time will vary based on crockpot model. When done, dulce de leche should be smooth and creamy with a rich caramel color.

DARK CHOCOLATE SHELL
Adapted from Doug Quint's recipe

Chocolate dip, that wonderfully waxy coating for soft-serve ice cream, is surprisingly easy to make at home and with this DIY version you can make it with top quality chocolate minus all the preservatives.

YIELD: ABOUT ²/₃ CUP

10 ounces 72% cacao dark chocolate, coarsely chopped
¹/₃ cup coconut oil

Add chocolate to a large microwave-safe bowl. Cover with waxed paper and microwave on high for 30 seconds. Stir and if the chocolate isn't completely melted, cover, and microwave in 15-second bursts, stirring in between until chocolate is completely melted. Whisk in coconut oil. Transfer to a clean large bowl and continue whisking until mixture reaches room temperature, about 5 minutes. Cover and refrigerate for up to 2 days.

O ne of the first gourmet food trucks to arrive in New York came courtesy of lawyer-turned-pastry chef Jerome Chang and his business partner, Chris Chen. As roommates, the two kicked around ideas about a food truck they should open, yet "the idea of gourmet desserts never really came around," explains Jerome. It wasn't until Jerome improved upon Chris's spreading Nutella on toast—by adding caramelized bananas and salt, a dish that would later appear on the opening menu—that the DessertTruck began to take form one day in October of 2006. But it did take a year to get everything together before they finally hit the road on October 30, 2007. "I had to do a lot of legwork," said Jerome, "it was really difficult to get information," mainly due to the lack of food trucks at the time. After clearing the common major obstacles out of the way, they were driving back from picking up their finished truck from a fitter in New Jersey, excited to finally get their show on the road, when the truck broke down right at the entrance to the Lincoln Tunnel. "That was sort of our first introduction to operating a truck in the city."

Despite the unwelcome introduction, they did luck out timing-wise. Since they were one of the first food trucks in New York City, their opening garnered much attention from the New York and national press. Within twenty-four hours of being open, the menu was highlighted on the famous site Eater.com, with reviews coming in from tipsters. They chose a quiet spot right outside New York University's Weinstein Hall with enough foot traffic to spread the word. "What was cool was whoever did come by and stop, was absolutely floored by it." Jerome's desserts showcased the skills he had gained from the French Culinary Institute, New Jersey's Copeland Restaurant, and in the kitchen at high-

> "He said, 'Wow, this is great. This would be great for a truck, for street food.' And that's where the idea came from." —JEROME CHANG

end Le Cirque. Bloggers and journalists focused on the creamy, custardy chocolate bread pudding that came with vanilla or bacon crème anglaise, or the decadent molten chocolate cake, or the bomboloni: fried balls of Italian brioche dough pumped full of Nutella or vanilla crème. Everything was truly a world-class gourmet dessert, off of a truck, for $5. The *New York Times* and *Food & Wine* featured articles on them, and around their one-year anniversary, they taped an episode of a new TV show with chef Bobby Flay. One customer even proposed to his girlfriend in front of the truck (she said yes).

Everything appeared to be coming up roses. But running a truck proved to be harder than it looked. In hindsight, Jerome relays, "It was almost a constant battle." The beginning of 2009 came with vendor permit issues that ultimately took the truck off the road for almost a year. The guys realized they could "make it a little easier on themselves" by having a storefront. They found one, named DT Works, on Clinton Street on the Lower East Side, a few doors down from the brunch hotspot Clinton St. Baking Company. Once the truck was back in service, they claimed their old spot rotation, only to find out one was illegal. With the streets proving hard, Jerome focuses his time on the store. If he were to head out again, he'd definitely "want a smaller truck." "I wish there were more chefs opening up trucks," he says. If the quality were the same as the fantastic desserts from DessertTruck, so do we.

GOAT CHEESECAKE WITH ROSEMARY CARAMEL, FRESH BLACKBERRIES, AND TUILE

Adapted from Jerome Chang s recipe

This dish quickly became one of the fancier treats available off of the DessertTruck. Make the caramel the night before to allow all of the savory rosemary flavor to infuse into the caramel, a great compliment to the tangy goat cheese cake.

YIELD: 4 (1 1/2 CUP RAMEKINS)

ROSEMARY CARAMEL

2/3 cup granulated sugar

2 1/2 cups light corn syrup

2 sprigs rosemary

1/3 cup warm water

Salt, to taste

GOAT CHEESECAKE

2 1/4 silver grade gelatin sheets

1 cup plus 2 tablespoons whipping cream

3/4 cup plus 1 tablespoon whole milk

3/4 cup granulated sugar

1/8 teaspoon salt

16 ounces fresh goat cheese

Juice of 1 1/2 lemons

TUILE

3 egg whites

3/4 cup confectioners' sugar

Salt, to taste

7/8 cup all-purpose flour, sifted

8 tablespoons melted unsalted butter

TO ASSEMBLE AND SERVE:

Blackberries

FOR THE ROSEMARY CARAMEL:

Combine the sugar, corn syrup, and water in a pot. Bring to a boil and immediately remove from the heat. Add the rosemary, cover, and let infuse overnight. The next day, reheat the syrup and cook until it reaches a medium-amber color. Whisk in the warm water and remove from the heat. Whisk in salt. Let cool and reserve at room temperature.

FOR THE GOAT CHEESECAKE:

Place parchment or wax paper rounds on the bottom of the ramekins. Place the gelatin sheets in 1½ cups water to hydrate (bloom) them. In a medium pot, bring the cream, milk, sugar, and salt to a simmer. Remove from the heat. Add the goat cheese to the mixture. Using an immersion blender, blend the mixture until very smooth, about 5 minutes. Take the gelatin out of the water, carefully squeezing any excess, and add to the goat cheese mixture while continuing to blend. Stir in the lemon juice. Transfer 1½ cups of the goat cheese mixture into each of the ramekins. Transfer the ramekins uncovered to the freezer for 6 hours, or until solid.

FOR THE TUILE:

Prepare a double boiler over high heat. In the top bowl, combine the egg whites, sugar, and salt. Whisk the sugar and egg whites until the mixture is lukewarm to the touch. Remove from the heat and whisk in the flour. Transfer the mixture to the bowl of a stand mixer fitted with the whisk attachment. Whisk on slow speed while gradually adding the melted butter until fully combined. Place in a covered bowl and chill.

Preheat an oven to 300°F. Line 2 baking sheets with silicone mats. Spoon about a half tablespoon of chilled batter onto a sheet, and spread the batter into a very thin shape resembling a comet with the back of the spoon. Repeat until the sheets are filled. Put in the oven and bake for 8 minutes, or until golden brown. Let cool to room temperature. Reserve in an airtight container.

TO ASSEMBLE AND SERVE:

Approximately 30 minutes before serving, remove the goat cheesecakes from the freezer and allow to thaw slightly in the refrigerator. Slip the finished cakes out of the ramekins by flipping them upside down into a bowl. If they get stuck, take a butter knife and cut around the edges to loosen. Drizzle with the caramel. Top each cheesecake with blackberries and a tuile.

BRIOCHE DOUGHNUTS

Adapted from Jerome Chang's recipe

YIELD: 25 DOUGHNUTS

⅓ cup lukewarm water (100 to 110°F)

1 tablespoon plus 2 teaspoons active dry yeast

1½ cups all-purpose flour

1½ cups bread flour

⅓ cup granulated sugar plus 2 cups for coating

5 large eggs, divided

½ pound (2 sticks) unsalted butter, cubed, cool but not cold straight from the fridge

2 quarts vegetable oil for frying

1 container (750 grams) of Nutella (you will need a plastic piping bag)

Pour the lukewarm water into the bowl of a stand mixer. Add the dry yeast and stir with a spatula until the yeast is completely suspended or until it looks completely dissolved.

To the yeast and water mixture, add approximately half of the either bread or all purpose flour along with about ⅓ cup of the granulated sugar. Loosely cover the bowl with plastic wrap and let it stand at room temperature for about 1 hour. It should begin to produce lots of bubbles.

On low speed and with the dough hook attachment, begin mixing the remaining flour and sugar into the sponge. Once most of the flour has been incorporated, add 2 eggs and allow them to begin incorporating with the rest of the dough. Add the remaining eggs and all of the salt and turn the mixer speed up to medium. Continue kneading the dough with your machine on medium until the dough begins to come together into a bowl and stops sticking to the sides of the bowl. Depending on the speed and power of your machine, this may take 10 to 15 minutes.

Once the dough has come away from the sides of the bowl, gradually add the cubes of butter. Keep mixing until the dough is uniform and smooth. Keep in mind that this dough will be slightly sticky and very soft.

Place the dough in a lightly greased container approximately 3 times the volume of the dough, cover, and let it rest in the refrigerator overnight. The dough will at least double in size.

Prepare a well-greased 18 x 12–inch baking sheet and set aside.

Punch down on your dough to remove the excess air. Take the dough out of its container and place it directly on a lightly floured counter. Sprinkle and spread a light dusting of flour on top of the dough. Using a lightly floured rolling pin, roll the dough out into a rectangle. The length and width of this rectangle do not matter, as long as it is at least 2¼ inches wide. Continuously sprinkle and spread flour on top of your dough while rolling out. Be sure to periodically flip it over, as well. Roll out your dough until it is ¾ inch thick. Using a chef's knife and a ruler, make small indentations to mark off 2¼-inch segments along two sides of the dough, one being the width and the other being the length. Using the chef's knife, cut out 2¼-inch squares of dough. Place the squares of dough on your baking sheet, making sure that there is approximately ¾ inch between squares and loosely cover the baking sheet with plastic wrap or a moist towel. Any dough scraps can be rolled into balls and allowed to rise as well.

Allow the dough to rise in a part of your kitchen that is no warmer than 100°F. Depending on how warm it is, the dough may take anywhere from 1 to 2 hours to rise. They are properly proofed when you gently press the top of the dough with a finger and the resulting indentation very slowly rises back up.

Preheat your fryer or a pot with the vegetable oil to 330°F. Prepare a container or baking sheet lined with paper towels. This will hold your finished product. Once the fryer is heated, place your doughnut squares in it. Let them fry on one side for about 3 minutes, or until golden brown, then, using tongs or a spider, flip them over to fry the other side for another 3 minutes, or until golden brown. Then using your tool of choice, remove your doughnuts and place them on the paper towels.

Line a flat pan with the 2 cups of sugar.

Fill a plastic piping bag with as much Nutella as it will fit. Cut a very small hole across the tip of the bag, approximately ½ inch in diameter or smaller.

Using a wooden skewer, stab each doughnut and whittle out a little space for the filling in the center of each doughnut. Squeeze Nutella into each doughnut until it just begins to fill up. Then coat each doughnut in sugar by dredging it in the pan of sugar.

Enjoy immediately or within one day. No refrigeration necessary.

In late 2009, David Schillace felt the urge to quit his corporate job and enter into the burgeoning food truck business. To help create the menu, he turned to his friend Thomas Kelly, who was at the time working in marketing and social media. Thomas had worked in restaurants part-time, did a fair amount of cooking at home, and had recently been playing around with "a fusion of southern American barbecue and Mexican." Playing around with Mexican food isn't too much of a surprise once Thomas lets you know that he loves the heat and the spice that comes from cooking with "dried Mexican peppers," and that he's done a number of culinary tour visits south of the border. It didn't take long for David and Thomas to come up with the menu for Mexicue. "Sooner rather than later [Thomas]

realized this was a pretty awesome idea that [Dave] had." During the late winter and early spring of 2010, Thomas worked on developing their menu while Dave got the business up and running, using a partner to help them navigate the New York City permits and licenses. By July, the truck was ready for business, but the guys weren't prepared for that all-important "very stressful and exciting first day."

They parked the truck on Park Avenue in the 50s—the heart of Midtown. "We thought it would be like a kind of slow build, cultivating a following." Instead, they had lines down the block. While one person served food to the masses off of the truck, the other would be running out to buy more supplies so they didn't run out. The lines caught people's attention, and with everyone liking the

> "We've taken two pretty accessible foods, Mexican and barbecue, and blended them together in new and interesting ways." —THOMAS KELLY

food, it was certain that they had hit upon the right concept. "We got some great press write-ups right away from all the usual suspects online, and before too long we got some of the write-ups from the traditional media." The hype hasn't stopped since. "It's been pretty much that same ride since we launched," which has led them to open two brick-and-mortar locations, one in Midtown and the other in Chinatown. But the continued success of the truck and the subsequent locations would not have come if it hadn't been for the customers. The truck and social media have allowed Dave and Thomas "to really engage with our customers a lot. Opening up a dialogue with our customers that I don't think exists necessarily in most restaurants." They can test out concepts, finding what works and what doesn't. As for working the streets, Mexicue tries to be a lover and not a fighter with testy old-school vendors. "We're trying to make friends here and not create enemies."

Their daily menu features a number of slider and taco filling options, including tender short rib, smoky brisket, or spicy BBQ beans. The guys did try to source a number of their products locally from New York City farmers' markets, but when that turned out not to be feasible, they decided to at least use local produce in seasonal specials. One particular special, the smoked mushroom taco, became a quick favorite with customers. Other specials can include a beet taco or the autumnal butternut squash taco. Having a home-base kitchen in the Chinatown store has allowed for more menu offerings, a popular one of which is their Green Chile Mac 'n' Cheese.

GREEN CHILI MAC 'N' CHEESE RECIPE

Adapted from Thomas Kelly's and David Schillace's recipe

Mexicue's Green Chili Mac 'n' Cheese isn't actually found on their truck, but rather comes from their store. The green chili sauce adds a wonderful spicy kick, and the mild Monterey Jack cheese melts into the perfect creamy sauce. This makes a great side dish for plenty of entrées, or something to just enjoy on its own.

....

YIELD: SERVES 6

2 tablespoons unsalted butter

2 tablespoons all-purpose flour

³/₄ cup milk

³/₄ cup heavy cream

2 cups elbow macaroni

¹/₃ cup canned green chilies, chopped

1 cup salsa verde (homemade or store bought)

8 oz cheddar cheese

8 oz Monterey Jack cheese

¹/₄ teaspoon fresh ground pepper

salt, to taste

Melt the butter in a pan and add the flour to create a roux. Cook over medium heat for 5 minutes, stirring constantly with a wooden spoon.

In a separate pot, gently bring milk and cream to a simmer. Add roux and stir with a whisk to combine. Gently simmer to thicken, about 15 minutes. Frequently stir with a rubber spatula to prevent bottom from burning.

Meanwhile, bring a large pot of water to a boil and add the elbow macaroni. Cook to al dente, strain, and return to the pot.

In another separate pot, heat green chili and reduce slightly to thicken, about 10 minutes. Add to cream sauce.

Add the cheeses, chilies, and pepper to the sauce, stirring until the cheeses melt. Pour all of the cheese sauce over the cooked hot macaroni and stir to combine.

Add salt to taste. Serve.

SMOKED MUSHROOM GRILLED QUESADILLAS

Adapted from Thomas Kelly and David Schillace's recipe

Mushrooms are like flavor sponges, so this recipe is a great for quick quesadillas that have huge smoke flavor. These instructions are for the oven, but these can also be grilled, just make sure to lightly brush olive oil or butter on the outside of the quesadillas. Barbecue sauce is the perfect topping for these, make yours spicy by adding some ancho chili powder and Mexican oregano for some extra kick.

....

YIELD: SERVES 4

12 ounces cremini and/or button mushrooms, cleaned and thinly sliced

3 tablespoons unsalted butter, melted

1 teaspoon kosher salt

¼ teaspoon ground black pepper

½ teaspoon chili powder

1 teaspoon dried Mexican oregano

10 ounces Monterey Jack cheese (about 3 cups)

4 (10-inch) flour tortillas

barbecue sauce, for serving

Preheat your oven to 325°F.

Combine mushrooms, butter, salt, pepper, chili powder, and oregano in a small bowl.

Place mushrooms in a tin foil pouch punctured with small holes, place on a cookie sheet, and place in the oven for 10 minutes.

Place the mushroom mixture in a medium bowl and mix with the cheese.

Lay two of the tortillas out on a large baking sheet and evenly distribute the cheese and mushroom mixture on each. Place the other two on top.

Place the quesadillas back in the oven for about 10 minutes until the tortillas are nicely browned and the cheese has melted.

Cut into wedges and serve immediately.

Oleg Voss discovered his culinary passions young during his high school days in Paris, yet he still tried to have a career in the supposedly more stable finance industry. In late 2007, he had a fleeting idea to open a schnitzel food truck in New York, but his career was about to take him to a position in Vienna. Then after the 2008 international banking meltdown, Oleg soon found himself jobless and headed back to New York. A Ukrainian immigrant himself, his family had come here soon after the Iron Curtain fell, and he's certainly known rougher times. He decided to use his culinary degree from the renowned French Culinary Institute rather than get back into finance and opened Schnitzel & Things in 2009, despite his lack of experience in running a small business. "We're a unique truck with a very different menu. We're the only ones doing this." And that worked to their advantage.

Shortly after the opening, people sought out Schnitzel & Things because not only were there delicious creations being served up by Oleg (with help from his mother's recipes), but also you were served one of the most generous portions around town. Regulars came to expect their schnitzel of choice pounded thin, covered with Japanese panko breadcrumbs, and fried fresh to order, to be a plate of meat atop various vinegary salad sides of their choosing. A regular platter is big enough to induce a late afternoon nap. Even when a fan won free schnitzel for a month and ate at the truck every day, their generosity continued after the month was up. "I thought they would make me pay, but they were like, 'whatever, here you go.'" Opening a brick-and-mortar shop was always in the works and happened in spring 2011. Most days, you can find Oleg's mom working the stove in the back, making sure the customers are getting some of the most delicious Eastern European food around, including their take on traditional Austrian potato salad.

"Best experience of my life. We're doing something right."

—OLEG VOSS ON THEIR VENDY NOMINATION

PORK SCHNITZEL
Adapted from Oleg Voss's recipe

Schnitzel is one of the most traditional Austrian dishes and here Oleg has added Japanese breadcrumbs, making it even crunchier than before. Don't be shy when pounding out your pork filets with a mallet—you want your pork to get as thin as possible.

YIELD: 4 SERVINGS

2 pork loin filets (about 5 ounces each)
2 tablespoons all-purpose flour
¼ teaspoon salt
⅛ teaspoon freshly ground black pepper
1 large egg
2 tablespoons whole milk
¼ cup dry panko (Japanese) breadcrumbs
2 tablespoons canola oil

Using a meat mallet or pounder, flatten the pork loin filets between 2 sheets of plastic wrap.

You will need 3 shallow bowls. In the first, combine the flour, salt, and pepper. In the second, combine the egg and milk, and then put the breadcrumbs in the third.

Coat the pork with the flour, then dip into the milk-egg mixture, and finally into the breadcrumbs, turning to coat.

In a large skillet on high heat, add the oil and add one pork schnitzel, frying each for approximately 2 minutes per side, or until cooked through. Serve immediately.

AUSTRIAN POTATO SALAD
Adapted from Oleg Voss's recipe

WARNING: This is not your mama's potato salad—unless your mama is from Salzburg. While classic American potato salad recipes tend to be chilled and mayonnaise-intensive, Austrian potato salad is served warm in a tangy vinaigrette. This difference makes perfect for summer picnics when refrigeration is not possible.

YIELD: 6 TO 8 SERVINGS

3 pounds Yukon potatoes, sliced in thin rounds
6 tablespoons olive oil
1 tablespoon white wine vinegar
1 tablespoon fresh lemon juice
2 shallots, peeled and finely diced
2 cloves garlic, peeled and minced
6 springs fresh flat parsley, coarsely chopped
salt, to taste
freshly ground black pepper, to taste

Add potatoes to a large pot and cover with water. Boil until tender, about 10 minutes.

In a small bowl whisk together olive oil, white wine vinegar, lemon juice, shallots, and garlic.

In a large bowl or serving dish dress potatoes with vinaigrette and sprinkle with parsley. Season with salt and ground black pepper to taste. It's ready to go once made and still warm, but can be eaten cold. Store in an airtight container in the fridge.

OUTE
BORO
SLIPPY'S

PLAIN
ONIONS $1.75
CHILI $1.85
SAUERKRAUT $1.85
RAW ONIONS & CHILI $1.75
KRAUT & ONIONS $1.90
CHEESE $1.90
CHEESE & CHILI $1.90
CHEESE, CHILI & $1.95
ONIONS $2.00
WALLYDOG (kraut, cheese, chili) $2.10
EVERYTHING $2.10

Cola
Cream
Root Beer
Sarsaperilla
Orange
Black Cherry
Sprite
Iced Tea
Yoo-Hoo

R

UGHS

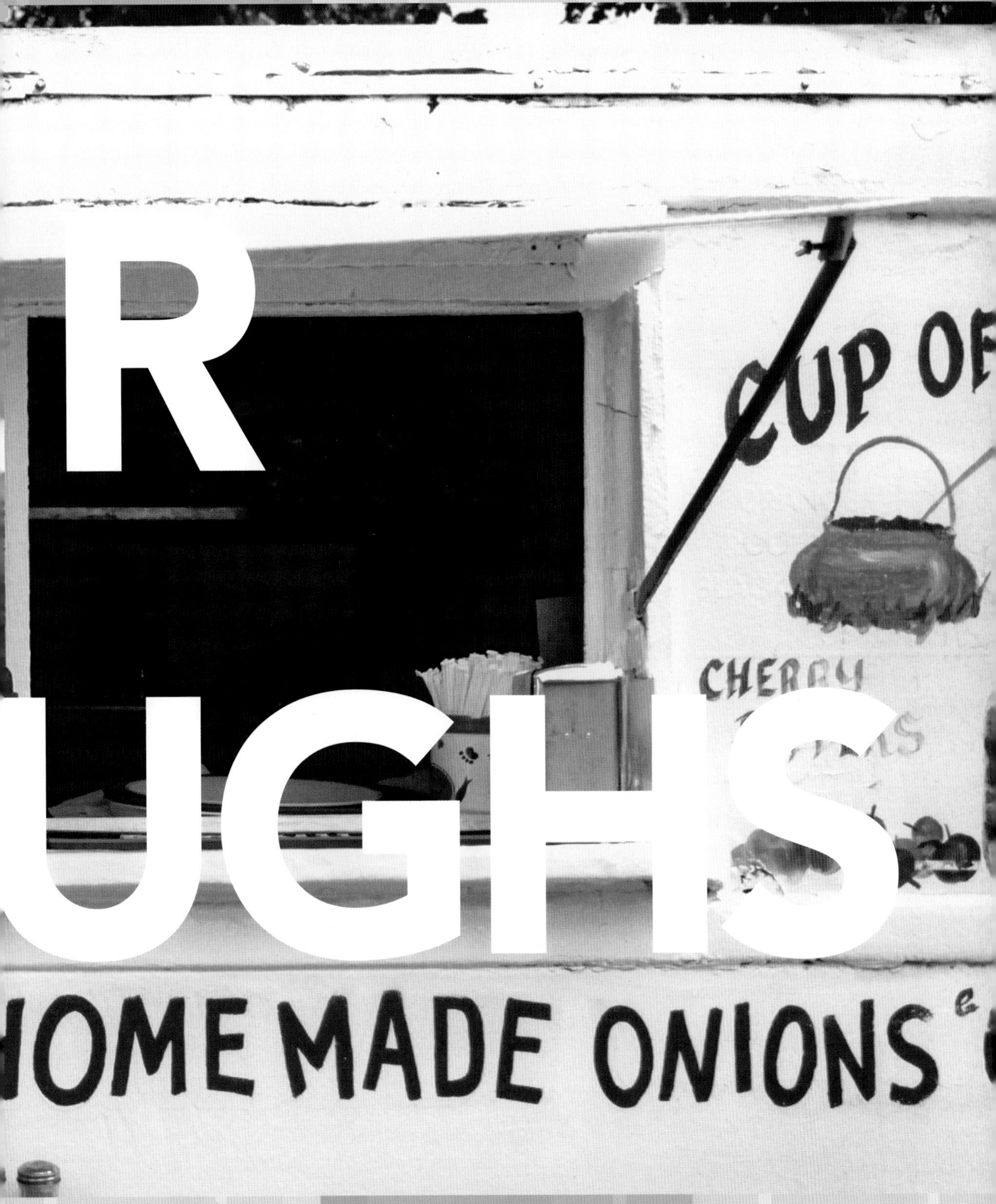

THE CHIPPER TRUCK

At 4:00 a.m., when session bands have played their last set and the bartenders have poured their last pint, the Woodlawn pub crowd spills out onto Katonah Avenue. But there's one more stop before the end of the night—the Chipper Truck. Run by Alice O'Brien Bermejo and her husband Valentino, The Chipper serves up fried fare seven nights a week from just after midnight until 5:00 or 6:00 in the morning. Alice works the window taking orders and chatting with regulars while Valentino mans the grill and fryers with military-like precision.

Like many of her customers in this predominantly Irish pocket of the Bronx, Alice speaks with a lilting brogue and a ready laugh. In Ireland no night on the town is complete without food to cap off the evening's revelry, so when the neighborhood's only twenty-four-hour diner shuttered, Woodlawn keenly felt the void. Inspired by the chip vans Alice remembered from her youth in County Leitrim, they opened the Chipper Truck in 2004. "When we used to go to a nightclub when I was younger, it was like a mile from the closest town. It was really out on its own," Alice explains. "A guy would come on a truck and sell food at two in the morning when the bars would close. You just had to. Food was the end of the night."

The Chipper quickly found a loyal following, a mix of cops and EMS workers on the night shift and young lads and lasses fresh from a night out. "This is what Woodlawn needed. They needed Irish food. Fast food. Good food. And he's great. He's a really good cook," Alice says, gesturing to her husband as he griddles up a couple burgers. Born in Puebla, Mexico, Valentino has worked his whole adult life making Irish food in restaurants and diners around Woodlawn. "I learn the Irish food, and I keep doing, keep doing," says Valentino. "Everyone was looking for me. They say this guy cooks good." Alice and Valentino met at an Irish restaurant where she was waitressing and he ran the kitchen. "When we had our first children, I stopped and he kept going. Then we just decided let's just do something for ourselves 'cause we weren't making it on our own. We had to do something, and this is it."

The menu offers up a dizzying array of late-night comfort foods—cheesesteaks and freshly made quarter-plus-pounders, along with Irish favorites like battered bangers sausages and boxtys, a traditional thick potato pancake native to the north midlands of Ireland. Made from Alice's mother's secret recipe, the boxtys are slightly crispy on the outside and fluffy and light in the middle. If latkes and mashed potatoes had an Irish love child, this would be it. A little bit salty, a little bit greasy but mostly just satisfying, they're ideal for soaking up a few Guinnesses.

"If the men were going out to work, they'd have it in the morning," Alice says. "It's a heavy feed that will keep them going for the day." Not surprisingly, chips are a big seller at the end of the night, and the Chipper Truck offers up a host of topping options. There's curry chips topped with a legitimately fiery tomato-based curry imported from Ireland, garlic cheese chips slathered in homemade garlic-loaded mayo that one regular calles "orgasmic." Alice favors the curry coleslaw chips with Valentino's freshly made Irish-style coleslaw, a chunkier, tangier 'slaw than its American cousin.

> "I just love it. I love the people. I love to see them enjoy the food. That's what it's all about. It's not just serving food. It's quality."
>
> —ALICE O'BRIEN BERMEJO

"No sugar in it," says Valentino, "just salt and vinegar and extra heavy on the dressing."

As the late-night crowd gathers, the jovial hum of regulars chatting mingles with the rhythmic sizzle and spatter of the hot oil. Valentino is preparing the taco chips, another import that Alice remembers from her teen years. "We make the taco meat like the Mexican tacos, but mix it with the Irish French fries," Valentino explains. Though the item was a bit slow to catch on, it's become one of their most popular sellers. In a single night, they can go through forty pounds of meat for taco chips alone. "Now all the American kids, they love it. They come here and they're like, 'taco chips! taco chips!' At four o'clock in the morning, you've got like ten orders of taco chips."

While virtually undiscovered outside the Bronx, the Chipper Truck is regarded as a neighborhood treasure. "Everybody knows us. It's not like we come to work here and then we live off someplace else. They see me walking down the street with the kids. They see me and Valentino. If we go out for a night we'll go here. We're part of the neighborhood, as well." The enthusiasm of their customers is unbridled. "This is my favorite spot," one cop confides as he waits for his bacon cheeseburger. "I love The Chipper. When I party around here, I come here all the time. I love it. It's good stuff. It sobers you up like that," he says with the snap of his fingers.

Orders are placed and filled in rapid succession. Valentino's a master at shorthand, but he longs to be back in the kitchen in the role of head chef. The Bermejos hope to one day open a restaurant to let Valentino's cooking shine. "But we'll never give up this," says Alice. "This is where it started."

BEER-BATTERED COD

Adapted from Alice O'Brien Bermejo's recipes.

Beer-battered cod is pub grub, pure and simple. While lager turns out an especially nice, light batter, you can use your own favorite beer to customize the flavor.

YIELD: SERVES 8

2 pounds cod filets

2 cups self-rising flour

½ teaspoon baking soda

½ teaspoon salt

½ teaspoon white pepper

1 large egg, lightly beaten with a fork

1 (12-ounce) bottle of beer (lager, preferred)

2 quarts canola oil for frying

Cut the cod filets into 2-inch-long pieces. In a large bowl mix flour, baking soda, salt, and white pepper. Whisk in egg. Slowly add the beer while whisking, stirring until just combined. Batter should be fairly smooth.

Heat 3 inches of oil in a large Dutch oven or deep fryer to 350°F.

Using heat-resistant tongs, dip fish pieces into the batter. Let any excess batter drip off, then carefully place pieces into the hot oil. Deep fry until fish is a deep golden brown then turn, using either the tongs or a shallow heat-resistant strainer, and fry until golden on the other side, about 1 to 2 minutes per side. Remove from oil with the tongs or strainer, and allow excess oil to drip off. Transfer to a paper towel or brown paper–lined rack to drain. Serve with French fries or chips.

PAN BOXTY

Preparing boxty batter is easy, but cooking the pancakes is a time-consuming process. Slow and low is the way to go with boxty. This recipe is all about having the patience to let the pancakes cook.

YIELD: MAKES 5 (8-INCH) BOXTYS

2 cups all-purpose flour

2 teaspoons salt

2½ cups whole milk

2 large eggs, lightly beaten with a fork

2½ cups Russet potatoes, peeled and grated (about 3 large potatoes)

2½ tablespoons unsalted butter, for cooking

Move oven rack to center position and heat the oven to 200°F. Place two large baking sheets in the oven.

In a large bowl, whisk together flour and salt. Whisk in milk and eggs until fully incorporated and batter is smooth. Stir in potato to distribute.

Add ½ tablespoon of butter in a 10-inch skillet or frying pan, and heat over medium. Be very careful not to let the heat get too high because the butter will burn, and that will make the boxty burn. Once butter is melted and bubbly add 1 cup batter, pouring to spread evenly over the pan. Reduce heat to medium-low and cook slowly until the top is nearly dry and the bottom is golden brown, about 7 to 10 minutes. Turn with a spatula and cook the other side to the same degree of doneness. Transfer boxty to oven to keep warm. Repeat until all the batter is used.

When Guadalupe Galicia came to the United States from Puebla, Mexico, in 1996, it was with tears in her eyes. She had come with her husband to find work and had left her sons, ages 2 and 3 behind. "I cried all the way. . . . I left my two children, what I love most. . . . I was supposed to have gone out to bring popsicles, and I hadn't returned." Guadalupe didn't want to leave Mexico, but she had to. There were no opportunities there for her family. When she arrived in New York, she took a job as a nanny caring for a couple's children six days a week, often for twelve hours a day, for only $400 a month. It was her sister who came up with the idea to sell the tamales. She said, "We would make one hundred. Fifty for her and fifty for me." Guadalupe had never made tamales before back in Mexico. Her family always bought them at the store. "I arrived when I was eighteen years old. I started cooking here. The need made me do it."

Guadalupe's sister didn't last long selling the tamales. "We sold them for one month, but she didn't like it," Guadalupe says. It was too much work to wake up at 4:00 a.m. . . . I had my children brought over, and I started selling my tamales." Her husband, the father of her sons and oldest daughter, Julie, "would drink and wasn't responsible at all." When he left the family, it was up to Guadalupe to provide for her children.

As a single mother of now five children, Guadalupe has faced challenge after challenge but kept her family together and provided for them with her hard work and ingenuity. "The police bother me a lot since I started in '99. Bother me a lot, two or three tickets a week. Others wondered why I wasn't taken away, and it was because I paid the tickets. I would go to the court. If I had the courage to go out and sell, then I could have the courage to go to the court."

Guadalupe sells both corn husk wrapped tamales and Oaxacan-style tamales which come wrapped in plantain leaves. Her flavors include: *rajas con queso* (chiles and cheese), green tamales with pork, red tamales with pork, *rajas con pollo* (chiles with chicken), sweet pineapple, and mole. She uses the same recipes that she created when she started the business. On Saturdays and Sundays from 7:00 a.m. until around 1 p.m., you can find her selling from a shopping cart in Bushwick at the corner of Knickerbocker and DeKalb. These days her oldest son, Marcos, is selling, too. "During the week my son is selling Monday, Tuesday. We are selling four days." Marcos graduated from high school in Bushwick and initially found work as a waiter, but he was wasn't making much, maybe $20 plus tips for 12 hours of work. Working for his mom made much more sense.

On the weekends, Guadalupe sells as many as 100 tamales a day. Tamales go for just $1.25 each. "I've only raised [the price] a quarter in the past two years," she says. "Those who buy $20 or more, I add *arroz con leche* free or a tamale." In many parts of Latin American *arroz con leche* is a rice pudding, but where Guadalupe is from in Mexico it's a hot sweetened beverage made with rice and milk that's typically served with tamales at breakfast. "There are many people who make the tamales but they don't make them well . . . sometimes I have seven

or eight persons waiting for my tamales, and they wait until they get them. They like my tamales."

How good are Guadalupe's tamales? So good that she's had more than one person offer to buy the recipe from her, saying, "'I'll give you $1,000 just for one day that you teach my wife,' but I say no that is my recipe not even if you give me $5,000. I will only give it to my children if one day they want to continue with the business." Guadalupe's sons don't even know the recipe, only her daughter, Julie, does, and Julie has plans. "My daughter now wants to open a restaurant because it's very cold on the street. It rains. She doesn't want to see me there,

but the rent with the food and bills—it's two thousand monthly, and I have to make them. Otherwise we will be thrown out. But I told her it's the way it has to be.'"

Guadalupe was named a Vendys finalist in 2011. In 2012, she received the Boot Strap Entrepreneur Award from Business Center for New Americans and the NYC Mayor's Office of Immigrant Affairs. But perhaps the highest praise comes from Guadalupe's youngest daughter, who tells her, "*I want to be like you—you make tamales, you have your children, you take care of them. I want to be like you.* So, first I say: *Be good at school and you'll be like me.*"

"If you are not in a good mood, the tamales won't cook."

—GUADALUPE GALICIA

BEAN AND CHEESE TAMALES

Adapted from Guadalupe Galicia's recipe

You can make these tamales a vegetarian affair by substituting vegetable shortening for lard. Guadalupe always uses Maseca® brand *masa harina*, or corn flour, which can be found in the international aisle in many supermarkets or at Latino grocery stores. Making tamales isn't hard, but it is a very time-consuming process and goes much more quickly with help. Get your friends together and make a party of it. The quality and size of corn husks can very greatly, so it's best to prep two packages of corn husks, just in case.

....

YIELD: 24 TAMALES

2 (3-ounce) packages of dried corn husks (about 50 to 60 corn husks)

3 tablespoons vegetable oil

½ cup fresh cilantro, finely chopped

4 cloves garlic, peeled and finely chopped

1 (29-ounce) can black beans, undrained

2 tablespoons salt

12 ounces whole milk mozzarella cheese

2 pounds *masa harina* (corn flour)

8 ounces lard or vegetable shortening, cut into ½ tablespoon–sized pieces

Add the dried corn husks to a large pot and fill with enough water to cover. Add a heavy plate to submerge the husks and soak for up to 2 hours to soften the husks.

In a medium saucepan, combine the oil, cilantro, and garlic, and sauté over medium heat until garlic is translucent and oil is fragrant, about 5 minutes. Add the black beans and ½ teaspoon salt. Cook over medium heat, stirring occasionally, until liquid has reduced by half, about 20 minutes. Remove from heat and transfer to a bowl to cool.

Cut cheese into 24 long thin, strips, approximately the width of a finger.

Mix the *masa harina* with the remaining salt. Use your hands to add the lard (or shortening, if you prefer), slowly adding about 3 to 4 cups of warm water mixing as you go to form a soft and only slightly sticky dough. The amount of water you'll need can vary based on the humidity, you don't want the dough to be too sticky or so dry that it's hard or crumbly. Turn dough out onto a a clean and flat surface and knead until the dough is well mixed and the lard or shortening are fully incorporated. Dough should be soft, slightly moist, but it shouldn't stick to your fingers.

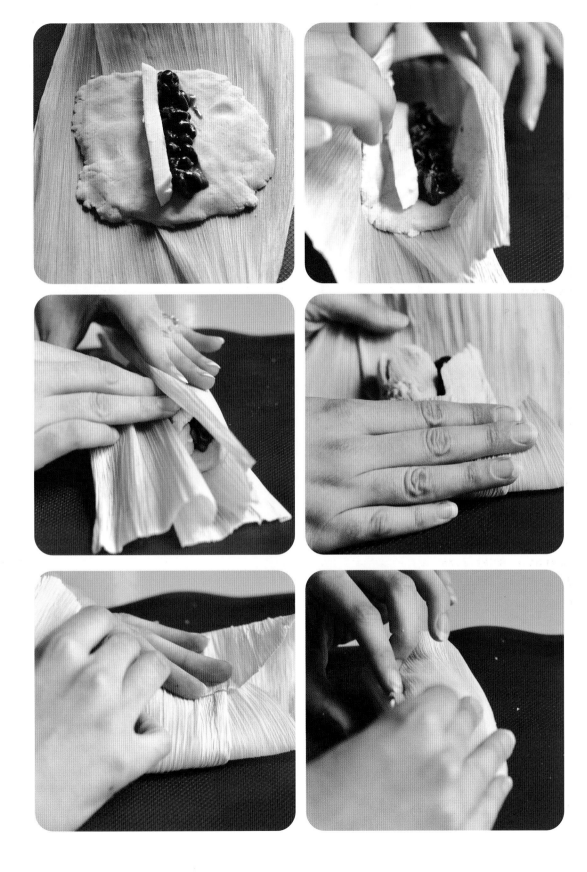

MAKING THE TAMALES:

Once the corn husks are softened, remove from water and pat dry with a towel. Examine your corn husks, separating the smaller or broken husks from the rest. Rip 48 long, thin, pieces, the small and broken husks set aside. These will be used as ties to seal your tamales and to line your steamer, or if you prefer you can use kitchen string or twine to close.

Divide the dough into 24 balls, slightly smaller than a tennis ball. On a flat surface lay out a large tamale husk. If your tamale husks are not wide enough to accommodate 4 inches of dough, double them up by laying one husk out narrow end facing down then lay another husk on top overlapping slightly with the narrow end facing up.

Take a ball of dough, center it on the corn husk and flatten it into a 4-inch square that's approximately ¼-inch thick. Spread a tablespoon of black beans lengthwise down the middle of the dough strip and place the cheese next to the black beans. Use the edges of the corn husk to draw the sides together, folding the dough and closing the tamale. If your tamale dough is at all brittle or delicate you can use the structure of the corn husk to lightly press the tamale dough and smooth it out. Fold the short edges of the corn husk inward, then fold the long edges, so that the husk forms a small packet around the dough, like an envelope. Tie the long pieces of husk (or string) around the husk to seal the tamale. Repeat with the rest of the dough and husks.

COOKING THE TAMALES:

In a large steaming pot, add water to just below the depth of the steamer. Line the steaming rack with leftover corn husks to protect the tamales from direct contact with the steam. Pack the corn husk packets tightly together on a steam rack above the water. Cover the pot with a lid and place over medium-high heat. Steam tamales for about 1 hour and 15 minutes to 1 hour and 30 minutes. When tamales are steamed completely the corn husk will release easily from the tamales. Serve immediately with *Jitomate* Salsa (page 213).

NOTE: Guadalupe likes to add a small piece of avocado peel in between the dough and the corn husk to give the tamales more flavor. Keep in mind that when the tamales are served, both the corn husks and the avocado peel (if used) should be removed *before* eating.

JITOMATE SALSA (MEXICAN COOKED TOMATO SAUCE)
Adapted from Guadalupe Galicia's recipe

This cooked tomato sauce gives pleasant brightness to the tamales but also works well in place of any traditional tomato sauce recipe with meat or pasta.

....

YIELD: ABOUT 2 CUPS

8 large red tomatoes

3 cloves garlic, peeled

½ of a medium-sized white onion

1 teaspoon salt

1 teaspoon cumin

2 tablespoons vegetable oil

In a food processor or blender add tomatoes, garlic, onion, and cumin and salt, then blend together. In a medium saucepan, heat vegetable oil over medium heat until hot but not smoking about 1 to 2 minutes. Add tomato mixture, reduce heat to low, and simmer uncovered, stirring occasionally for 40 minutes. Store covered in refrigerator for up to 2 days.

On Saturdays and Sundays from April to late October the ball fields of Red Hook Park come alive with soccer players, their fans, and the legendary pan-Latin Red Hook Food Vendors. For decades the vendors operated on the edges of the park selling their home-cooked wares—fire-grilled corn dusted with salty *cotija* cheese, chile and lime-doused mango slices, enormous freeform tortillas known as *huaraches*, and ceviche among other Mexican, Guatemalan, Salvadoran, Colombian, Dominican and Ecuadorian specialties. In an age of convenience cooking, the Red Hook vendors prepare traditional recipes from scratch, no shortcuts. Today the Red Hook Food Vendors Association boasts three Vendy Award winners among its members. For ethnic food lovers, the sheer con-centration of delicious diversity is unparalleled.

Originally settled by the Dutch in the 1600s, Red Hook was a bustling industrial neighborhood and shipping center until the 1960s, when the dock jobs dried up and unem-ployment and crime rose. By the late '80s *LIFE* magazine called the neighborhood "the crack capital of America." It was in this depressed environment that the ball fields came to be. Red Hook happened to be the home of one of only a few fields in New York large enough to accommodate the semi-professional soccer leagues of the recent Central and South American immigrants. "This was the center of the soccer playing scene in Brooklyn," says César Fuentes, Executive Director of the Red Hook Food Vendors Association. The vending

scene began in 1974, a spontaneous outgrowth of the *Liga Guatemala*, the most competitive and popular of the four soccer *ligas* that played in Red Hook. Soccer drew crowds, and the earliest of the Red Hook vendors—some of them spectators themselves—recognized an opportunity. Equipped only with a table, a grill, ingredients and perhaps a tarp for shade, these original vendors offered created flourishing family businesses. Success attracted competitors. Before long, the ball fields had grown into an open-air food market similar to those one might find in Central and South America. The food was fresh and inexpensive and captured flavors of the homelands the vendors and their customers had left behind. The Red Hook vendors thrived. And by the late '90s the ball fields were discovered by foodies who ventured out to the remote neighborhood specifically for the cheap, authentic eats.

For over three decades the ball fields enjoyed minimal interference from city regulators. Fierce competition ensured quality control; vendors serving excellent food were rewarded with long lines, subpar vendors found themselves replaced by those who could do better. But when gentrification ultimately came to Red Hook, the vendors faced the threat of extinction. The upscale supermarket, Fairway, moved into the neighborhood as did furniture superstore IKEA. As the neighborhood grew tonier, the humble market didn't fit some people's vision for a revitalized Red Hook. After decades of being effectively unregulated by the city, in 2007, changes in the permitting requirements for the park forced the vendors to have to bid to retain the permits they had held for years and increased enforcement by the Department of Health

caused the vendors to invest in mandated costly mobile units—carts and trucks. Led by César, a grassroots movement to "Save the Soccer Taco" rallied. The vendors began their 2008 season with a long-term permit, but the feel was different. Gone were the weathered tarps and tables. Gone, too, were some of the vendors unable or unwilling to make the changes and afford the significant investment to upgrade to a truck or cart. Once again the vendors are gearing up for a fight to remain at the ball fields. Their six-year vending permit is up for renewal in 2013 and nothing is guaranteed. As César puts it "The big question is, 'are we going to be able to be around for the next six years?'"

Yolanda Ceron is the last of the original Red Hook vendors. A seamstress by trade from Cali, Colombia, her foray into selling food came as a happy accident. "She came here once to watch a soccer game, and she brought some food," her daughter, Yezenia Ceron, explains. "Somebody asked her if she was selling food because nobody was selling food and she said, 'OK, yes.' That's how she started."

At the time, Yolanda worked in a sewing factory in Brooklyn. "She saw that what she was making in the factory she made here in one day. And she had to pay a babysitter because of me and my brother, so she was wasting more of her paycheck on daycare instead of being with her kids." After starting her own business at the ball fields, Yolanda was able to spend the week with her children while still making money over the weekend. In the beginning, it was mainly Yolanda and her husband working the business. Says Yezenia, "My grandma came

for a couple of years when I was younger. My grandma would be on one side, and my mother would be on the other side." Yezenia has been working at the ball fields with her mom for about six years, along with her sister and her dad. Though she'd help her mother with the prep around the house as a kid, "when I was young I would go to the park or the beach, anywhere else but here."

The Cerons specialize in traditional Colombian dishes—both white-corn and sweet yellow-corn *arepas*, *chicharrón* (deep-fried pork belly), golden fried yucca, and chorizo. With their crispy, cornmeal exteriors and melt-in-your-mouth-tender filling of beef, potato, and onion, Yolanda's Cali-style empanadas rise above the ordinary into the realm of the ethereal. "We usually only have beef, but now we have chicken, and we have cheese also, so we're going to see how that works out," says Yezenia. The *bandeja paisa,* or Colombian platter—a mixed plate that includes rice, beans, sausage, fried egg, fried

"She says on the day she dies she wants her ashes thrown around here. She loves the park." —YEZENIA CERON

pork, steak, and an *arepa*—is especially popular, as are their *papas rellenas*, deep-fried, braised beef–filled potatoes.

For about ten years Yolanda left the ball fields to concentrate on Maison Valluno, a restaurant that she opened in Brooklyn on Fort Hamilton and 37th Street. But she couldn't stay away forever. Says Yezenia, "She used to miss the park because it was only the weekend—meanwhile the restaurant was every day." When Yolanda had the restaurant, she was isolated most of the time in the kitchen, a far cry from the constant interaction with her customers that she had at the ball fields. "It's a hassle, but she likes it. That's why we're here. If it wasn't for that, we wouldn't be here."

The demographics have changed as different Latino groups have come and gone from the neighborhood. These days far fewer Colombians come to the ball fields. Years ago there used to be a Colombian soccer team. Now the teams are primarily Mexican and Guatemalan, and many of the Colombians have decamped from Brooklyn to Queens and New Jersey. "Years ago it used to be Friday, Saturday, Sunday, and it was all Spanish people. Now it's totally different." While some vendors have resisted the changes, Yezenia appreciates not having to lug the grills around and deal with all of the setup and cleanup from the old days. "To me, it's cleaner on the trucks. We don't have to pick up and load . . . over here it's more clean, more organized. You just close the door and leave."

PORK EMPANADAS

Inspired by Yolanda Ceron.

Colombian empanadas are typically filled with *guiso*, a stewed pork or beef mixed with tender diced potatoes and spices. Leftover *guiso* is wonderful heated up on its own or served over rice. To make the empanada dough you need a special pre-cooked yellow corn flour known as *masa instantánea* that can usually be found at the grocery store among the Latino specialty items. P.A.N.® brand is imported from Latin America and works especially well.

YIELD: MAKES 16 EMPANADAS

FOR THE FILLING:

2 tablespoons extra-virgin olive oil

½ medium white onion, finely minced

3 cloves garlic, peeled and minced

½ teaspoon dried oregano

½ teaspoon dried thyme

½ teaspoon cumin

½ teaspoon Kosher salt

½ pound boneless pork country ribs, cut into 1 inch strips

3 medium white potatoes, diced

2 cups chicken stock

Add oil, onions, garlic, spices and salt to a large frying pan or cast iron skillet, sauté over medium-high heat, stirring occasionally until oil is fragrant and onions and garlic are beginning to turn translucent, about 3 minutes. Add pork and potatoes, stirring occasionally until pork is browned, about 5 minutes. Add chicken stock and reduce heat to medium low, stirring occasionally and cook until liquid has reduced almost completely, about 40 minutes. Potatoes should be very tender. Transfer mixture to a large bowl and remove pork pieces. Coarsely chop pork and stir to reincorporate with potato filling. Cover and refrigerate while you prepare dough.

FOR THE DOUGH:

2 cups yellow *masa instantánea*

1 teaspoon salt

3 tablespoons vegetable oil

2 cups water or chicken stock

....

In a large bowl, mix *masa* with salt until thoroughly combined. Add in vegetable oil and 2 cups water or chicken stock to form a dough that's soft, but not too sticky. Let dough rest for 20 to 30 minutes–then form into 16 golf ball sized balls.

Lay out a sheet of plastic wrap and place dough ball on top. Gently flatten the dough into a circle about 4 inches in diameter and approximately ¼ of an inch thick. Add a tablespoon of cooled filling and use the plastic wrap to draw the left side of the empanada over the right side to form a half circle shape. Press lightly against the plastic wrap to completely seal the empanada around the edges, make sure there are no holes or torn spots on your empanada so it fries properly. Set aside on a large plate and repeat with the remaining dough balls.

Heat 3 inches of oil in a large Dutch oven or deep fryer to 350°F. Using heat-resistant tongs, add the empanadas one at a time, cooking no more than three at once. Fry until exterior is crunchy and golden brown, about 3 to 5 minutes. Using tongs or a heat-resistant strainer, remove empanadas from oil and transfer to a paper towel lined plate. Let cool for a couple minutes and then serve with Ají (page 220).

AJÍ (COLOMBIAN SALSA)

This spicy Colombian salsa is typically served with empanadas, but you may want to make extra to have on hand for grilled meats, hamburgers, and sandwiches. The traditional way to eat Colombian empanadas is to bite off the tip of the empanada and then spoon some ají over the open end. Don't be ashamed to add a bit more ají as you work your way through the empanadas, you won't be the only one.

YIELD: ABOUT A CUP

4 scallions, whites and greens coarsely chopped

½ cup cilantro, coarsely chopped

½ medium white onion, coarsely chopped

¼ cup white vinegar

¼ cup lime juice (about 2 limes)

¼ cup extra-virgin olive oil

1 jalapeño, seeded and coarsely chopped

½ teaspoon salt

Add all ingredients to the bowl of a food processor or blender. Process on high for about a minute or until smooth. Serve with Pork Empanadas (page 218). Store covered in the refrigerator for up to 2 days.

ed Hook Ball Fields veteran vendor, Esperanza Ochoa, emmigrated from Guatemala in 1983. Like many of her fellow food truck vendors, she first came to the Red Hook Ball Fields as a customer when a friend and fellow Guatemalan suggested that it would be a good place for her to sell food. "When I came, there were maybe two other people selling—way out there, far off," says Esperanza. During the week, Esperanza worked as a seamstress, and on the weekends she would come to the soccer fields to vend. In those days there was a large contingent of Guatemalans who would come to the fields to watch the soccer games and socialize, and Esperanza cooked all the specialties they missed from home: pork and chicken tamales, *chiles rellenos* (battered and fried peppers stuffed with meat and cheese), *carne adobada* (adobo-marinated meat), sweet fried plantains, and a bright and tomato-packed *ceviche* with shrimp and mixed fish. Esperanza recalled the early days of the ball fields and the rustic outdoor-*mercado*-feel of the place: "I would bring the food in pots and put them on the bench and sell from there. Then I started to make a wood fire and cooked in front of the people,

until one day the health department arrived and said things had to change—it was very pretty back then, it is still pretty."

Esperanza's husband, Juan, and her sons help her out, but primarily she does all of the prep and cooking. It's hard and time-consuming work. The food is prepared fresh with traditional methods—no modern shortcuts, and that was, and is, part of the delight of the ball fields. Just one of Esperanza's

"The people were Guatemalan, so I cooked what we eat, in the style of our country—tamales de puerco y de pollo, chiles rellenos, carne adobada, plátanos fritos." —ESPERANZA OCHOA

tamales—which come wrapped in green Maxan leaves instead of corn husks—can be a substantial meal on its own. Hearty and filling, they're homey and comforting, like a hug from your Guatemalan grandmother.

Everything changed in 2007 when the department of health got involved. "The health department said we must sell from a truck. They said it was for health reasons, but nobody was sick from my food. It was freshly cooked, and the people would eat it—from the fire to the client. It would be different if I brought the food already cooked or if it had been frozen for days, but everything was fresh," she says. When the health department made their demands, it was hard. Vendors who had sold for years without incident retired. "Many people complained. We jumped, we screamed, but it was impossible," she laments. Faced with the prospect of closing their business or complying with the city regulations, the Ochoas invested in a small truck,

with a tight yet efficient kitchen. And while Esperanza's food is as good as ever, these days with the city involved, things are different. "You pay more, and the sales are not as good. Before the people could watch us cook and they say that was part of the fun—people miss that." When asked about the future of the vendors and her predictions for five years down the line, Esperanza is direct: "Most won't be here because the expenses are too much. Just for parking it is $400 a month—the truck has to park in the commissary." All the expenses—from the permits to the parking—add up. "I have to clear $1800 for the eight days of work in the month. If we could get more permission [to sell other days] we could do it. . . . I think if we had two or three days out more we could make it." Still Esperanza tries to remain optimistic. "I hope it gets better because it doesn't make sense to go into debt to lose money and not make a living . . . You have to have faith because God doesn't abandon us."

SHRIMP CEVICHE

Adapted from Esperanza Ochoa's recipe

One of the best deals at the Red Hook Ball Fields is without a doubt the *ceviche*, a lime juice–cured seafood that comes in pint-sized-containers for just over $10. Perfect as an appetizer for a summer meal, this dish is a guaranteed crowd pleaser.

....

YIELD: SERVES 4

1 pound large or medium raw shrimp, peeled and deveined

2 ½ cups fresh lime juice (about 20 limes)

½ medium white onion, julienned

½ teaspoon salt

¼ cup fresh cilantro, minced

2 cups fresh tomatoes, diced

hot sauce, to taste, for serving

Rinse shrimp and place in a large nonreactive bowl. Add 2 cups lime juice and stir to ensure shrimp are covered with juice. In a medium non-reactive bowl add onion and salt and marinate with remaining lime juice. Cover and refrigerate both bowls for three hours.

Just before serving, add onions, cilantro, tomatoes, and hot sauce, if desired, to shrimp. Serve cold.

At the corner of Bay Street just off Clinton Street, one of the first sights to welcome visitors to the Red Hook Ball Fields is the Vaquero Fruit Truck. Run by Everardo Vaquero, his wife Maria, and their children, the truck opens early on the weekend, providing breakfast and drinks for soccer players. "They come to drink coffee, eat breakfast—they come hungry," says Everardo's daughter, Kenia. The Vaquero's shiny silver truck is plastered with a large sign showing off their extensive line of iced drinks and proclaiming "Refrescate!" It's both a command and a promise. Whether you opt for the watermelon *agua fresca*, *agua de Jamaica*, a vivid red hibiscus flower-based iced tea or a creamy *horchata*, a sweet rice milk drink—you'll soon find yourself totally refreshed.

Everardo emmigrated from Puebla, Mexico, in 1963 and initially found work here as a maintenance mechanic. He worked for twenty-four years until the company closed. "[My parents] used to come here to watch the soccer games," says Kenia. They started thinking maybe there was something they could sell, too. "I had to find a way. If you don't work, you don't eat," says Everardo. Working at the ball fields is a family affair. Kitty-corner from the Vaqueros truck is the Country Boys Truck, which is run by Everardo's sister, Yolanda Martinez, and her husband, Fernando. While the Country Boys concentrate on food—tacos, *huaraches*, quesadillas—the Vaqueros sell complementary products: fruits, drinks, and snacks like *elotes*—grilled corn on the cob that's brushed with mayonnaise, spritzed with lime, then dusted with cayenne and sharp and salty *cotija* cheese.

In many Spanish-speaking countries, *arroz con leche* often refers to rice pudding, but in parts of Mexico it can also refer to a hot rice-and-milk drink that is typically enjoyed at breakfast with tamales. Alas, because of permit regulations, the Vaqueros can't sell the two together: "The health department are very strict with what we sell, so we can't sell tamales," says Kenia. Even without the tamale accompaniment, their *arroz con leche* is a nice morning alternative to coffee. If you're feeling too hot for a warm beverage, their *agua frescas* are always popular. The watermelon drink, which consists just of liquefied watermelon with ice (and a squirt of lime, if desired), is like slurping the essence of summer through a straw. With mostly light and summery offerings, the Vaqueros do their strongest business during the warm months. When the Sol Goldman public pool is open across the street, swimmers hit the ball fields for food after working up an appetite, flooding the vendors with customers.

While some lament the loss of the old days and the way the ball fields used to be, the Vaqueros are happy with the physical transformations they've witnessed in Red Hook over the past twenty-five years.

"Now it's cleaner, more peaceful . . . Now it's pretty,"

—EVERARDO VAQUERO

"When we started, there was a lot of violence. It was ugly. It was a lot of garbage, prostitution, drugs," says Kenia. Everardo doesn't mind the transition to the truck. "For us it's easier, but for the people, they liked it better when it was outside," he says. Everardo can peel, cut, and prepare hundreds of pounds of fruit with great ease and speed. Doing the majority of the prep work for the day only takes him one to two hours. "He's fast. He's so accustomed to it," says Kenia. During the off-season Everardo and his wife travel back to Mexico and spend five months there for some well-deserved R & R. "He gets to relax at home," saya Kenia.

E | **GF** | **V**

HORCHATA (SWEET RICE MILK)

Adapted from Everardo Vaquero's recipe

While there are many different variations of *horchata*, the version that the Vaqueros sell is the *tres leches* of *horchatas*. Like the Mexican cake of the same name, their recipe calls for three types of milk: evaporated milk, whole milk, and sweetened condensed milk. The result is a frothy, creamy, lightly sweetened drink that makes for a great way to beat the heat.

....

YIELD: SERVES 6

1 cup long-grain rice, uncooked

1 cinnamon stick

4 cups boiling water

8 ounces evaporated milk

2 cups whole milk

8 tablespoons sweetened condensed milk

1 teaspoon vanilla extract

½ teaspoon ground cinnamon

In a medium bowl add the rice and the cinnamon stick. Pour the boiling water over the rice. Cover and refrigerate for 4 hours or up to overnight.

Remove the cinnamon stick from the rice water. Add the rice water and evaporated milk to a blender. Pulse mixture for 1 to 2 minutes to grind the rice—rice should be very finely ground. Strain mixture over a large pitcher and discard and any remaining rice. Stir in the whole milk, sweetened condensed milk, vanilla extract, and cinnamon. Serve over ice. Refrigerate leftovers in an airtight container for up to 1 day.

ELOTES ASADOS (GRILLED CORN)

Adapted from Everardo Vaquero's recipe

One of the most popular items at the Vaqueros' truck is the *elotes asados*, grilled corn that's dressed with lime juice and mayonnaise (or butter), then dusted in sharp and salty *cotija* cheese crumbles.

....

YIELD: SERVES 4

4 ears of corn with husks

1 lime, cut into 4 wedges

2 tablespoons mayonnaise or butter

¼ cup *cotija* cheese, crumbled

cayenne pepper, to taste

Preheat the oven to 350°F and move oven rack to the center position. Place corn, still in the husks, on the oven rack. Cook for 25 minutes. Remove corn from oven and let rest for 3 to 5 minutes, until they are cool enough to handle. Peel back and remove husks, and transfer corn to a broiler pan. Broil for 3 to 5 minutes per side, until corn is nicely browned and some kernels have blackened. Remove from broiler, let cool slightly, rub with a lime wedge, then brush each cob with mayonnaise or butter. Sprinkle with cheese and dust with cayenne, if desired. Serve immediately.

> **TIP:** To make *elotes* on the grill: remove corn from husk and place directly on the heated grill. Cook, turning occasionally until corn is tender and slightly charred, about 5 to 7 minutes.

> **TIP:** At the Red Hook Ball Fields the Vaqueros serve their *elotes* on 8-inch wooden skewers, which make them a little easier (and a little more fun!) to eat. If you want to serve your *elotes* on wooden skewers, be sure to soak the skewers in water for 30 minutes prior to placing corn on the skewers—right before you put them in the broiler.

Anyone who's ever been to the Red Hook Ball Fields can tell you that the Country Boys' line is always among the longest. No matter the hour, no matter the weather, if you want food from the Country Boys, you're going to have to wait. As the winners of the 2009 Vendy Award, they are known citywide and internationally for their *huaraches*, large handmade, oblong corn tortillas filled with refried beans and topped with your choice of meat or vegetable and chopped lettuce, *cotija* cheese, sour cream, guacamole, and pico de gallo. But Fernando and Yolanda Martinez weren't always master cooks. In fact they learned on the job.

Fernando first came to the park as a player. "A friend invited me to come to the park to play. I was young and liked soccer. I came and played and noticed there were people selling." Fernando quit playing to dedicate himself to building the business. They didn't have much in the way of startup funds, just enough to buy a few tables: one for the grill, one for their vegetables, and one for their customers.

Watching Yolanda prepare the handmade tortillas is strangely calming. No matter the line, she's as unflappable as a Zen master. But she didn't start out that way. Says Fernando, "It was very difficult for her to learn. She was practicing for about a month and finally. She has no problem now." In the early days of their business, they would travel to Mexico at the end of every year to pick up advice for how to improve their food and technique. On a busy weekend they serve as many as a thousand huaraches. "I never imagined that. When we started we were happy with 100 to 150. Two hundred were too many."

Prior to starting their business at the ball fields, Fernando and his wife worked in clothing factories in the city. "It was always our idea to have our own little business. We even bought sewing machines, and we started sewing at home. . . . We would work from Monday to Friday in sewing, and Saturday and Sunday we would come to the park to sell." The Martinezes are no longer taking sewing home. "Now we dedicate ourselves completely to this. Thank God we are doing well. For the past five years business has increased a lot."

Between the shopping, cleaning, and cooking, their prep work takes all week. Keeping the business running is a family affair. Yolanda and Fernando are

"We started from the bottom with only one little table and one grill, my wife and I, alone. We sold very little. $300 to $400, which was a lot for us, but little by little about four years into it, the business started to take off." —FERNANDO MARTINEZ

joined by their three sons, and Fernando adds, "almost the majority of my brothers are here." With so many Martinez men involved in the business, you might think that they are the namesake "Country Boys," but actually it's the name that came with their truck. When the city stipulated that the vendors needed to be in trucks or carts to continue vending, all of the vendors rushed to find their vehicles. Fernando found a truck that was outfitted with everything, including a name. "When I bought the truck, I asked the owner if he was continuing with this work, and he said he was not continuing, he was going to retire." The owner told Fernando, "'I sell you the truck and that's the end for me.'" Fernando liked the name, so he got the former owner's permission to continue using it.

Over the years, the menu at the truck has changed very little. The most notable addition is the "quezahuarache," a hybrid of a *huarache* and a quesadilla (basically a huarache with melted moz-zarella in addition to crumbly *cotija* cheese). Huaraches at the ball fields do differ from those served in Mexico: "We have added a lot of things—the lettuce, the pico de gallo, and the gua-camole—that people here like a lot." These additions came as they saw their clientele begin to change. These days there's less of a soccer community than in years past. "They come to play and leave. Sometimes they bring their own lunch. Well, I understand with the economy it's not easy." In years past, most of their clients were Mexican and Central American, but "now 80 percent are white—Hispanics, less . . . We know that the non-Hispanics are very conscious of healthy food—they like vegetables especially, very little meat—that's why we started using more vegetables, lettuce, pico de gallo, guacamole." In addition to the traditional meat toppings of spicy chorizo, *cecina* (salted dried beef), *chicharrón* (crispy pork skin), and chicken, they also have lighter vegetarian toppings like zucchini, mushrooms, and spinach.

The notoriety from their Vendy win has helped them secure ever-growing legions of fans. During the summer months, there's "always a line of ten to fifteen persons. And the boys can't get a rest—that [award] has been very helpful." Despite the long hours and nonstop work, Fernando still enjoys the ball fields, especially "the fellowship with those who work with me and those who come to buy." He's been bowled over by the support of local politicians: "They came when we were having the problems with the city—when they wanted to throw us out— many people to support us, many political leaders— Schumer, Nydia Velázquez, Sara Gonzalez, so that has been helpful." 2013 marks the last year of the Red Hook Vendors permit for the parks, and there is uncertainty as to what the future holds—if the vendors will be able to secure another long-term permit from the city, if the current vendors will want to return. Fernando says, "At least if we are four or five that could stay together, we will see what we do." In the meantime, the Country Boys have expanded their presence to the Smorgasburg, a weekly outdoor artisan food market in Williamsburg and "Mister Sunday," a Sunday afternoon and evening outdoor music and dance party in Gowanus.

Long term, Fernando and Yolanda hope to open a restaurant in Red Hook, but if not there, then in nearby Park Slope or Sunset Park. "Once we have a restaurant, we will feel more at peace," he says. Even if they expand to a restaurant, they don't have plans to leave the truck behind. "This will keep on being like my good luck charm. I have a lot of faith on this truck, this place."

CHORIZO HUARACHES

Adapted from Yolanda and Fernando Martinez's recipe

These enormous, oblong, handmade tortillas are filled with a little bit of refried beans and are easily one of the most popular dishes at the Red Hook Ball Fields. A single *huarache* requires two paper plates to contain it (and in most cases two eaters to devour it). It doesn't take many ingredients to make *huaraches* but it does take practice to make them well. The Martinez family was entirely self-taught, they learned in true trial-by-fire fashion at the ball fields.

Huaraches can be delicate and if the bean filling begins to burst through as you're rolling it out, pinch a piece of dough from the ends to patch the holes and continue rolling out the *huarache*. Fortunately *huaraches* are covered with layers of beans, meat, veggies and cheese so if your results don't match the perfection of the Martinezes' versions, it's unlikely anyone will notice between greedy bites.

YIELD: 6 HUARACHES

1 pound Mexican chorizo

16 ounces (about 3½ cups) *masa harina* (corn flour)

1 teaspoon salt

1 cup refried beans, divided

½ cup vegetable oil, for frying

1 small head iceberg lettuce, coarsely chopped

5 medium tomatoes, diced

½ medium white or yellow onion, thinly sliced

5 teaspoons fresh cilantro, coarsely chopped

½ cup *cotija* cheese

recipe continues

Heat a large cast-iron skillet on high for about 5 minutes. Remove chorizo from their casing and add to the pan. Reduce heat to medium-high and fry chorizo, breaking it into small pieces with a spatula as it cooks. Cook until browned and crispy, about 5 minutes. Remove from heat and drain off grease. You can reserve grease to fry *huaraches*, if desired.

Place the *masa harina* in a large bowl and mix with salt. Slowly add about 2¼ cups water and mix with hands to reach right consistency. The dough should be soft but not sticky, and you may need to use more or less water. Form 6 roughly palm-sized, egg-shaped balls. Press your fingers into the center of each one by hand into circles to form a deep trench in the center so the ball of dough resembles a canoe. Add ½ teaspoon of beans to the middle of each ball of dough and pinch the dough to seal and restore the egg shape. Place dough on a large sheet of plastic wrap and press gently to flatten then cover with another large sheet of plastic wrap and use a rolling pin, to stretch the stuffed dough to form a large oval about ¼-inch thick. Add 1 to 2 tablespoons of vegetable oil (or reserved chorizo grease) to a flat grill or large cast-iron skillet and heat over medium-high for 1 minute. Carefully place *huarache* onto heated surface for about 3 minutes, flip over, and grill for another 2 minutes or until both sides are golden brown.

Spread with a couple of tablespoons of remaining refried beans. Top with chorizo, chopped lettuce, tomato, onion, cilantro, and *cotija* cheese.

QUEZAHUARACHE

Same process as the *huarache*. While the *huarache* is still on the grill, sprinkle mozzarella cheese over it and let melt for another 2 minutes. Then add the meat and vegetables to your liking.

R afael Soler and his wife, Reina Bermudez-Soler, have put *pupusas*—a traditional, handmade Salvadoran corn cake stuffed with a variety of fillings—on the culinary map. They've appeared on *The Martha Stewart Show* and the Food Network. They've won the coveted Vendy Cup, but no matter what accolades they receive, they'll never forget their humble beginnings at the Red Hook Ball Fields and their first sale, which ended up *costing* them money.

Rafael and Reina had been coming to the ball fields to eat and have fun. One of Reina's uncles was a vendor there, and when he decided to retire, he offered Rafael the opportunity to take over his business. Rafael had to meet with the other vendors to get approved, but the transition was a quick one.

"We went to the meeting, and there was no objection," Rafael says. "I took [the] place on Thursday, and on Saturday I would have to sell—I didn't know anything, only Dominican food—so I started selling roasted meats and whatever I could sell."

Rafael was nervous and excited that first day. "Nobody knew me in the park. I was the only colored person, and it caused a bit of commotion seeing who the new people were. That first day was a cold day, and we took coffee [to sell.] The customer just wanted coffee and only had a twenty-dollar bill. I didn't know I was supposed to make change. My first customer—I will never forget—it was a free coffee!"

Rafael and Reina each have their own responsibilities, though Reina's son, César Fuentes—

Executive Director of the Red Hook Food Vendors—says, "To give honor where honor is due, my mom is more like the visionary, and Rafael, he's got the flavor." The business soon began to draw a following. "The most interesting thing was that the people who came the first week were the same people who were coming the third week. And they would all ask, 'Why don't you do this dish from Guatemala, or that dish from Colombia?' So, I said to my wife, 'We are going to have to diversify more.'" In the early days, their main specialties were Dominican-style meats, but when they added *pupusas* from Reina's native El Salvador, sales really took off. As César describes it, "The *pupusa* is the national dish—it's akin to what the tacos are for Mexicans." For Salvadorans, *pupusas* are what Reina calls an "Every day, every time food . . . if you go to El Salvador basically on every corner there is a *pupuseria* . . . a place where you come and enjoy *pupusas*." As the popularity of their *pupusas* grew, so did Rafael's association with the dish. "My name was changed. Now they call me, 'Mr. Pupusa.'"

Prior to starting their business at the ball fields, Rafael had been a tailor. "I would make pants, and then I went on to cutting the cloth for clothing. I had learned that in my country. In the '80s and '90s, the one who knew how to cut patterns was like a doctor in my country. So, I felt very good. I wore suits, and in those days I earned $15 to $16 an hour, which was money in those days. Once in the United States, and as jobs in the garment business moved overseas, it was harder to make a living practicing his craft. "When this opportunity came about, I couldn't say no," Rafael said. "I said to my wife, 'We have to make our destiny.'"

Over the past ten plus years, the destiny of the Red Hook area itself has changed, too. "We feel very proud that many changes have happened in the Red Hook area. . . . It has grown a lot, and we feel we are part of Red Hook's growth," says Rafael. But that growth was not without challenges. "The problems came when the health department thought we could make many changes in a short time." It wasn't possible to comply with all of the city regulations while working under the old conditions of charcoal grills in an open-air setting. "Two of the oldest vendors were out because we had to make an immediate investment," Rafael says. The Solers didn't have the money to buy a new truck, but they were able to scrape together enough to buy a secondhand truck so they could continue at the ball fields.

As a non-Salvadoran, Rafael is less wedded to tradition when it comes to *pupusa*-making, which has allowed for some innovation. "I came up with the chicken *pupusa*. It wasn't known here, nor in El Salvador. I introduced it. I thought if I cook the chicken so well, why can't I make the *pupusas* with chicken?" When their customers started to change, Rafael adapted the *pupusas* to suit them. "The people from Manhattan started to come to the park," he says. Many of the newcomers were vegetarians. "I had a bright moment, and we started to work more with the bean," says Rafael. "We work with the fish, with jalapeños, zucchini, spinach, and all vegetables." As the demand for the *pupusas* has soared, the Solers have created three platters to introduce customers to a taste of other Latin specialties like *plátanos manduros*, fried ripe plantains. Rafael is particularly fond of the sample platter "because I can't leave my *tamales* out. They are the best—that platter has everything, the *pupusa*, the *tamale*, chorizo, fried ripe plantain, sour cream, and jalapeño."

Besides working the ball fields from April through October, the Solers have set up shop at the Brooklyn Flea year-round. "Mr. Eric [Demby, cofounder of the Brooklyn Flea] invited us—all of us vendors [to sell food]. . . . We had a meeting, among the vendors—many didn't come, because they didn't think the mix in the flea market would work." Only two vendors from Red Hook decided to participate, the Country Boys and Solber Pupusas. In the beginning, they shared a ten-foot by ten-foot space. The lines were massive, and each earned their own spot at the market. Rafael says that the organizer told him, "'As the flea market grows, in the same way the possibilities for you grow.' Whenever he opens another flea market, he wants me to be there."

"Every day we are adding new flavors always mixing new ideas, new recipes so they are more unique." —RAFAEL SOLER

PUPUSAS REVUELTAS (PORK AND CHEESE PUPUSAS)
Adapted from Reina Bermudez-Soler's recipe

Pupusas, filled, griddled corn cakes, are a traditional Salvadoran dish dating back hundreds of years. In recent times, the form has been adapted to suit modern tastes—the Solers even have a pepperoni-filled pupusa! Even with filling innovations there's little that can be done to improve the classic *pupusas revueltas*. Filled with a mix of seasoned ground pork and cheese, these are among the top sellers at the Red Hook Ball Fields.

One of the secrets to the filling is a touch of Adobo seasoning. Reina prefers the Goya® variety with pepper.

YIELD: MAKES 24 PUPUSAS

FOR THE FILLING:

½ pound ground pork

2 medium tomatoes, peeled, seeded, and coarsely chopped

4 cloves garlic, peeled

¼ large red onion, coarsely chopped

½ teaspoon dried oregano

2 tablespoons olive oil

½ tablespoon adobo

½ cup beef stock

1½ cups mozzarella, shredded

FOR THE DOUGH:

1½ pounds (about 5¼ cups) *masa harina* (corn flour)

¾ teaspoon salt

1½ tablespoons vegetable oil, plus more for pan frying

4 to 6 cups lukewarm water

FOR SERVING:

Curtido (page 240)

Salsa Fresca (page 240)

½ cup sour cream

¼ cup pickled jalapeños, if desired

TO PREPARE THE FILLING:

Add the pork, tomatoes, garlic, onion, oregano, and adobo to the bowl of a food processor. Pulse several times to mix, then process until puréed.

In a large pan or cast-iron skillet, add olive oil. Heat oil for a minute then add the meat mixture and sauté over on medium-high heat, stirring occasionally until meat is browned, about 5 minutes. Add beef stock, then reduce heat to medium-low and let it cook uncovered, stirring occasionally for about 40 minutes, or until the meat is still moist but most of the liquid is reduced. Remove from heat and transfer to a medium bowl. Cover and refrigerate while you prepare the *pupusa* dough.

MAKING THE PUPUSAS:

In a large bowl, use your hands to combine the flour, salt, and vegetable oil. Slowly add the water and mix until dough is soft and manageable (doesn't stick to your hands).

Form dough into 24 balls that are slightly larger than a golf ball. Pressing between your hands, start to flatten each, taking care to preserve the roundness. When flattened into a circle approximately 3 inches in diameter and ¼-inch thick, put 1 tablespoon of the cheese and 1 tablespoon of the pork mixture in the middle and gently bring the sides up in order to form a ball again, pinching to shut. Once you have the ball you gently flatten by slapping back and forth between your hands (imagine you are playing patty-cake).

Heat a large cast iron skillet over medium-high heat for 1 to 2 minutes. Add 1 to 2 tablespoons of vegetable oil to grease the skillet. Working in batches place the *pupusas* on the heated surface and fry for 3 to 4 minutes on each side, or until *pupusas* are golden brown and crisp. Serve with a generous helping of *Curtido* (page 240) and *Salsa Fresca* (page 240) and a dollop of sour cream and pickled jalapeños, if desired.

ZUCCHINI PUPUSAS

Adapted from Reina Bermudez-Soler's recipe

As more vegetarians have discovered the Red Hook Ball Fields the vendors have adapted their menus to cater to their dietary needs. The garlicky, sautéed zucchini filling for these pupusas makes a great side dish on its own.

YIELD: 24 PUPUSAS

FOR THE FILLING:

2 tablespoons olive oil

1 tablespoon garlic, mashed

1½ cups zucchini, shredded

1½ cups mozzarella, shredded

FOR THE DOUGH:

1½ pounds (about 5¼ cups) *masa harina* (corn flour)

¾ teaspoon salt

1½ tablespoons vegetable oil, plus more for pan frying

4 to 6 cups lukewarm water

FOR SERVING:

Curtido (page 240)

Salsa Fresca (page 240)

½ cup sour cream

¼ cup pickled jalapeños, if desired

In a large frying pan or skillet add olive oil and garlic and sauté over medium-high, stirring occasionally until oil becomes fragrant and garlic turns translucent, about 3 minutes. Add the zucchini and sauté, stirring occasionally until zucchini is tender and lightly golden brown. Remove from heat and transfer to a medium bowl. Cover and refrigerate while you prepare the *pupusa* dough.

MAKING THE PUPUSAS:

In a large bowl, use your hands to combine the flour, salt, and vegetable oil. Slowly add the water and mix until dough is soft and manageable (doesn't stick to your hands).

Form dough into 24 balls that are slightly larger than a golf ball. Pressing between your hands, start to flatten each, taking care to preserve the roundness. When flattened into a circle approximately 3 inches in diameter and ¼-inch thick, put 1 tablespoon of the cheese and 1 tablespoon of the zucchini in the middle and gently bring the sides up in order to form a ball again, pinching to shut. Once you have the ball you gently flatten by slapping back and forth between your hands (imagine you are playing-patty cake).

Heat a large cast-iron skillet over medium-high heat for 1 to 2 minutes. Add 1 to 2 tablespoons of vegetable oil to grease the skillet. Working in batches, place the pupusas on the heated surface and fry for 3 to 4 minutes on each side, or until pupusas are golden brown and crisp. Serve with a generous helping of *Curtido* (page 240) and *Salsa Fresca* (page 240) and a dollop of sour cream and pickled jalapeños, if desired.

CURTIDO
(SALVADORAN PICKLED CABBAGE)
Adapted from Reina Bermudez-Soler's recipe

Pupusas are commonly served with *curtido*, a bright and crispy Salvadoran-style 'slaw. This recipe doesn't take much time to prepare, but you need to make it at least a day ahead to allow the cabbage enough time to pickle slightly in the vinegar. If you love spicy foods, add jalapeño slices to give this a fiery edge.

YEILD: 6 CUPS

5 cups white cabbage, shredded
1 cup purple cabbage, shredded
1 cup white vinegar
1/2 teaspoon dried oregano
1/2 teaspoon salt, or to taste
1 jalapeño, seeded and cut into thin rounds
   (optional)
1 teaspoon black pepper (optional)

Mix all the ingredients with 1 cup water. Refrigerate in an airtight container for at least one day before serving. Store in the refrigerator for up to 2 weeks.

SALSA-FRESCA
(TOMATO SALSA)
Adapted from Reina Bermudez Soler's recipe

Light and bright, this easy homemade salsa traditionally accompanies *pupusas*, but it also works well with tacos, burritos and nachos.

YEILD: ABOUT 3 CUPS

8 medium tomatoes, peeled, seeded, and
   chopped
1 medium-sized red onion, chopped
1 green pepper, seeded and chopped
2 cloves garlic, peeled
1/2 teaspoon salt
1/2 teaspoon black pepper

Purée all ingredients and 1/2 cup water in a blender or food processor.

Pour into a medium pot and bring to a boil over medium-high heat. Reduce heat to medium-low and simmer uncovered for about 10 minutes.

Serve warm or at room temperature. Refrigerate leftovers in an airtight container for up to 3 days.

The El Olomega sports a sign that says "since 1990," but that's not exactly true. "My mother and father started," says co-owner, Marcos Lainez. "I mean we put on our sign 1990, but it was well before that. We just didn't want to look so old." Technically Marcos's uncle, Carlos Ayala, was the first to start vending in the family. "He kept telling my mother, 'Oh you should go there because they are not selling pupusas and those that were weren't good.'" Marcos's mother, Teodora (known as Esperanza), started coming with his aunt, Ana Maria Ayala. They had a single small charcoal grill and were happy to make $50 to $75 dollars in sales. "That was a lot of money," says Marcos, "better than staying at home."

The truck is named for the Lainez family's hometown in El Salvador, and *pupusas* are their must-try item. From the truck's large serving window, customers can watch as a trio of ladies (on busy days, sometimes it's a quartet or quintet) hand shape each *pupusa*, slapping the soft masa dough between their hands to form a flattened circle that's then filled with meat or vegetables and cheese before being shut, reflattened, and griddled. The *pupusas* come in a range of flavors, including chicken, bean and cheese, and spinach, but the most traditional are the *pupusas revueltas* which are stuffed with spiced ground pork, beans, and melty mozzarella cheese, the latter ingredient being an American innovation to the *pupusa* form. In El Salvador they use a different cheese, "a cheaper cheese," says Marcos. "It doesn't taste the same. Ours tastes better." The *loroco* and cheese ones are Marcos's personal favorite. "It's a flower. You might be skeptical about it. You might wonder what a flower tastes like. Some people think that it tastes like okra. I don't think so. I think *loroco* has its own taste. I love it." For newbies, Marcos has some advice: "We

"Everything is handmade. Nothing is precooked or from the shelf."

—MARCOS LAINEZ

tell people to get two flavors so you'll like at least one. You can't go wrong with pork and cheese or chicken and cheese." One of the delights of the *pupusas* are the accompaniments—the *curtido*, a crunchy, briny homemade slaw made of red and white cabbage and *salsa de tomate*, a bright and tangy tomato sauce.

Those who lament the loss of the "old ball fields"—the open-air atmosphere of the tents and tarps and in-your-face grills that allowed customers to see the whole preparation process from start to finish—will be comforted to know that the Lainez family is still using their old grills. They're just installed in a new space. In fact their entire truck was retrofitted to suit their needs. They purposely made sure their wide window put the food at eye level. "That's what people like here. . . . People need to see in order to buy. If you don't see the food, you don't know what it is and don't want to buy." Still, Marcos misses the close interaction that the old setup afforded. "The environment is not the same. It was better before because you had the communication with your client. You were standing right next to them. They were watching you, really close. Now you're enclosed in the box."

Marcos and his wife helped his mother at the ball fields for years, but it was the increased city regulations for ball field vendors that spurred him and his sister, Janet, to take over the family business. "We live in Red Hook. I said, 'Look my parents have been there for so many years. You can't just leave'. That's why my wife, my sister, and me got together and formed a corperation as required by law because we wanted to protect our own." A medical

photographer by day and a jack-of-all-trades on the weekend, Marcos handles repair jobs, as well as their growing online presence on Facebook, Twitter, and their own site. "I cook, but not the *pupusas*. For some reasons, Salvadoran men don't make *pupusas*. You'll never see a man making *pupusas*. They would ask what is wrong with this guy. It's a *machista*, thing. . . . Here all the chefs are men."

In years past it was the soccer leagues that brought the crowd to the fields. These days it's more likely that the people are coming just to eat. "The better teams moved over to Caton," says Marcos referring to another set of soccer fields by Prospect Park. "They were really great for us because they had a lot of fans." Over time as the customer base changed, so did the menu: ". . . the Americans wanted different vegetables. So we began to add different items to the menu." Zucchini, spinach, and *loroco* are bestsellers for vegetarians, but even with the changes, the demand for the pork and cheese holds strong.

It takes all week to stay on top of the needs of the business, and the weekends are brutally long. "Saturday and Sunday for us is like 6:00 a.m. to 12 midnight," Marcos says. "I'm the last one to get home because I have to go and park the truck. I get home at 11:30 to 12:00. Then again the next day. I have to make sure the truck is ready for the day so that when they come it's ready to cook."

Monday is spent cleaning, and Tuesday the cooking starts again. Even with all the challenges and the long hours, the family is proud of their hard work and their longevity at the ball fields. "We survived. We're still here. That's what counts."

CHICKEN PUPUSAS

Adapted from the Lainez family recipe

Though pork and cheese are the most traditional of the *pupusas*, ground chicken also works well. Serve these with *Salsa Fresca* (page 240) and *Curtido* (page 240), and if you like heat, add some pickled jalapeños and carrots. *Pupusas* are made of *masa harina*, corn flour treated with lime. The Lainez family recommends Maseca® brand flour.

YIELD: MAKES 24 PUPUSAS

FOR THE PUPUSA FILLING:

1 cube chicken bouillon

½ pound lean ground chicken breast

1 cup tomatoes, coarsely chopped (about 2 ½ small tomatoes)

½ cup yellow onion, coarsely chopped (about 1 small yellow onion)

½ cup green bell pepper, coarsely chopped, seeded (about ½ a large green pepper)

¼ cup flat parsley, coarsely chopped

1 clove garlic, peeled

½ teaspoon salt

½ teaspoon black pepper

2½ teaspoons olive oil

xxx cheese, shredded

1½ cups mozzarella

FOR THE DOUGH:

5¼ cups *masa harina* (corn flour)

4 to 6 cups lukewarm water

¾ teaspoon salt

½ cup vegetable oil

In a large pot add 5 cups of water, chicken bouillon, and ground chicken. Bring water to a boil over medium-high heat and boil chicken uncovered for about 40 minutes or until chicken is fully cooked and water has reduced to just a few tablespoons. Cover and refrigerate chicken to cool to room temperature, approximately 20 minutes. When cooled, place chicken in food processor to break up any clumps. Transfer to a medium bowl and set aside.

Add tomatoes, onions, and green pepper to food processor or blender with parsley, garlic, salt, and pepper. Pulse several times until all ingredients are finely chopped.

In a large frying pan heat olive oil over medium-high. Add tomato mixture, reduce heat to medium and lightly fry for 5 minutes, stirring occasionally . Then add chicken, stirring to thoroughly combine. Cook for 20 minutes over medium heat, stirring occasionally, then remove from heat, cover and refrigerate until chicken cools to room temperature.

MAKING THE PUPUSAS:

In a large bowl combine corn flour, salt, and 4 to 6 cups of warm water.

Mix with your hands until a soft dough forms. Divide the dough into 24 golf ball–sized balls.

Form the *pupusa* by flattening the ball of dough by slapping it between your palms to form a circle approximately 4 inches in diameter and about ¼ of an inch thick. Add a tablespoon of chicken filling and a tablespoon of shredded cheese to the center and carefully draw the sides together to close and seal. Gently flatten the dough with the meat inside to form, slapping it between your hands again to form a circle approximately 4 inches in diameter.

Heat a griddle or a large cast-iron skillet over medium-high temperature, add 1 to 2 tablespoons of oil and working in batches cook *pupusas* until golden-brown spots appear, about 3½ minutes each side. Serve with *Curtido* (page 240) and *Salsa Fresca* (page 240).

PLATANOS FRITOS
(SWEET FRIED PLANTAINS)

In El Salvador a typical breakfast present on nearly every kitchen table is the platanos fritos. Be sure to select plantains that are already yellow not green plantains. For best results, wait until plantain peels have turned entirely black, which means they are completely ripe.

In a large frying pan or skillet, heat the oil over medium-high. Slice the plantains in half and fry until they turn golden brown, about 3½ minutes per side. Serve with refried beans and sour cream, if desired.

YIELD: SERVES 2

2 tablespoons olive oil or vegetable oil

2 ripe plantains

1 cup refried beans, for serving

¼ cup sour cream, for serving

Humberto Carrillo first discovered the Red Hook Ball Fields through another vendor, his good friend, Marcos Lainez, owner of El Olomega Truck. "I introduced my mother to them, and they asked, 'why you don't come here, find something to sell?'" Humberto says. "So my mother started selling those fried tacos. That's how she started here. That was like, maybe eighteen years ago." Humberto's mother, Maria Estella Carrillo, soon branched out to other traditional items popular in Guatemala's *mercados* or open markets—dishes like tamales filled with meat or sweet corn, *rellenitos* (fried sweet plantains filled with refried beans or pastry cream and *atol de elote*, a popular) hot sweet corn drink. The cart's name embodies their menu—*antojitos* means snacks, and *chapines* is an informal term Guatemalans use to describe themselves. There are very few Guatemalan restaurants in New York, and expats longing for a taste of home know to come here get their fix.

Time and age began to take their toll on Maria Estella. The long hours of standing in the hot weather were becoming too much for her. Eventually the family convinced her to retire. "She still want to go, but she can't," Humberto says. For the past few years, the stand has been operated by Humberto and his wife, Reina. Preparing to sell is a week-long process. "We start Monday doing the shopping, then start cooking during the week. This is just the end," says Humberto. So much of their business depends on the weather, which is always hard to predict during the week. "We can't predict. We always prepare. . . . It's not like you know, put it in the freezer and take it out or just go to the store and buy it in the store." In the tight confines of their cart, Humberto and Reina stick to their duties. "She prepares the food, and I fry it. Once it's done, I serve. . . . She make everything. I'm the helper."

Tamales are especially popular and one of Humberto's favorites. Guatemalan *tamales* are larger than their Mexican counterparts, and the *masa,* or cornmeal filling, has a wetter, creamier texture. Back in Guatemala, tamales are sold from people's homes on Fridays or Saturdays. "When they sell them, they got a little red light on the house," Humberto says. "You see a little red light there, it's because they sell the tamales." Another one of the more unique items on their menu is the *pacaya*, the flower of a palm tree native to Guatemala. The flower itself has a tentacle-like appearance. Reina batters and deep fries it, then serves it taco-style over corn tortillas, topped with a tomato sauce and garnished with onions and cilantro. It's an acquired taste, slightly sour, slightly bitter, and Humberto admits that it wasn't his favorite as a child. "At my house with my mother, she always cooked it, but I

"This is native-style, from-Guatemala—cooking. It's not stuff you can buy in the stores. I wish! It would be easier, but you can't."

—HUMBERTO CARRILLO

never ate it." These days Humberto eats it with lots of lemon.

Over the years Red Hook has changed considerably. "We used to have a lot of Guatemalan customers here. But everything changed. Before it was the Spanish people at the park. A lot. But it changed. Where did they go? Who knows. Just a few, they keep coming. Everything changed." While the Pan-American soccer league once was the big draw to the park, the soccer teams have changed, too. "Now on Saturdays it's a Guatemalan league. They lost a lot of teams because they don't give out good *premios* [prizes] at the end of the season. So they moved someplace else. I think they moved to Prospect Park." The loss of the better teams also meant the loss of their fans, who would buy food from the vendors to enjoy while they took in the game. In years past, Saturday was the bigger day for sales, but not anymore. "On Sundays, it's better; the Mexican league is better. It used to be on Saturdays; now it's on Sundays."

While the Latino customers may be dwindling, the reputation of the Red Hook vendors has spread to the foodie community. Posts about the food at the ball fields began cropping up on Chowhound.com as early as 1999, and as the food blogosphere exploded, word of the Red Hook Ball Fields spread to adventurous food lovers around the city. Humberto remembers when the foodies first came: "They start buying one order; they split it with five or whatever. There was no money for us. They like it now, so now it's like they buy one order for each one. Before they used to buy one order and taste it. Now it's better."

Even with the foodie crowds, the business is not what it used to be, and many of the vendors are

still trying to recover their investments on the carts and trucks that the city required them to purchase to comply with the Department of Health code. Upgrading from a bunch of folding tables with grills to a food truck cost some vendors upward of $30,000. The Carillos were fortunate that Humberto works in a junkyard that used to buy repossessed carts from the city by the lot. Around the time of the changes, there were two carts that came into the yard. "One was nice; you have nothing to do with it, just to clean it. So I talk to my boss; I want that one." When the day came to purchase the cart, they had already sold it. "Then they got this other one, but this was all beat up. So I redo that one. I pay $7,000 to redo it." Unlike some of the other vendors, the cart isn't the Carrillos's sole source of income. "I work. I don't live on this . . . this is extra money, and actually I always tell her, 'That's your money; it's not my money.'"

Working in close quarters in the summer sun is a challenge. "I don't even know if we are gonna continue doing this. . . . Sometimes we feel like cats inside there fighting. You know the summer heat is hot! The people, you get nervous, you get stressed there. Sometimes I feel like I just want to go and leave. She got patience. I can't." All of the Red Hook vendors have known each other for years. Some are friends. Some are relatives. But in the end they're all independent businesses. With the increased regulations imposed by the city—from the various permits to the cost of parking at the commissary throughout the year and the rising costs of everything from ingredients to gasoline—it's hard to say what the future will bring. "We got ten vendors here. Everyone want to do some things; some people don't want to do things. It's very hard. We are together, but we are not together. . . . some of us agree, some of us disagree, but we'll see."

ATOL DE ELOTE (GUATEMALAN SWEETENED HOT CORN DRINK)

Adapted from Reina Carillo's recipe

During the early spring and fall, the shoulder months of the Red Hook vendors' selling season, the Carrillos serve *Atol de Elote*, a popular, sweetened, hot corn-and-milk beverage from their native Guatemala. This cinnamon-flecked beverage instantly warms you up and is ideal for taking the chill off on those mornings you'd much rather stay in bed.

....

YIELD: SERVES 4

2 cups of sweet corn kernels (about 4 ears)

2 cups whole milk

½ cup granulated sugar

1 cinnamon stick

½ teaspoon vanilla extract

1 teaspoon cinnamon, for serving

Cut corn off cob and add kernels to a blender or food processor with 1 cup water. Purée mixture until smooth, about 2 to 3 minutes. Transfer mixture to a large saucepan and add milk, sugar, cinnamon stick, vanilla, and an additional cup of water. Stir to dissolve sugar, then bring the mixture to boil over medium-high, stirring constantly. Reduce heat to a simmer and cook, stirring occasionally for 20 minutes, until mixture has slightly thickened. Remove from heat, discard cinnamon stick. Pour into 4 mugs for serving and sprinkle with cinnamon, if desired. Serve immediately.

Y ou say smoothie; Victor Sosa says *licuado*. But when the drinks are as refreshing as the ones at the Sosa Fruit Truck, there's really no need to mince words. Just point and order. You can't go wrong.

After ten years in business Victor is a street-vending veteran, but at the Red Hook Ball Fields, where some vendors have been for over twenty years, he's still the new kid on the block. Like the Vaquero Fruit Truck across the way, Victor and his wife, Santana, sell fresh-cut fruit, *elotes*, and a variety of cold drinks. On the surface, the trucks may seem similar, but if you take a closer look at the menu, you'll see some differences. For starters the Sosas have *licuados,* or what some call *batidos*, smoothie-like beverages made with a milk base and lots of fresh fruit. The *licuados* at Sosa Fruit come in papaya, strawberry, and mango, and they very much live up to their "blended wonders" tagline on the menu.

The *elotes*—corn on a stick brushed with mayo and then dressed with lime, *cotija* cheese, and cayenne pepper—are prepared *al gusto* or "to taste." If you don't like the char from grill, you can have the corn boiled instead. Their *horchata*, a sweetened rice drink, is especially rich from the ground almonds used to prepare their version of the iced drink.

Victor started his business with one product: mangoes. "The idea was to sell something, so I started selling mangoes, no food only fruits," he says. He still does a brisk mango trade, going through cases upon cases of the green and sweet varieties each weekend, with the green mangoes being the more popular of the two. Victor offers his fresh-cut mangoes with chile powder, freshly squeezed lime juice, and a touch of salt—just the way they are served by street vendors in Mexico. Victor doesn't skimp on the lime, and he definitely doesn't use bottled juice from concentrate. The effect is sweet, salty, sour, spicy, and just plain good.

Like many of his fellow vendors, Victor emigrated from Puebla in Central Mexico. In addition to the fruits and drinks, he also sells nuts, dried pumpkin seeds, and *jamoncillo de pepita*, a traditional fudge-like candy made from ground pumpkin seeds and sugar. Each bar of *jamoncillo* is accented with a stripe of vivid pink dye, making it visually arresting, as well as a sweet and satisfying little snack.

Like many of his fans, Victor mourns the loss of the days at the ball fields when they had the open air *mercado*-feel of a Latin American food bazaar. "Before, we didn't sell from the truck. We sold from a table. There were no trucks," he says. Gone are the weather-worn tarps and tables where visitors could watch the food being prepared right in before their eyes. Upgrading from simple folding tables to fully equipped mobile kitchens has been a big investment for the vendors, and it's hard not to be discouraged when the crowds have been thinning with the passing years. "In previous years there were more people . . . many people came before, not now. Before, there were more people playing [soccer]. Now there are just a few."

"They [the changes] are bad because you invest a lot but don't make a lot."

—VICTOR SOSA

WATERMELON AGUA FRESCA

Inspired by Victor Sosa's recipes.

One of the most popular beverages at the Red Hook Ball Fields is the Watermelon Agua Fresca, a simple and utterly refreshing drink consisting of blended watermelon, ice, and a spritz of lime. Add a splash of rum or vodka for a light and fruity summer cocktail.

....

YIELD: SERVES 4

8 cups seedless watermelon pieces, cubed

2 tablespoons lime juice (about one lime), if desired

....

Add the watermelon, lime juice, and 3 table-spoons cold water to a blender. Pulse for a few seconds to break up the watermelon, and then blend on high until smooth, about a minute. Serve over ice.

CHILE MANGOES

Green mangoes with lime, chile powder, and salt are the soft pretzel of Mexican street food. In major Mexican cities you can find vendors pushing little shopping carts stocked with cases of mangoes and their fixings. The Sosas began their business at the ball fields selling mangoes, and the Chile Mangoes remain one of their most popular items.

....

YIELD: SERVES 1

1 green mango, peeled and cut into wedges

2 tablespoons lime juice (about 1 lime)

salt, to taste

½ teaspoon cayenne pepper or ancho pepper, or more to taste

....

Place cut mango into a bowl for serving. Toss with lime juice, then sprinkle with salt and cayenne pepper to taste. Toss to coat and serve immediately.

The lunch menu at Fauzia's Heavenly Delights cart is always a surprise, sometimes even for Fauzia herself. "Every morning after I finish cooking, I handwrite my menu," says Fauzia Abdur-Rahman. "Sometimes I will have one thing in my mind, and by the time I get to work and finish cooking, there might be two changes on the menu." It's the surprises and Fauzia's "nouveau-Caribbean" food that have kept lunch crowds coming back for going on twenty years. Lunch offerings from her cart might include Jamaican curry chicken, tofu tikka, spicy stewed black beans with coconut milk, creamy butternut squash soup with mushroom, roti, and her sinfully good Nilla® wafer–laden banana pudding. "The customer likes the element of surprise. They come to the cart, and it's not just grilled chicken, rice and vegetables," she says. A self-proclaimed "freestyle cook," Fauzia credits Indian, Asian, Mexican, African, and West Indian influences, saying, "I'm Jamaican, but my food crosses all boundaries."

Fauzia speaks about food with such eloquence and passion, it's hard to believe that when she first came to this country she didn't know how to cook anything. Fauzia and her sister came to New York from Jamaica to visit her aunt for a summer of fun in 1978 and fell in love with the city. "We were just mesmerized by 42nd Street and all the lights, you know?" Fauzia says. When it came time to go home, her aunt asked her, "'Why are you going back to Jamaica to your father's house? You're twenty years old, why don't you just start your life?'" So Fauzia stayed. Despite having two years of college, she wasn't exactly qualified for most of the jobs open to her as a new immigrant. Coming from her father's home, where they had two servants, "I didn't cook. I *did not* cook. I didn't wash, I didn't do absolutely nothing." She eventually found a job at a Jewish nursing home in Riverdale bringing in around $35 per week. Her life turned around when one of her friends hooked her up with Kelly Girl Service, a temporary staffing agency, where suddenly she was being tapped for long-term assignments and working for $19 to $20 per hour.

Fauzia had another change in fortunes after her son was born in 1984. After several years struggling as a working single mom, her own mother sat her down and told her that she needed her own business. Fauzia's mother spent the whole summer teaching her to cook. They started with the basics: codfish cakes and sorrel, a popular drink in the Caribbean. With her mom's help she ventured out for her first selling experience at an African American festival in Newark. Despite being woefully underprepared—"We got down there, we realized we didn't have a table. . . ."—they sold out. At her

"People know quality. New Yorkers? Oh please, New Yorkers have the most sophisticated palate in the world." —FAUZIA ABDUR-RAHMAN

next event, they added a few more items to the menu, and the business grew from there. Fauzia wanted to expand her business and get a cart, but she had a decent job working for the city in the Department of Finance. She was scared to leave, so she kept cooking as a side business.

Meeting her husband Amin inspired Fauzia to begin cooking more vegetarian dishes. "To me it was so much easier to cook. It didn't take a whole lot of time. I could make it really nice and flavorful." With the support of her husband, Fauzia applied for a Bronx-specific vending license when her maternity leave for her second son ended and cashed out an insurance policy. "It was just enough—$5,000—and the cart cost $4,500." Fauzia and her husband lived in Manhattan and didn't know the Bronx at all. After getting chased away from a spot outside Lincoln hospital, they found their home outside the district attorney's office on the corner of 161 Street and Sheridan Avenue—and have been there since February 21, 1994.

Fauzia arrives at her spot at 8:30 in the morning and prepares everything fresh on the truck. Lunch starts at 11:00 a.m. and finishes up when she's sold out, usually around 4:00 or 4:30 p.m. They used to sell out by 2 p.m., but recently they've faced some tough competition from a new market nearby that "went around to all the different businesses and they basically got an idea about what everybody sells and opened up a big megastore and put everything in there . . . when you walk in there it's one-stop shopping." While the new market has put a temporary dent in Fauzia's business, it would take a lot more to get this 2008 Vendys Award finalist down. In 2012 she started summertime vending as part of the concessions on Governors Island, bringing her eclectic food to a whole new audience. "My philosophy is if I'm not going to eat it,

I'm not going to give it to you. It has to be *the best*."

Fauzia takes interest in her customers and keeps up after them, like the young boy who would come to the cart to talk to her after his mother passed away. "I would say, 'You know what, you bring me your report card. For every 85 you get $5. Anything over 90, you get $10.' That's what I did with my kids. I said to myself, *maybe his mom would do that.*" For her older customers who can't make it out to the cart anymore, Fauzia has her husband bring them meals. Cook and confidante, Fauzia is a treasured member of the community. "It's not just about food," she says. "When you talk at my cart, the metal absorb it. Nothing is revealed."

JAMAICAN CURRY CHICKEN

Adapted from Fauzia Abdur-Rahman's recipe

One of the most popular dishes at Fauzia's Cart is her curry chicken. Made Jamaican-style with lots of spices, plenty of ginger and garlic, the thick sauce is ideal for spooning over rice. Fauzia serves this with her Sautéed Mixed Vegetables (page 256). One of the secrets to this curry is "seasoned salt" a mix of salt, herbs and seasoning.

YIELD: SERVES 6

½ teaspoon turmeric

½ teaspoon cumin powder

1 tablespoon seasoned salt

¼ teaspoon black pepper

1 teaspoon garlic powder

Pinch of dried or 1 sprig fresh thyme

1 tablespoon Jamaican curry powder

1 teaspoon fresh ginger, grated

½ large onion, coarsely chopped

1 scallion stalk, white and green parts finely chopped

3 cloved garlic, peeled, and minced or crushed

2½ pounds boneless, skinless chicken legs and thighs, cut into bite-sized pieces

3 tablespoons olive oil

3 cups cooked white or brown rice, for serving, if desired

Mix all of the ingredients, except for the chicken and olive oil, in a large bowl. Add chicken to the bowl and thoroughly rub ingredients into the chicken.

Cover and marinate the chicken in the refrigerator for 1 hour.

Add olive oil to a large cast-iron skillet or Dutch oven. Place seasoned chicken with marinade in the skillet. Add 1½ cups water and cook over medium heat, stirring occasionally, for 45 minutes to 1 hour, until chicken is cooked and sauce has reduced. Serve over rice, if desired, with Sautéed Mixed Vegetables (page 256).

SAUTÉED MIXED VEGETABLES

Adapted from Fauzia Abdur-Rahman's recipe

Fauzia's flavorful vegetable sides are a big draw with her lunch crowd and super-easy to prepare at home. Serve this with Jamaican Curry Chicken (page 255)

YEILD: SERVES 4

1 (10-ounce) package frozen mixed vegetables (peas, corn, string beans, etc.), thawed

1 medium white onion, diced

1 teaspoon garlic powder

2 tablespoons olive oil

½ medium cabbage, shredded (about 3 cups),

1 teaspoon dried basil

½ teaspoon salt, or more to taste

pinch or two of black pepper, or more to taste

In a large cast-iron skillet or frying pan, sauté mixed vegetables with onion and garlic powder in oil over medium-high heat, stirring occasionally for about 5 minutes or until vegetables are cooked and tender.

Add cabbage and basil. Cover and steam over medium-high heat for an additional 3 to 5 minutes, until cabbage is tender, being careful not to overcook cabbage. Add the basil, salt, and pepper.

L eaving behind the comforts of his family and homeland to stay with an uncle, Fares "Freddy" Zeidaies arrived in America as a bright-eyed 15-year-old Palestinian and tried to stay out of the trouble that can easily befall any teenager growing up in New York City. "I went to school for one week. I couldn't, packed it up." Instead, he began working, bouncing from one job to the next, including opening a deli in Long Island City in 1995. By 2002, he had noticed that none of the falafel and *shawarma* resembled the kind found in his homeland, giving him the idea to open a food cart selling just that. Though opening a cart in Astoria was harder than ever—"being Middle Eastern and coming off of 9/11. It was

hard." After procuring the license, permit, and cart, Freddy set a goal for himself to be the top New York City street vendor and was willing to even use guerilla marketing tactics to get customers to his cart, which is appropriately named King of Falafel and Shawarma. "I would stand around eating my falafel," preying on customers using Astoria's Broadway subway station or visiting the neighborhood watering holes, chatting up other patrons. "What I sell in one hour, I used to sell in one day" back then. It took about a year of relentless marketing for the cart to finally take off, and a decade later, he still gets excited when people praise his cart. "I remember the first Yelp review we got—it was so exciting," he recalls.

> "My goal from day one was I wanted to be number one."
>
> —FARES "FREDDY" ZEIDAIES

Just being at Freddy's cart is usually an experience in and of itself. He loves blasting Middle Eastern music and dancing with his regulars, all while keeping up conversations and, of course, making you food. If the wait's long or if you stop by near the end of a shift, you can bet on getting a free falafel appetizer to subdue your hunger. He brought this experience to the Vendy Awards as a finalist in 2007 and 2009 before winning the Vendy Cup and People's Choice award in 2010. During the 2009 Vendys, Freddy's efforts to sway the judges and audience included having a belly dancing show halfway through the festivities. Just the thought of it makes him laugh. "In 2010, I said none of it. I'm just going to show up." That year, he made sure that the judges' entrées were made to order, plated correctly, and generous with food: relying on his food, not his gregarious personality, to perform for him.

The Vendys win and ensuing praise definitely boosted Freddy's confidence in his career choice, but to him it all comes down to making his customers happy. "Being with the people. You serve them, you see them smiling," and that's what keeps him going six days a week. Freddy will concur that he wouldn't be able to handle opening the cart again. "It was hard. I don't have the energy now that I did then." Luckily for us, he doesn't have to.

FALAFEL

Adapted from Fares "Freddy" Zeidaie's recipe

Falafel is the Middle East's biggest contribution to street food culture. It began appearing on New York streets during the latter half of the 20th century during a large influx of immigration from the region. To complete this dish, layer the falafel, pickled turnips, lettuce, and tomato in a fresh pocket pita, and smoother with tahini and hot sauce. Though be sure to use dried chick peas and not canned since you want the nuttier flavor without the moisture.

YIELD: MAKES 24 FALAFELS

1 cups dried chickpeas (garbanzo beans)

½ medium-sized onion, quartered

1 teaspoon turmeric

1 teaspoon paprika

½ teaspoon cardamom

½ teaspoon nutmeg

1 clove garlic, peeled

3 sprigs of fresh parsley

1 teaspoon salt

1 teaspoon ground cumin

1 teaspoon ground coriander

½ teaspoon red hot pepper flakes or 1 whole hot chile pepper

1 teaspoon baking soda

3 cups vegetable oil for deep frying

Pick out foreign matter from the peas before placing them in a large bowl, cover generously with water and soak uncovered, at room temperature overnight, adding more water if necessary.

Drain peas, and place them along with the other ingredients and 2 tablespoons water in a food processor. Pulse until the peas are finely ground, about the size of couscous. Roll about 1 tablespoon of the batter into a ball between your palms. Heat the oil in a large heavy-bottomed pot to 350°F. Carefully deep fry each ball until golden brown, about 5 minutes each. They will fall to the bottom and rise during the frying. Serve hot stuffed in a pita or by themselves, covered in tahini sauce.

PICKLED TURNIPS RECIPE

To add a pop of color to white pickled turnips, Freddy throws a beet into the mix. The hot pink turnips then brighten up every falafel sandwich he serves.

YIELD: 1 QUART

1 large beet

1 pound turnips, peeled and sliced into sticks

2 large cloves garlic, thinly chopped

1 cup water

1 cup white vinegar

1½ tablespoons salt

Sterilize a quart-sized jar.

Separately cook both the beet and the turnips in boiling water. Boil the beet until tender, remove from the water, peel before allowing to cool, and slice into rounds. Boil the turnip sticks for 3 minutes, remove, and cool.

Combine the water, vinegar, and salt in a medium pot and bring to a boil. Meanwhile, place alternating layers of the turnips and beets, with the garlic scattered throughout, in the jar.

Fill the jar with the boiling vinegar mixture and seal. Store in a warm place for 10 days. Once the finished jar has been opened, place it in the refrigerator.

When a friend suggested to Galdino "Tortas" Molinero that he should sell the Mexican sandwiches known as *tortas* in Flushing Meadows Park during Sunday soccer games, he didn't believe much would happen. It was just a way for the injured restaurant worker to make some extra pocket money during his time off from work. That first day out though, he ended up selling all twenty tortas he had made in less than twenty minutes. He brought more the next week, only to sell out again. Only then did he realize he was onto something.

Tortas first arrived in New York from Mexico City in 1986, leaving behind his first wife and three small boys. After a few years bouncing back and forth between Mexico and New York, he found work as a dishwasher and was quickly promoted in the kitchen. He continued in the restaurant industry for years, including one stint as a sushi chef—"I don't even like fish!" Then one day on his way to work in New Jersey, he got into a serious accident that left him with leg injuries that required surgery and rehabilitation. It was during his recovery period that his friend Hector approached him about selling tortas during the weekly soccer games. "I had no money; I had nothing," so Hector bought him the supplies he needed to sell the tortas on the sidelines. Business was so good that even after return-

ing to work in catering, he continued to sell tortas in the park on Sundays.

Once he was well enough to travel, Tortas headed down to Mexico on a vacation to visit his family. While he was there, another friend Francisco propositioned him with the cost of a pushcart to sell the tortas from. "Everybody knows you sell tortas and you do good business," Francisco told him. He agreed and started using the cart on Sundays, while a friend worked it during the week. Tortas watched his friend struggle to manage both the restaurant and the cart during the week, so he decided to quit his job and buy the permit for the cart. Tortas Neza, opened on 111th Street and Roosevelt Avenue in 2002. The cart did well enough to allow Tortas to buy a brick-and-mortar space in Woodside in 2009, but that would only last for two years. After closing the restaurant, he went back to vending on the streets, reopening Tortas Neza in December of 2011.

For his menu, Tortas named his sandwiches after Mexican *fútbol* (soccer) clubs using the most popular sandwich combinations from his days in Flushing Meadows. His personal favorite is the Tortas Neza, a monster of a sandwich filled with cheese, ham, breaded chicken, and *queso de puerco* (aka headcheese). His customers, though—who run the gamut from teenagers stopping by for a quick bite to eat on the way home to area construction workers to yuppies making the trip out on the rumbling overhead 7 train—seem to like every sandwich on the menu. The unifying ingredients found in most of his sandwiches are the chunks of avocado, lettuce, and tomato, as well as quick spreads of mayo and refried beans on the bread. But most importantly, Tortas gives each sandwich a finishing grill upside down "because the customers like it. It's different." It's a sheer balancing act to avoid losing the filling straight onto the grill, so only try this trick if you dare.

TORTA PUMAS

Adapted from Galdino "Tortas" Molinero's recipe

Torta Pumas is Tortas Neza's truly signature sandwich. It's a five-meat Goliath of a sandwich, complete with the standard toppings of lettuce, tomato, and refried beans. *Quesillo* is a fresh Oaxacan-style cheese available at Latino grocery stores; if you can't find it, we recommend regular Oaxaca cheese or Monterey Jack cheese. If you're a little squeamish of head-cheese, be sure to seek it out freshly made from a quality butcher—they'll have the best-tasting variety.

....

YIELD: SERVES 2

Canola oil

1 chicken cutlet, pounded thin

¼ cup all-purpose flour

2 chicken hot dogs, scored every half inch

½ link of Mexican chorizo

2 eggs, beaten

2 tablespoons Mayonnaise

1 Portuguese, bolilo, or telera roll, sliced in half
    and toasted

2 tablespoons refried beans

3 slices headcheese

6 slices of ham

2 ounces *quesillo* cheese, shredded

1 large lettuce leaf, shredded

½ large tomato, sliced

Heat canola oil to 350°F to 375°F in a deep, heavy pan. Coat chicken with flour before dropping into the hot oil. Fry chicken until done, about 7 minutes. After removing chicken, place the two hot dogs in the pan and fry them until golden, turning them once, about 5 minutes.

While the meats are frying, squeeze the chorizo out of its casing into a separate warmed pan and fry on medium-high heat. Once it has browned and released its oil, pour the eggs into the pan, carefully incorporating the chorizo into the eggs as they scramble, about 3 minutes Once combined, flip the eggs to cook on the other side.

ASSEMBLY:

Spread mayonnaise on the bottom half of the roll and refried beans on the other. Place the fried chicken cutlet on the bottom, topping it with the sliced meats, the cooked chorizo and egg, and the hot dogs. Top with a generous helping of the *quesillo* cheese, lettuce, and tomato. Serve immediately.

TORTA CHIVAS

Adapted from Falino "Tortas" Molinero's recipe

The Torta Chivas is quite possibly the best breakfast sandwich ever created, and the perfect thing to wake up to after a rough night.

YIELD: SERVES 2

½ link of Mexican chorizo

3 eggs, beaten

2 tablespoons mayonnaise

1 Portuguese, bolilo, or telera roll, split in half and toasted

2 tablespoons refried beans

2 or 3 sliced jalapeños

1 large lettuce leaf, shredded

½ large tomato, sliced

Squeeze the chorizo out of its casing into a warmed pan and fry on medium-high heat. Once the chorizo has browned and released its oil, about 5 minutes, pour the beaten eggs into the pan, carefully incorporating the chorizo into the eggs as they cook. Once the eggs have cooked on both sides, about 3 minutes each, remove from the heat.

Spread mayonnaise on the bottom half of the roll, the refried beans on the top. Place the egg and chorizo on the bottom, topping them with the sliced jalapeños, lettuce, and tomato. Serve immediately.

POLICANO'S ITALIAN SAUSAGE

You know a truck is going to be good when you see a paddy wagon packed with cops, clown car–style, pull up for lunch. Such is the case with Policano's Italian Sausage truck, an East New York institution since 1978. Started by Joseph Policano, the truck has been helmed by his cousin and current owner, Doug Policano, since the '90s.

While food trucks in Manhattan jockey for parking spots on a daily basis, Policano's has been parked on Linden Boulevard at 79th Street, just on the border of Brooklyn and Queens for over three decades. Eight lanes of traffic whiz by, and behind the truck lies an undeveloped eight-acre lot that's

been tied up in legal struggles for years. Foot traffic is nothing like the busy streets of Midtown, but Policano's itself is the destination. Rocking a SAUSAGES license plate, the truck is old-school Italian all the way and covered with hand-lettered phrases like "Eat Sausage, Be Happy," "Saus-eech his own!" (a play on the Neapolitan dialect pronunciation of sausage), and "Ahhhh . . . the freshness of it all!" The red, white, and green Italian flag flutters in the breeze beside the good old star-spangled banner.

While most trucks have just a takeout window on the side, the whole back of the Policano's truck is open like an Italian street fair sausage stand, so cus-

tomers can see all the action. Five-pound coils of hot sausage and sweet sausage made from top-secret seventy-five-year-old family recipes sit side by side with thinly sliced onions and mixed bell peppers on a flat-top grill that spans the width of the truck. There's a kind of ballet to the preparation. Sausage, peppers, and onions cover most of the grill, while hot dogs and knishes occupy some territory in the right hand corner. Doug readies orders and chats with customers all while keeping a close eye on the sausages, turning them at just the right time to ensure the proper char. "It's just the standard recipe for sausage and peppers," says Doug. "We don't use no oil, no nothing. Everything's natural from the grill, just the juice from the sausages. Everything here is based on the juice. That will make the onions brown. You want to roll it. You want to put a dog in it. Everything. We call it the glaze."

The menu is simple: sausage and peppers (hot and sweet), hot dogs, and knishes (the rock stars of classic New York street fare), but the variations on those few menu items is impressive. Between the hot and sweet sausage, it's no contest. Says Doug, "Sweet is way more popular. Sweet is two to one." The perennial bestseller is "sweet with the works" (sweet sausage, onions, peppers, hot peppers, mustard, ketchup, barbecue sauce, hot sauce, salt, and pepper), but you can also get a "double" (two sausages in one bun) or a "dunk-a-roo," where the bread gets a dip in the left corner of the grill to soak up some of the sausage grease.

Really hungry? Try Doug's own invention, a knish sandwich known to regulars as "the rib-sticker," a hunger-busting combo consisting of a butterflied sausage, laid flat in the middle of a split knish and topped with the works. Doug concocted the sandwich as a kid working on the truck. "It's real, filling, sticks to your ribs," he says. One bite of the rib-sticker and you'll wonder why you hadn't thought of a sausage and potato sandwich before (and why every sandwich isn't served on a crisp-on-the-outside, pillowy-soft-on-the-inside knish).

Regulars don't need to say a word. As soon as they step into Doug's line of sight, he starts prepping their orders. His son, Michael, works the side

"I'm blessed with the best customers in the world from East New York. The best. Love East New York. We've got an expression 'ENY 'til we die.'"

—DOUG POLICANO

takeout window with a precision that betrays his military training, packing the sandwiches and sodas in red-and-white bags that say "Policano's King of Italian Sausage." In addition to your standard soda selection, they also carry classic New York beverages: Manhattan Special, a sweetened espresso soda based out of Brooklyn since 1895, and Dr. Brown's, a kosher soda company started in the city in 1869.

The customers are loyal and appreciative. Whenever anyone leaves a tip, Doug and Michael shout "subway," a nod to Doug's Italian immigrant grandparents, who, as he explains, "never had any money, so when they got some, they'd shout 'subway' because that meant they had enough to at least take the train."

As for his success, Doug is humble. "I don't say it like I'm the best—it just comes with the territory. I just let my cooking speak. So, if it goes that way and it works out that way, it's good." Though the concept is simple, Policano's longevity—not to mention the length of its lunchtime lines and legions of fans—are a testament to hard work and commitment. "The reason why you see us online as the best is because there's two things that are real important: really good ingredients and consistency. That's the key to any real business success." At Policano's there's no slacking; there's no time for being off his game. Doug wants his customers to have a great experience every visit: "If you go to a restaurant or you come see Dougie's sausage, you're going to eat fifty times here, you're going to be so happy. That one time you get a bad sandwich, you're going to walk away and you're going to say, *I got a bad sandwich.* You'll always remember that one time. I don't want you to remember that one time. So we try to make the first sandwich and the end sandwich of the day the same way."

OLD-SCHOOL SAUSAGE AND PEPPERS

Forget about pizza. Forget about pasta. If we're talking Italian American *street food*, sausage and peppers is where it's at. Go to any street fair in the summer, and the odds are good there will be at least one—if not two or three—sausage and pepper stands grilling up onions and mixed bell peppers with your choice of hot or sweet sausage. Every Southern Italian family has their own recipe for sausage and peppers. While the Policano's sausage recipe is a closely guarded family secret, in the end, it's all about using good ingredients and making use of that juice from the sausages. Seek out the best authentic Italian sausage you can find from a butcher. This easy recipe for sausage and peppers at home comes from co-author, Alexandra Penfold's mom, Pamela Parrella, and was passed down by her grandmother, Maria Esposito Parrella.

YIELD: SERVES 4

3 tablespoons extra-virgin olive oil

3 large cloves garlic, peeled and crushed

1 teaspoon dried basil

1 pound sweet Italian sausage

1 large white onion, thinly sliced

1 red bell pepper, seeded and cut into strips

1 green bell pepper, seeded and cut into strips

4 Italian hoagie rolls, split lengthwise

In a large cast-iron pan or skillet add olive oil, garlic, and basil. Sauté for 1 to 2 minutes over medium heat to flavor the oil. Add sausage and cook until browned on the outside and sausages are cooked through, about 20 minutes. Once sausages are cooked, remove from pan, reserving oil in pan. Set sausages aside to cool slightly. Add onion and peppers to the pan and sauté over medium heat until onions are tender and translucent. Once sausages have cooled enough to handle, slice sausages into coin shapes, about a ¼ of an inch thick and return to pan. Reduce heat to low, stirring frequently, until onions are completely browned, about 20 to 30 minutes. While onions are cooking, set oven rack to center position and preheat the oven to 300°F. Place split rolls on a rimmed baking sheet and warm for 10 minutes. Divide sausage and peppers among rolls and serve immediately.

S kippy's Hot Dogs is a beloved Staten Island institution that locals revere as one of the best places to get a dog in the five boroughs. Started by Robert "Skippy" Bellach and his wife, Jane, the truck has been headed up by their granddaughter, Dawn LaVigne, since 1983 and celebrating its golden anniversary in 2012. Not much has changed since the early days. Dawn still drives the cheery red-and-white 1956 Harvester International Metro van her grandfather spent two years outfitting by hand. She still serves virtually the same menu as when the truck opened: snappy Sabrett® natural casing all-beef hot dogs on fluffy buns with your choice of toppings that range from the standard ketchup, mustard, onions, and sauerkraut to melted Velveeta cheese and Skippy's famous homemade onion sauce and chili. "I don't sell anything else," Dawn says. "My grandfather taught me if it's not broken, don't fix it."

Adventurous eaters pick the "everything"—loaded with cheese, sauerkraut, cooked onions, raw onions, and chili—while purists can go for the "plain," which is just a tube steak in a bun. The most popular order, however, is the chili cheese dog served mild. Everything is done according to Dawn's grandmother's top-secret recipes, though she'll admit, "I changed the chili just a little. 'So sorry, grandma!'" she says, looking skyward.

Nobody's noticed, and in fact, these days it's the chili that's a big draw. "When my grandfather ran the truck, it was all about the onions. . . . Now I sell more chili than I do onions—thank the Lord because I cut a hundred pounds of onions by hand." Dawn won't reveal how many hot dogs she sells in a day, except that she "drives home alone."

Dawn is a real dyed-in-the-wool New Yorker, and her family has been here longer than the Statue of Liberty. She can trace her Staten Island roots back to 1873, when her great-great-great-grandparents Wilhelm and Wilhemina Bellach immigrated to New York. The truck parks on a surprisingly tranquil and grassy spot just off of busy Hylan Boulevard between Seaver and Stobe Avenues, which once was part of the Bellach farm before large pieces of land were sold off during the Great Depression. Dawn lives in the family home, a house her grandfather built, just five blocks away. It's a short commute for the trusty truck, but as the years have gone by, traffic's gotten worse. Says Dawn, "One day it took me twenty minutes to get to work!" Still, the truck rolls on. "I have an awesome mechanic, my cousin, and he actually makes parts. He takes parts off of his '55 Chevy and converts them to fit on here because you can't find parts anymore. That's the only reason I'm still running."

The truck itself is covered with stories. Every year it gets a paint job on the Fourth of July. "Everybody laughs at me and says Rust-Oleum® is holding the truck together. I'd like to do a

Rust-Oleum® commercial. That's all I want to do, a Rust-Oleum® commercial, 'cause I have thirty years' worth of paint on here." The front right window has an etching of her grandparents that Dawn commissioned. Her grandfather's reaction? "Well, you know your grandmother's on there, I guess it's okay." The back door sports the names Devin and Vinny, along with a heart and their anniversary date. Devin is one of Dawn's cousins, and Vinny worked at the beer distributor down the block. Dawn did a little matchmaking, and now they're married with beautiful twins, a boy and a girl. "See that table out there?" Dawn says, pointing to an enormous blue-and-yellow picnic table. "I built that when I was twelve. Me and my grandfather built it. I was going to take it down two years ago 'cause it was in really bad shape, and one of my customers, his name was Danny Schnell, said to me, 'You aren't taking that table down. I've been sitting on that table since I'm in preschool.' And him and his friends came and fixed it."

A peek in the back reveals a tiny 1960s stove and steam table and an antique cash register dating back to 1901 that Dawn purchased from a customer. The space is tight, but Dawn is used to it. Watching her expertly whirl around, pivoting to add chili and a stripe of cheese, is mesmerizing. She can knock out a dozen dogs in no time flat, while catching up with her regulars and never losing her rhythm. The truck operates Monday through Satur-

"Who's got a better job than me? I've got people telling me they love me all day long." —DAWN LAVIGNE

day, unless it's raining. Monday through Wednesday, she usually finishes up around 3:00 or 3:30 p.m. Thursday through Saturday, she tries to stay until 4:00 pm or until she sells out. It's the customers who keep things interesting. "Everybody talks about the way people are. People are the way you treat them. I never have a bad customer. . . . I know everyone who comes here, and if I don't know them, I *want* to know them. They become a part of my family."

Most patrons are longtimers, some since childhood. Dawn's easy way with people makes you want to be a regular. She has a ready laugh and a smile and a "hi, baby" for everyone. While she might not remember everyone's name, she remembers their orders. "I've been working here since I was eleven years old. I used to work with my grandfather. I don't even know what else to tell you. Every day is fun. Every day somebody new comes by, it's a new story."

Her grandfather started the truck as a business for her grandmother. "They came out here, and on the first day they didn't sell a hot dog—not one. So when they pulled in the yard, they were like, 'hot dogs for dinner!' They were raising nine kids at the time. That's the big joke in the family. And, no, we don't eat hot dogs for dinner," says Dawn. Rocky beginnings aside, Skippy's soon grew into a thriving business. "My grandmother worked for the first five years, and then he fired her. That was a huge fight, but she had a heart problem, and he didn't want her working. But she did all of the behind-the-scenes work—she did all the cooking." Dawn's grandmother passed away when she was a young girl, but she enjoyed a close relationship with her grandfather growing up. "Before she died, my grandfather never did any of the cooking, or the serving, by the way. And when she died, in his suit—she knew she was sick, she knew, she had a heart attack, she wouldn't go for the operation—she had the onion and chili recipe in the pocket of his suit."

With twenty-seven grandchildren, Skippy had an army of helpers. "Everybody got a shot working the truck," Dawn explains. "I shouldn't say this but my cousin—and I'm gonna to say it—used to sit up there and read her book while he worked, and it drove him crazy." Still with Dawn it seemed fated. "I knew from the minute that I stepped on this truck that this was going to be my purpose. I knew this was why I'm here." As much as food brings people to the truck, it's more than that; Dawn brings people together. "Everything on this island has changed. . . . I'm the only thing left from way back when that hasn't changed. I know someday I'm going to have to, but common courtesy, respect, you know, that's all part of it, and you get that when you're here. There could be a bunch of strangers that come here, and when they eat they sit on that one table—I won't put another table—and they're friends when they leave."

LOCATIONS & CONTACT INFORMATION

For vendors without set locations, just tweet them to find their location for the day.

MANHATTAN

KELVIN™ NATURAL SLUSH CO. TRUCK

@KELVINSLUSH • kelvinslush.com/

GELŌTTŌ CART

NORTHWEST CORNER OF WASHINGTON
SQUARE PARK, APRIL THROUGH OCTOBER

WOOLY'S ICE

PIER 17 AT SOUTH STREET SEAPORT

APRIL THROUGH OCTOBER

@WoolysIce

A-POU'S TASTE

LIBERTY STREET AT BROADWAY

@Apouspotsticker

DONATELLA'S MEATBALL WAGON

184 EIGHTH AVENUE

@DonatellaArpaia

N.Y. DOSA

WASHINGTON SQUARE SOUTH

VERONICA'S KITCHEN

FRONT STREET

UNCLE GUSSY'S

SOUTHEAST CORNER OF EAST 51ST STREET AT
PARK AVENUE

unclegussys.com • @UncleGussys

EGGSTRAVAGANZA CART

NORTHEAST CORNER OF EAST 52ND STREET
AT PARK AVENUE

@ETRAVAGANZA

HALLO BERLIN

54TH ST AND 5TH AVENUE

halloberlinrestaurant.com

BIRYANI CART

SOUTHWEST CORNER, WEST 46TH STREET
AND SIXTH AVENUE

biryanicart.com

KWIK MEAL CART

SOUTHWEST CORNER, WEST 45TH STREET
AND SIXTH AVENUE

PATACON PISAO

WEST 202ND STREET, BETWEEN NINTH AND
TENTH AVENUES

pataconpisaony.com

CHIMICHURY EL MALECÓN

204 SHERMAN AVENUE

@ChimiElMalecon • chimichuryelmalecon.com

MISS SOFTEE

@hi_im_chrissy

KIMCHI TACO TRUCK

@KimchiTruck • kimchitacotruck.com

WAFELS & DINGES

@waffletruck • wafelsanddinges.com

THE TREATS TRUCK

@TheTreatsTruck • treatstruck.com

COMME CI COMME ÇA

@chefsamirtruck • chefsamirtruck.com

LUKE'S LOBSTER
@LukesLobsterNY • lukeslobster.com

BIÀN DĀNG
@biandangnyc • biandangnyc.com

COOLHAUS
@CoolhausNY • eatcoolhaus.com

THE CINNAMON SNAIL
@VeganLunchTruck • cinnamonsnail.com

BIG D'S GRUB TRUCK
@bigdsgrub • biggrub.com

GREEN PIRATE JUICE TRUCK
@juicepirate • green-pirate.om

MORRIS GRILLED CHEESE
@MorrisTruck • morrisgrilledcheese.com

VAN LEEUWEN ARTISAN ICE CREAM
@VLAIC • vanleeuwenicecream.com

BIG GAY ICE CREAM TRUCK
@BigGayIceCream • biggayicecream.com

DESSERTTRUCK
@DessertTruck • desserttruck.com

MEXICUE
@Mexicue • mexicue.com

SCHNITZEL & THINGS
@schnitznthings • schnitzelandthings.com

BRONX

THE CHIPPER TRUCK
237TH STREET AND KATONAH AVENUE, WOODLAWN

FAUZIA'S HEAVENLY DELIGHTS
161ST STREET AND SHERIDAN AVENUE, CONCOURSE VILLAGE

@Fauzia_Cart

BROOKLYN

TAMALES GUADALUPE
KNICKERBOCKER AVENUE AND DEKALB AVENUE, BUSHWICK

CERON COLOMBIAN TRUCK
CLINTON STREET AND BAY STREET, RED HOOK

OCHOA TRUCK
CLINTON STREET AND BAY STREET, RED HOOK

COUNTRY BOYS
CLINTON STREET AND BAY STREET, RED HOOK

SOLBER PUPUSAS
CLINTON STREET AND BAY STREET, RED HOOK

@solberpupusas • solberpupusas.com

EL OLOMEGA
CLINTON STREET AND BAY STREET, RED HOOK

@elolomega • elolomega.com

CARRILLO ANTOJITOS CHAPINES
CLINTON STREET AND BAY STREET, RED HOOK

SOSA FRUIT TRUCK
CLINTON STREET AND BAY STREET, RED HOOK

VAQUERO FRUIT TRUCK
CLINTON STREET AND BAY STREET, RED HOOK

QUEENS

KING OF FALAFEL AND SHAWARMA

29-10 BROADWAY, ASTORIA

@kingfalafel • thekingfalafel.com

TORTAS NEZA

111TH STREET AND ROOSEVELT AVENUE, CORONA

POLICANO'S ITALIAN SAUSAGE

79 LINDEN BOULEVARD, OZONE PARK

policanositaliansausage.com

STATEN ISLAND

SKIPPY'S HOT DOGS

HYLAN BOULEVARD BETWEEN SEAVER AND STOBE AVENUES, DONGAN HILLS

WHERE TO BUY

Most of the ingredients listed in the recipes are easily found at any grocery store, but here is a list of our favorite places in New York City to shop at, including a few that accept online orders.

DUAL SPECIALITY STORE

91 FIRST AVENUE

NEW YORK, NY 10003

(212) 979-6045

MEAT

192 5TH AVENUE

PARK SLOPE, NY 11217

(719) 398-MOOO (6666)

HERITAGE MEAT SHOP

120 ESSEX STREET

NEW YORK, NY 10002

(212) 539-1111 • heritagefoodsusa.com

KALUSTYAN'S

123 LEXINGTON AVE

NEW YORK, NY 10066

(800) 352-3451 • kalustyans.com

O. OTTOMANELLI & SONS PRIME MEAT MARKET

285 BLEECKER STREET

NEW YORK, NY 10014

(212) 675-4217

PATEL GROCERY

5303 4TH AVENUE

BROOKLYN, NY 11220

(718) 748-6369

FLEISHER'S GRASSFED AND ORGANIC MEATS

61-05 WOODSIDE AVENUE

WOODSIDE, NY 11377

(718) 651-5710 • fleishers.com

SAHADI'S

187 ATLANTIC AVENUE

BROOKLYN, NY 11201

(718) 624-4550 • sahadis.com

THE MEAT HOOK

100 FROST STREET

BROOKLYN, NY 11211

(718) 349-5033 • the-meathook.com

Acknowledgments

Many hands and hearts went into making this book but first and foremost it would not have been possible without the generous outpouring of support of the vendors. You inspire us with you hard work and dedication and it's an honor to be able to share your stories.

We could fill a whole other book with our many thank yous. Here are a few of the many people who cheered us on, lifted us up and helped us along the way...

The incredible team at Running Press headed up by our awesome editor Jennifer Kasius and designer, Joshua McDonnell. Thank you for bringing this book to life.

Our rock star agent, Susan Ginsburg of Writers House for seeing the potential our proposal back when and guiding us each step of the way. Special thanks to her right-hand gal, Stacy Testa for her support and insight.

Our fantastic photographers Clay Williams and Donny Tsang who braved five borough outings at all hours of the day and night to capture the vendors hard at work.

Sean Basinski at the Street Vendor Project and Helena Tubis, Managing Director of the Vendy Awards for their assistance and encouragement.

Brian Hoffman and Cindy VandenBosch of Turnstile Tours for everything they do to support vendors and all the spontaneous moments of assistance.

Jeff Orlick and Joe DiStefano, the kings of Queens, for their hours of working, eating, and walking (and sometimes translating.)

Gluten-free guru and author, Elizabeth Barbone for going through our recipes and advising us on our recipe labeling.

We wouldn't have been able to finish this book were it not for the life-sustaining coffee and wi-fi from Steeplechase Coffee and countless sandwiches and take-out roasted chickens from Brancaccio's Food Shop in Kensington to keep us going.

Our extraordinary pals spread throughout all corners of the internet, especially Zach Brooks for believing in us from the very beginning.

Our friends and families who have put up with two years of canceled plans, jam-packed weekends, being photoshoot models, and repeat recipe testing marathons. Bonus points for those who came out to be our taste testers. Extra bonus points for the ones who helped with the dishes, you know who you are.

FROM SIOBHAN....

Much love to Momsie, for being the best mom she can be. If it hadn't been for you, we would have never moved back to New York and none of this would have ever happened. I loves you!

Extra shout out to Rob and Meagan for being the best brother and sister a girl could have. I owe you much bourbon and a new router.

Bonus hugs to Christine, the bestest best friend I could ever wish for. I literally wouldn't have made it this far without you. Thank you, from the bottom of my heart.

Thank you to my nephew, Brendan, for letting me miss most of his tenth year on this planet. I promise to make it up to you because I love you so much!

Thank yous and missed beers are owed to many people, mut mostly to my awesome cousins Lauren and Jackie; Janine; Pam; Melanie and Chris; Vega; my boos Rachel and Mo; Melissa Z; Molly, Dave and Kimber; Mamacita; everyone who helped me at The Meat Hook and The Brooklyn Kitchen; and my NYU classmates and professors.

Of course, extra special bonus thank yous to Donny, Clay, and Alex to infinity.

Lastly, thank you to the four generations of Wallaces who put New York in my blood. I can only hope this makes you proud, Dad.

FROM ALEXANDRA . . .

There's not a single member of my family that didn't pitch in to help throughout the process. I have so many reasons to be thankful and grateful.

Thanks especially to my mother and father who never doubted that I could do anything that I set my mind to. I wouldn't be here without their love and support (not to mention recipe testing and consultation).

To my brother for joining on scouting missions and watching my little one while I was in the final push.

To my mother-in-law and father-in-law for translating and transcribing interviews, having patience with my Spanish, and allowing me to take over their kitchen for weekends at a time.

To Lisa, my brother-in-law, sister-in-law, Jill, and Max for recipe testing. To Tia and my tamale-wrapping nieces and nephews for their help in the kitchen.

To Gen, Kristina, Lucy, Cara, Chloe, and Kristy for the right words at the right time.

To Siobhan, Donny and Clay for one of the most incredible adventures of my life. We did it! It's a book!

And last but certainly not least to my incredible husband and son for absolutely everything.

PHOTO CREDITS

SOURCES

"Ban in Rockaways on Hawking Signed." *The New York Times* 17 Aug 1938: 21. Print.

"Best Street Food in New York is the 'Wurst'." Narr. Jesse Baker. *Weekend Edition. NPR.* Natl. Public Radio. 13 Nov 2005. Radio.

"Horn & Hardart Scooter Rolls into Bryant Park." *The New York Times* 17 Sep 1966: 19. Print.

Basinski, S, et al. *Vendor Power! A Guide to Street Vending in New York*, 2009. Print.

Dubner, S. "Street Treats." *New York* 23 Dec 1991: 96-97. Print.

Ferrier, P, Russell Lamb. "Government Regulation and Quality in the US Beef Market." *Food Policy* 32 (2007): 84-97. Print.

Handelman, D. "The Wurst Luck." *New York* 14 Dec 1987: 42. Print.

Keeley, C. "Effects of the Immigration Act of 1965 on Selected Population Characteristics of Immigrants to the United States." *Demography* May 1971: 157-169. Print.

Mackenzie, C. "Curb Food Markets Boom." *The New York Times* 18 Aug. 1935: SM17. Print.

Magolis, M. *Little Brazil: An Ethnography of Brazilian Immigrants in New York City.* Princeton: Princeton University Press, 1994. Print.

Maitland, L. "Most Street Food Vendors Find Revisions in Rules of Little Help." *The New York Times* 1 Aug 1978: B3. Print.

Quinzio, Jeri, "NOTABLE EDIBLES: The Ice Cream Sandwich—Born on the Bowery and Eaten by Economists," *Edible Manhattan*, July-August 2012. Print.

Roberts, S. "New York 1945; The War Was Ending, Times Square Exploded, Change Was Coming." *The New York Times* 30 Jul 1995: Sec 13, Page 1. Print

Schumach, M. "Neighborhoods: Changes Tear at the Old West Side." *The New York Times* 2 Oct 1970: 36. Print.

Sheraton, M. "The Pleasures of Outdoor Eating: Dining à la Cart on Avenue of Americas." *The New York Times* 27 May 1981: C1. Print.

RECIPE INDEX

SUBJECT AND NAME INDEX

NEW YORK

à la Cart